Down Home and Uptown

Down Home and Uptown

The Representation of Black Speech in American Fiction

Sylvia Wallace Holton

Rutherford • Madison • Teaneck
Fairleigh Dickinson University Press
London and Toronto: Associated University Presses

© 1984 by Associated University Presses, Inc.

Associated University Presses
440 Forsgate Drive
Cranbury, NJ 08512

Associated University Presses
25 Sicilian Avenue
London WC1A 2QH, England

Associated University Presses
2133 Royal Windsor Drive
Unit 1
Mississauga, Ontario
Canada L5J 1K5

Library of Congress Cataloging in Publication Data

Holton, Sylvia Wallace.
  Down home and uptown.

  Bibliography: p.
  Includes index.
  1. American fiction—History and criticism.
2. Black English in literature.   3. Afro-Americans in
literature.   4. English language in literature.
5. Speech in literature.   6. Black English.   I. Title.
PS374.B63H64   1983   813′.009′3520396073   82-48270
ISBN 0-8386-3130-4

Printed in the United States of America

For Milne

Contents

Preface

At the beginning of the fall semester of 1971, I joined the faculty of the Department of English Studies at Federal City College (since 1977 the University of the District of Columbia). At that time, the institution was beginning its third year of life as the "land grant college" of the District of Columbia. The faculty and student body were predominantly black.

Almost immediately I found myself engaged in lengthy discussions, both in conversation and at English Department faculty meetings, that turned around the subject of "Black English." These discussions were theoretical, highly political, only occasionally practical, but always passionately argued. Such questions as whether the department should teach Black English or Standard English in the classroom, whether white teachers should correct the grammar of students who wrote in Black English, and whether it was socially beneficial for black students to learn Standard English at all, were disputed for lengthy afternoons.

No conclusive decisions were ever reached, and many linguistic theories were called upon to support each position. But little evidence was offered concerning the presence of Black English as a literary language, although that presence is obvious and very important in American literature.

The idea for this book took shape when I came to realize how little was really known concerning the important questions surrounding the presence of Black English as an American literary language. Although I had for a long time been interested in developments in applied and historical linguistics and in dialect study, my primary commitments were literary. Thus I decided that my book would be directed at a literary audience. That literary audience would need an introduction to the phenomenon of Black English as it is variously identified and "explained" by linguists. Yet, since no previous study had been undertaken, my first commitment must be to an account, chronologically presented, of the ways in which Black English has been used for literary effect over the years of development of American fiction. Only then could I venture upon the more speculative critical considerations that shape the latter part of my study.

I particularly wish to thank both my students and my colleagues in the

Department of English Studies at Federal City College/University of the District of Columbia for their encouragement and advice. I am also deeply grateful to Janet McKay of the University of Maryland and Ralph Fasold of Georgetown University, who helped clarify a number of linguistic points. The librarians and staff of the Library of Congress and of Widener Library helped me locate and accumulate the many books and materials I needed. Virginia and Benjamin Fairbank literally gave me shelter while I worked for several weeks at Harvard University in the summer of 1975. Charles E. Beveridge, Ian Ousby, Robert F. Sayre, and R. Baxter Miller read the manuscript and offered many helpful criticisms and suggestions from a variety of points of view. Eli Rosenfield's help with the Index was indispensable. Ruth Doerflein typed the manuscript with intelligence, patience, and amazing precision. Most of all, I wish to thank my husband, to whom this book is dedicated, for sharing his knowledge of American literature with me and for steadily directing my attention to the final goal.

Introductory Note

My intention in this book is to examine the ways in which Black English dialect has been used in American fiction and the literary effects its use has generated. During the nearly two centuries that Black English speakers have been vocally present in American fiction, the writers who have recorded their speech have developed various tactics for its representation. Each of the various tactics used can suggest assumptions and reinforce prejudices concerning the black characters whose speech has been recorded in fiction. Thus certain tactics have acquired political implications; they have been repeated or replaced by new tactics as subsequent writers have agreed or disagreed with the assumptions or prejudices implicit in a particular type of dialect representation.

Interest in Black English as a linguistic phenomenon was largely a concern of the late 1960s and early 1970s. Although much research of a theoretical nature was undertaken in this period, many people in the field of education were particularly interested in the application of this research to the curricula of urban school systems with predominantly black students. Few literary scholars and critics had then or have yet seen the possibilities that the study of Black English as a linguistic phenomenon offers to an understanding of the way dialect has been used in fiction for literary effect.

In order to understand the implications involved in the representation of Black English speech in a literary context, the reader must first come to an awareness of the origins of the Black English dialect and to a comprehension of the various theories concerning the history of its development. With that background the reader will be ready to perceive the distinguishing features of Black English as a distinctive dialect spoken by black Americans and to comprehend the range of possibilities for its representation in American fiction.

The first two chapters of my study consider the backgrounds and linguistic identity of American Black English. The first chapter sets forth the dominant theories concerning the origins, development, and present autonomy of Black English as a linguistic phenomenon. The second chapter reviews the linguistic studies of Black English undertaken in the 1960s and 1970s and describes those phonological, grammatical, lexical, rhetorical, and rhythmical features that are today generally associated with Black English speech by linguists. With this background the reader will be sufficiently informed so that he can understand the linguistic implications of the literary investigation that follows.

The third chapter begins the literary discussion with a consideration of the ways in which the speech of American blacks has been represented by writers of American fiction. By examining the dialect fiction of the pre- and post-Civil War periods and culminating in the *fin de siècle* local color fiction, I identify the conventions of representing Black English dialect that came to be established in nineteenth-century American fiction. The fourth chapter considers the years of change in the tradition—the years between 1900 and 1940. During this period an increasing number of black writers, particularly those associated with the "Harlem Renaissance," who perceived and resisted the assumptions inherent in the now-established tradition of Black English dialect representation in fiction, turned to new procedures; white writers also experimented with new techniques so that they might express their new awareness of black characters and their consciousness. The fifth chapter, which deals with the last forty years in American Black English dialect fiction, considers the results of those early explorations in method. Here I describe a period of radical literary experimentation and innovation, as black and white writers, unconvinced by the traditional procedures of dialect representation, and brought up in a time of awareness of and pride in racial origins, sought to identify in their fiction the uniqueness, distinction, and symbolizing power of Black English dialect.

The changes in dialect representation have generated significant implications for the narrative structures of dialect fiction. In Chapter 6 I explore the relationship between the Black English speech of fictional characters and the speech, either Standard English or Black English, of a fictional narrator. I conclude with a consideration of the possibility of the emergence of Black English dialect as a literary language—as a language that can itself serve as an autonomous medium for fictional narration.

Any first consideration of a literary phenomenon ignored by critics and literary historians over a period of nearly two hundred years must by its very nature be cursory and selective. It is not possible here to consider all the important linguistic studies of the dialect that have been published over the past twenty years, nor is it conceivable that I would hope to identify, much less to discuss, the literally thousands of examples of representations of black American dialect in two hundred years of American fiction. Many of our major writers of fiction have recorded Black English speech in classic novels, yet many of these novels have been ignored in this study. On the other hand, I have discussed at length novels and fictions that have no particular critical or historical significance but that in some way seem typical or of interest because of the method of dialect representation their authors employ. This book is not meant to be a literary history. It is intended as the first look at what to my mind is an important phenomenon too long ignored in American fiction, a phenomenon that has already left its distinguishing mark on the shape of American fiction and may well continue to do so.

Down Home and Uptown

Black English: Origins

SEVERAL decades before Alex Haley presented America with his bicentennial gift[1] and excited the imaginations of black Americans with stories of the romantic as well as tragic origins of their forefathers and mothers, linguists had been searching through historical and literary records, seeking to determine the origins of the language of these people, the origins of what we have come to know as Black English.

As an identifying phrase, "Black English" is relatively recent. But the variety of English to which it refers is as old as the institution of slavery in the New World. Other terms have been used to describe the variety of English spoken by black people—"Negro dialect," "Non-Standard Negro dialect," "Black language," "Black English Vernacular," "Merican," "Pan-African Language in the Western Hemisphere," and, most recently, "Ebonics." Each term registers different connotations: those containing "Negro," commonly used before the 1960s, now sound dated, old-fashioned, and demeaning; those containing "black" convey more contemporary and positive meanings. Ever since the "Black Pride" movement of the 1960s, "black" has been the term that most black Americans, certainly those born after 1940, have chosen to refer to themselves. It is an adjective that has come to connote strength and unity to black people. And to refer to the speech of these people, "Black English" or "Black English dialect" is preferred by most contemporary linguists.

Although some may find the term unfortunate—perhaps itself an oxymoron—it is of sufficiently common currency so that to seek a substitute would be eccentrically scrupulous. Furthermore, the term generates important positive connotations. "Black English" recognizes the positive term of identity chosen by black people: "black," and it accurately labels the predominant, although not exclusive, language family, "English," with which the speech of black Americans is associated. It is a term that covers the whole range of black speech, from the time blacks were thrust unwillingly on American soil and began to struggle to communicate in a foreign tongue to the present, when English is spoken by blacks of all social classes (except, of course, for those, primarily the educated, who speak Standard English).[2]

The term "Black English dialect" more specifically identifies the speech of black people as a dialect, a subdivision of the language family, English. Since everyone can be said to speak a dialect of one kind or another, this term accurately identifies the variety of English that many black Americans speak.[3] The term "Black language," which is used occasionally, poses a different problem. It implies that blacks communicate in a linguistic system that is unique and separate from English. Anyone who listens to blacks speaking will recognize immediately that, although there are clear differences from Standard English in Black English speech, what he hears is unmistakably a variety of the English language. Furthermore, the term "Black language" refers to the sociopsychological considerations that shape the acts of verbal communication initiated by Black American speakers. Since the characterization of "Black language" would lead to sociohistorical and psychohistorical considerations much too extensive for the scope of this study, and because the term is misleading for linguistic reasons, "Black language" will be only occasionally and obliquely treated.

There are other Black English compounds that refer to specialized subdivisions of Black English. "Black English Vernacular,"[4] for instance, has come to refer specifically to the colorful speech of urban black youths, usually male (the speech of urban black females has not been separately studied), most of them dropouts from schools, who spend much of their leisure time "rapping" on the streets of New York, Detroit, or Chicago. In their speech can be found some of the most original and creative examples of language in America today. "Cultivated Black English," or "Black Standard English" is frequently used to describe a more formalized black speech, the black equivalent of White Standard English, the type of speech often heard uttered by black preachers or government officials. Many blacks, of course, speak a Standard English that is indistinguishable from "white" Standard English. These people, most linguists would say, do not speak Black English; however, some of them may be able to speak it when they wish to, in informal or intimate situations.

A few linguists remain dissatisfied with the term "Black English," and have tried to suggest alternatives. "Merican" is one of these terms. But if the language of black speakers is "Merican,"[5] then what does one call the variety of English that Mexican-Americans, or Puerto Ricans, or Boston Irish, or New York Jewish speakers speak? All of these varieties are just as "Merican" as Black English. "Pan-African Language in the Western Hemisphere,"[6] yet another suggestion, is lengthy and clumsy when uttered in its entirety and unpronounceable when reduced to its acronym, PALWH. Still another term that has been suggested is "Ebonics,"[7] a fusion of "ebony" and "phonics," words whose Greek etymologies only confuse the issue of dialect origin.

The heated dispute among linguists over the preferred term for describing the speech of black people seems confusing, and perhaps even silly, to the layman. Unfortunately, one is never far from political overtones when discussing any subject that deals with blacks in America. And black linguistics, largely because much of the research has been done by whites, is at the center of the political arena. Each of the terms used to describe black speech that is discussed here makes its own political statement. But of all those suggested, "Black English" seems to be not only the most linguistically accurate, but also one that carries with it predominantly positive connotations.[8] Although it may be necessary to define different types or categories of Black English, there seems to be no need to create a new term.

Over the years linguists and scholars have offered different interpretations of the data available concerning the origins of Black English. The oldest position taken is that of the Anglicists, whose views on language reflect the attitude of whites toward blacks during the first half of the twentieth century. But today, when their position is challenged by more recent linguistic research, it seems to lack validity. Basically, the Anglicists were aware that the African slaves placed on Southern plantations spoke a number of African languages. The lack of a common language made communication difficult. From the slaveholders' point of view, however, this diversity of speech was an advantage, for it also made organized rebellion difficult. The Africans spoke many different languages, but since English was the language of the owners and the white overseers, the burden was on the slaves to communicate in that language. They did so, but—as does anyone who is thrust into a situation in which a totally unfamiliar language is spoken—they adapted the new language to the characteristics of their native tongue. The Anglicists, however, none of whom admitted to familiarity with any African language, assumed that as the years passed and generation followed generation, the Africans' and, by then, the Afro-Americans' proficiency in English increased—to such an extent that all traces of the original African languages disappeared. The Anglicists took the position that those blacks who came to America in the seventeenth and eighteenth centuries learned their English from British overseers, of rural British yeoman stock. In places where the blacks were geographically and socially isolated, as in the Sea Islands of South Carolina and Georgia, their descendants tended to preserve in their speech archaic forms of peasant British English, which their ancestors had spoken. Their English was imperfectly spoken, but, according to the Anglicists, its peculiarities were English, nevertheless. Guy B. Johnson, in an article published in 1930, explains the accepted Anglicist view of the origin of Black English speech:

> But this strange dialect turns out to be little more than the peasant English of two centuries ago, modified to suit the needs of slaves. From Midland and Southern England came planters, artisans, shopkeepers, indentured servants, all of whom had more or less contact with the slaves, and the speech of these poorer white folk was so rustic that their more cultured countrymen had difficulty in understanding them. From

this peasant speech and from the "baby talk" used by masters in addressing them, the Negroes developed that dialect, sometimes known as Gullah, which remains the characteristic feature of the culture of the Negroes of coastal South Carolina and Georgia.[9]

Gullah, which the Anglicists considered a "frozen" form of early British English, can still be heard in parts of the Sea Islands today. The speech of black people from other regions, however, sounds quite different. Most blacks had more contact with white society and formal schooling than did the Sea Islanders. And these blacks continued to adopt Anglicized speech forms. There is no doubt that the language black Americans use today is English, even though there may be some obvious contrasts with standard usage. It is these points of contrast—phonological, grammatical, and lexical—that the Anglicists insisted can be traced to English origins.

Thus the Anglicists assumed that any differences between the speech of blacks and the speech of whites could be attributed to the preservation of early rural English dialect characteristics. They adamantly rejected all suggestions of African language ancestry and insisted upon clear Anglo-Saxon origins of all distinctive features of Black English speech. The naiveté of this position in the light of recent linguistic evidence is astounding. The error, expounded for at least forty years, was based on a false hypothesis that was never tested—because none of the proponents of the Anglicist position was familiar with African languages.

John Bennett, one of the earliest of the Anglicist scholars, revealed his highly developed literary imagination when he wrote about Gullah. He was particularly intrigued with the similarities he found between Gullah and Shakespearean English.

> This dialect spoken by low-country plantation negroes is strangely akin to the English dialects; quite as akin to England's provincial dialect as was the best English spoken in the Southern States, settled in William Shakspere's days, or immediately thereafter, to the English of Shakspere's plays.[10]

Fourteen years later, in 1922, in his collection of Gullah folk tales from South Carolina and Georgia, Ambrose Gonzales identified 1,700 Gullah words in his glossary. But these, he maintained, had no connection with Africa.

> The words are, of course, not African, for the African brought over or retained only a few words of his jungle-tongue, and even those few are by no means authenticated as part of the original scant baggage of the Negro slaves.[11]

George Philip Krapp, one of the most highly respected linguists of his day, reiterated the idea of English origins in 1924.

> In one very important respect, however, the Negro is not a foreigner and an outcast: his language is finally and completely English.[12]

And later,

> The Negroes, indeed, in acquiring English have done their work so thoroughly that they have retained not a trace of any native African speech.[13]

One can note in these excerpts a tone of condescension as the white scholar bends over backward to compliment the black by telling him he has learned his adopted language, the language of the master class, very well, and, like a good immigrant, appropriately forgotten his African linguistic past. Unfortunately, however, the "liberal" white had not done his linguistic homework, and therefore could not speak from a position of linguistic authority.

In the foreword to a book entitled *Gullah,* by Reed Smith, published in 1926, Stanhope Sams describes Gullah in the following words:

> Gullah, that quaint linguistic mongrel of the black folk of the Carolina-Georgia coast and sea-islands, an English dialect molded by the lips and genius of African slaves.[14]

Sams continues by praising the work of Reed Smith:

> He has worked out the laws and analogues that unconsciously wrought this quaintly beautiful transformation of English through the mentality and spirit of the slaves in Southern homes. He has placed Gullah upon the plane with our great dialects,—Irish, Scottish, and some of the English idioms.[15]

Again, the white man's praise for the black man's Anglicized speech predominates.

At least Reed Smith, the author of the book Stanhope Sams introduced, recognized that Black English speech found in the South Carolina Sea Islands in 1920 sounds quite different from English. Even so, he was still committed to the Anglicist argument for English origins.

> What the Gullahs seem to have done was to take a sizable part of the English vocabulary as spoken on the coast by the white inhabitants from about 1700 on, wrap their tongues around it, and reproduce it changed in tonality, pronunciation, cadence, and grammar to suit their native phonetic tendencies, and their existing needs of expression and communication. The result has been called by one writer "the worst English in the world." It would certainly seem to have a fair claim to that distinction. To understand it requires a trained ear, and at first blush it is equally unintelligible to white people and colored people alike.[16]

In 1935, when Cleanth Brooks published his study of the Alabama-Georgia dialect, he accepted completely the argument concerning the English origins of Black English speech; he also saw few, if any, differences between black and white dialects. As he said, "The dialect of both white and negro . . . is substantially the same."[17] Here again we see an ideological assumption behind the linguistic statement: if blacks speak like whites, their assimilation into the dominant society will be assured eventually. Political realities, however, did not follow the linguistic patterns in logical fashion.

One of the latest of the Anglicists, Mason Crum, who published his book *Gullah* in 1940, has a great deal of respect for African traditions remaining in the Sea Islands of the South Carolina coast. As he says in his preface, "It is significant that nowhere on the continent can a purer African culture be found."[18] Furthermore, he discusses in some detail the African etymology of the word *Gullah*. Unfortunately, however, when he begins to discuss the Gullah dialect itself, his predisposition toward African influence is overcome by the books and articles he has read concerning the English origins of Gullah speech. Relying heavily on the ideas of Bennett, Krapp, and others, he says: "Gullah is predominantly English, a true English dialect; in fact, more truly English than much of the English spoken in America today."[19] Later in the same chapter, however, he cannot resist his instinctive sense of the African presence: "While the body of the dialect is English, its spirit is African."[20] In his discussion of Gullah, Crum's own "spirit" seems to be in tension with the established position that he reiterates. If he had only trusted his own instincts, he might, instead of being one of the last of the Anglicists, have led the group of researchers convinced of African influence on Gullah who were inevitably to follow.

As it turned out, that role would be filled by Melville Herskovits. With the publication of Herskovits's book *The Myth of the Negro Past* in 1941, the Anglicists could no longer maintain their insular linguistic position. Herskovits, who had worked with Gunnar Myrdal on historical and sociological background material for *An American Dilemma* (1944), was appalled at the naive but self-confident statements reputable scholars were willing to make concerning the linguistic origins of Black English speech—without any knowledge of African languages and very little knowledge of the historical and geographical movements of black people from the time they left Africa as slaves until their descendants found themselves unappreciated and resentful in the middle of the twentieth century. According to Herskovits, most of what was accepted as common knowledge about the Anglicized nature of Black English speech was pure myth, myth that needed to be replaced with reliable scholarly research into African languages.

That the cautions which enlightened considerations of scholarly method dictate have not been observed by students whose concern has been with tracing African survivals in the vocabulary and phonetics of Negro speech is thus apparent; that work based on closer acquaintance with African tongues as well as with various dialectal manifestations of English is needed before adequate analyses of the linguistic acculturation of the Negro are to be made is the only conclusion that can be drawn at this time.[21]

In effect, Herskovits overturned the Anglicist position with a single blow. Thereafter, the research into African languages that had been needed for so many years could no longer be avoided.

The first important linguistic work to reflect Herskovits's position, Lorenzo Dow Turner's *Africanisms in the Gullah Dialect*, appeared in 1949. Turner's historical research[22] concerning the Sea Island area uncovered a number of facts that helped to explain the linguistic situation he found there. Turner estimated that at least 100,000 slaves were imported directly from Africa to South Carolina and Georgia before 1808. They came primarily from the west coast of Africa, from the area between Senegal and Angola. Specifically, these countries were "Senegal, Gambia, Sierra Leone, Liberia, the Gold Coast, Togo, Dahomey, Nigeria, and Angola."[23] Slaves from these countries brought with them a number of languages, of which Turner identified twenty: "Wolof, Malinke, Mandinka, Bambara, Fula, Mende, Vai, Twi, Fante, Gã, Ewe, Faon, Yoruba, Bini, Hausa, Ibo, Ibibo, Efik, Kongo, Umbundu, Kimbundu, and a few others."[24]

After January 1, 1808, the Slave Trade Act, which made it illegal to import slaves into the United States direct from Africa, went into effect. Despite the illegality, there is evidence that a few slaves continued to be imported to the Sea Islands. Even during the eighteenth century more slaves had come to the South Carolina and Georgia coasts direct from Africa than from the West Indies, mainly because duties were considerably higher on the slaves from the West Indies than on those from Africa. Thus the Sea Islands seemed to be an area settled largely by blacks of pure African origin. And the whites, because of the intense heat and high rate of malaria, stayed away as much as possible. In 1808, on Edisto Island, there were 236 white people and 2,609 slaves, or a ratio of approximately ten blacks to one white person.[25] The situation that resulted, then, was a geographically isolated colony of slaves, the majority of whom had come directly from Africa. Turner explains the linguistic consequences:

> The African speech habits of the earliest Gullahs were being constantly strengthened throughout the eighteenth century and the first half of the nineteenth by contact with the speech of native Africans who were coming direct from Africa and who were sharing with the older Gullahs the isolation of the Sea Isands—a condition which obviously made easier the retention of Africanisms in that area than in places where Negroes had less direct contact with Africa and lived less isolated lives. One should not be surprised, therefore, to find among the Gullahs today numerous African customs and speech habits.[26]

In his book Turner records approximately 4,000 Gullah words, each with an African etymology. And he cannot resist pointing out the inadequacies of Ambrose Gonzales's earlier list of 1,700 Gullah words, for which he had assumed English etymologies. Turner had reason to be proud of his work; he presented overwhelming evidence for the African roots of Gullah. Ever since 1949, when his book was first published, linguists interested in the history of Black English have had to come to terms with Turner's data.

Although the pure Anglicist position disappeared suddenly after the publication of the works of Herskovits and Turner, there was still a group of linguistic scholars who, although they admired Turner's works and accepted the African etymologies for a number of English words, believed that Black English speech reflects to a large extent the region of the United States in which black speakers were born and brought up. These dialect geographers, led by Hans Kurath and Raven McDavid, examined Standard and Non-Standard forms of American speech, samples taken from both black and white speakers. They discovered that many of the characteristics often regarded as typical of Black English speech were also found in other Non-Standard American dialects and to their considerable amazement, even in a dialect spoken in Newfoundland![27] One of the more recent members of this group, Juanita Williamson, uses various examples both from literature and from "real life" to convince her readers that there is essentially no difference between black and white speech of a given geographical region.[28] Blacks will speak one way in one part of the country and another way in another part of the country, just as whites do. For Williamson, Black English is clearly a variety of English whose remaining African roots are shared by speakers of other Southern or Non-Standard dialects.

The other side of the debate, which at times becomes quite heated, is represented by linguists who consider themselves the direct descendants of Herskovits and Turner. These linguists call themselves "creolists," although neither of their mentors, neither Herskovits nor Turner, ever articulated a clear creolist argument for the development of contemporary Black English. The creolists, of whom William A. Stewart and J. L. Dillard are probably the most outspoken,[29] frequently attack the positions taken by the dialect geographers.

In order to validate their linguistic findings, the creolists not only familiarized themselves with the original languages the slaves spoke, but also hypothesized about the ways in which the original languages were changed and modified as the slaves moved away from the cultural and linguistic sphere of African influence and into an American sphere. The creolists claimed that Black English must be regarded as a language separate from American English; it has a separate history and was subject to a different pattern of development. They specified four stages through which the language passed:

1. Native African language
2. Contact with English > pidgin
3. Pidgin > creole
4. Decreolization

Although the stages hypothesized occurred chronologically, it is impossible to assign specific dates for the conclusion of one stage and the beginning of the next. Language is a curious and mysterious phenomenon. Changes take place almost imperceptibly. But in most cases it is very difficult to attribute a specific linguistic change to a specific occurrence. It is impossible, then, to determine exactly at what point the change from the pidgin to the creole occurred, or when the process of decreolization began. Certainly the stages overlap to some extent. The discussion that follows, then, is not tied to specific dates, although, whenever possible, it does attempt to correlate historical events with linguistic change.

As long as the slaves remained in Africa, one can assume that they were proficient in the language of their community. Those who remained within the confines of the linguistic community probably spoke either a "pure" version of the language or a variety that was least affected by any outside influences. But those who did business with Africans from other language groups, or with Portuguese or other foreign traders, inevitably felt the necessity for communicating in a common language. The "common language" that resulted was called a pidgin—a language that combined and simplified two or more different languages when they came in contact with one another.

A pidgin has a number of distinctive features. First of all, the forms of expression are greatly simplified. One can assume that the original purpose of the speakers is to conduct business or to give or receive orders, and not to express intimate emotions or to proliferate a literature. Simplicity of expression is mandatory. Therefore only the most necessary grammatical indicators are preserved. The vocabulary is a mixture of the languages involved.

At first the pidgin that the creolists hypothesize as the ancestor of Black English probably had a Portuguese base, since a Portuguese pidgin was the most widely used trading language along the West African coast from the mid-fifteenth century to the end of the sixteenth. Then, during the seventeenth century, as the English began to replace the Portuguese as the dominant traders, English words began to infiltrate the Portuguese pidgin. Thus, during the seventeenth and eighteenth centuries, the most extensive period of slave exportation from Africa to the New World, communication between the Africans and the Europeans in a pidgin language with a Portuguese-English-multiple-West-African language base seems probable.[30]

Since there were so many languages spoken along the west coast of Africa, it is impossible to isolate a single language as the primary African source for the pidgin that was eventually imported to the New World.[31]

However, despite this linguistic multiplicity, the West African languages tended to share many structural features of grammar and syntax, even though their vocabularies were quite different. The structural similarities, then, simplified the problem for the Africans of acquiring another language—in this case, English. They could retain much of their native grammar and syntax and impose upon that basic structure the vocabulary of English.

As long as the Africans remained in Africa and dealt with English speakers in a business relationship, the pidgin probably reflected a balance of sorts between the languages. But once the Africans were put on the slave ships and were under the domination of an English-speaking crew and thereafter of English-speaking slave owners and overseers, the English influence on their speech became increasingly more dominant. Furthermore, because the slaves from different parts of western Africa, who spoke a myriad of different languages, were all mixed together, there were presumably only a few people for an individual slave to talk to in his native tongue. In order to communicate he was virtually forced to speak a pidgin. Very soon one pidgin—with an English component—became the *lingua franca,* the common language, of the slave community.

The theory that the pidgin from which Black English was descended was derived from a trading language is the most widespread of the theories of origin. But two others, perhaps in combination with the trading-language theory, have also been suggested. One is that the pidgin originated as a native African language in homes of mixed marriages—between European males and African women—while the blacks were still in Africa. The third theory proposes that when two languages come in contact with one another, the characteristics that survive are those which offer a compromise between the deep structural characteristics and the surface structures of the two contact languages.[32]

Whatever the assumed source of the pidgin that preceded Black English, "the age of the pidgin" probably lasted until the slaves were well established on plantations in the New World. This language, as it was heard in America, has been described by a number of travelers, literate slaves, and plantation owners. Frederick Douglass, for instance, who was born a slave around 1817 in Maryland, describes the language of slaves on an isolated Eastern Shore plantation where he spent his youth.

> There is not, probably in the whole South, a plantation where the English language is more imperfectly spoken than on Col. Lloyd's. It is a mixture of Guinea and everything else you please . . . there were slaves there who had been brought from the coast of Africa. They never used the "s" in indication of the possessive case. "Capn Ant'ney Tom," "Lloyd Bill," "Aunt Rose Harry" means "Captain Anthony's Tom," "Lloyd's Bill," etc. *"Oo you dem long to?"* means "Whom do you belong to?" *"Oo dem got any peachy,"* means, "Have you got any peaches?" I could scarcely understand them, so broken was their speech.[33]

The language Douglass characterizes here is almost certainly an example of what linguists would call a pidgin—spoken by slaves who had been directly imported from Africa. John W. Blassingame attempts to establish the terminal date for the use of what he calls the "African-English patois," probably equivalent to the "pidgin" Douglass describes:

> In most areas of the South traces of African languages disappeared after two or three generations. As long as fresh Africans were imported during the eighteenth century, however, some African linguistic patterns were retained by blacks even when they spoke English. The end of the African slave trade in the last quarter of the eighteenth and early years of the nineteenth centuries ended the African-English patois in the quarters—and after 1830 in most places.[34]

After the first generation of slaves had died off and importation of slaves direct from Africa was stopped, there was very little opportunity for renewed African influence, either of a cultural or of a linguistic nature. The language these descendants of the original slaves spoke was no longer a second language but rather the language they knew best; it had become their "first language." At this point, in linguistic terms, the language was no longer a pidgin; it had become "creolized."

A pidgin can be distinguished linguistically from a creole by the function each type of language serves. A pidgin, a simplified form of expression created by two people or groups of people whose native languages are mutually unintelligible, generally has a simplified syntax in which word order is rigid and redundancy is reduced. A pidgin often lacks passive constructions and reversed-order questions. And because of the reduction of complexity, it lacks ways to express connotative information and ways to provide for stylistic variations and individual expression. When a pidgin-speaking people reach a point in their acculturation at which they wish to express more than the simplified expressions required for basic survival, or when they wish to express more subjective, abstract, philosophical, or literary ideas, they will presumably expand the capacity of the language so that it can adapt itself to their needs. The vocabulary will increase and the grammatical formulas for expression of certain ideas will be expanded. At this point, when the speakers consider the language satisfactory for expressing their needs, they will find increasingly little use for their original first language and will thus replace it with the more versatile, by now creolized pidgin. Now their first language is a creole.

A creole language, then, is a more regularized, systematic language than a pidgin; it is a language that develops from a pidgin, but is used as the first language of the speakers in a particular area. It may continue to expand its vocabulary as the result of contact with the dominant language, in this case, English, but it will also be significantly different, largely in structural features, from the dominant language.

Specifically, creole languages tend to have a number of characteristics that can be considered simplified when they are set beside similar modes of expression in the dominant language. Usually, for instance, a creole language has very few inflections. Furthermore, in the grammatical context, there may be no endings to indicate plurality, case, gender, tense, mood, or aspect. Instead, the creole may add a separate word that will indicate plurality or identify the tense used, if that is absolutely necessary. Often, too, the copula or helping verb *to be* is omitted, as in *him good.* In the area of phonology, creole speakers tend to avoid consonant clusters and to favor consonant-vowel-consonant patterns. In a word like *desk,* for instance, the creole speaker will very likely reduce the final consonant cluster and pronounce the word as if it were spelled *des.*[35]

Linguists accepting the creolist hypothesis conjecture that Black English in its creole stage probably possessed a number of features similar to other creole languages. However, given the relative isolation of blacks in this country—geographically, socially, and vocationally—it is difficult to imagine, as Dillard does, that the same type of English-based creole could be found throughout the country. Certainly it must have been extremely difficult to identify a "Standard American Creole." The relationship between Standard English and Black English can perhaps best be illustrated by imagining a continuum, with the West African languages on one end and English on the other. Along the continuum speakers of the creole—those most isolated from English influence and undoubtedly preserving more African speech forms—would be placed closer to the "African end," and those more closely associated with English speakers and preserving more recognizable English forms in their speech, would be placed closer to the "English end." Undoubtedly, as the years pass and as Black English speakers continue to be exposed to English influence, more and more will move toward the English end of the scale. As the English influence on the creole speakers continues, one can assume a continual process of "decreolization," for the speakers will gradually, but inevitably, adopt a language more and more similar to that of the dominant language group.

According to the creolists, decreolization, the final stage in the development of contemporary Black English, is a process that is still going on. Decreolization can be said to occur when a creole language remains in contact with only one of the languages that has helped to create it.[36] As a result of this increasing and overwhelming influence, the creole will gradually begin to resemble this original language, which also presumably has a higher prestige than the creole. In the case of the development of Black English, contact between Black English creole speakers and Standard English speakers has increased over the years. Since English has been (at least until very recently) the language of greater prestige, the creole tends to assume gradually the features of Standard English. But the creole speakers also hold onto the grammatical structures that are the most ingrained and those for which the rules of application are easier than in Standard English.

The regularization of the third person singular present tense of the verb, so that the final -*s* of the Standard English form *(he walks)* is omitted *(he walk)* and thereby made to conform to the rest of the present-tense conjugation, is but one obvious example.

As its speakers continue to have contact with Standard English, the distinctive features of the creolized Black English dialect will presumably continue to disappear. The process of decreolization of Black English, then, is far from completed. And indeed, it will only be completed if and when Black English disappears and Black English speakers adopt the Standard English speech to which they are constantly being exposed.

Specifically, then, the creolists assume that Black English developed as a result of the pidginization-creolization-decreolization process. They believe it is possible to trace the roots of the present Black English dialect, that of speakers in the northern cities as well as of speakers in the rural South, back, through Gullah, and through various pidgins, to Africa.

Thus the existence of Gullah is very important to the creolists' position. J. L. Dillard, for instance, believes that all contemporary black American dialects are "related historically to Gullah."[37] Despite the diversity of the routes the slaves followed in coming to America, whether they came directly from Africa or stopped for varying periods of time in the West Indies; despite the differences between their times of arrival in America, whether it be some time in the sixteenth, seventeenth, eighteenth, or nineteenth centuries; despite the differences in the terms of their employ, whether they were originally field hands or house servants, Dillard asserts that the speech forms of all American blacks can still be traced through Gullah back to West Africa. Dillard's position is difficult to prove. He attempts to do so, however, by analyzing the vocabulary and syntax of Black English as it is recorded in early literary texts. Although he makes a good case for his hypothesis, the records are very sparse and it is necessary for him (and for his followers) to make a very long leap from the evidence concerning Gullah that has been tabulated to the speech of blacks from different parts of the country. The study of Gullah, then, for the creolists, represents a microcosm of the study of Black American English. But as yet there has not been adequate proof that the same linguistic influences that affected Gullah, the language of an isolated and largely homogeneous racial and speech community, also affected the speech of those blacks who were settled in various areas of the mainland and many of whom eventually moved to the northern cities.

Despite the fact that in stating his creolist position Dillard has strongly opposed the English-origin supporters, he has entitled his own book *Black English,* a title that, perhaps somewhat ironically, calls attention to the English origins of the dialect. The inconsistency is disturbing, but it may also point out that Dillard's true position is not so extreme as he sometimes states it.

Interestingly enough, in one of his most recent publications, Dillard seems to have modified his position somewhat. He warns the creolists against making the same mistake the Anglicists made by attempting to determine specific Anglican sources for Black English speech characteristics. Likewise, says Dillard, the creolists must not attempt to isolate "too direct influence from Africa." He continues, "Seldom is it possible to trace a feature to Africa, especially to a given area or tribe, with any confidence."[38]

The creolists' theory is attractive for political and educational reasons, for if it could be proved that current Black English was a direct descendant of African—as opposed to English-speaking—ancestors, American blacks would have a linguistic basis for their sense of racial pride. Moreover, if schoolteachers were aware that the derivation of Black English was different from the derivation of Standard American English, they would have to approach the teaching of English differently from the traditional way—which too often assumes that Black English dialect is a deficient form of Standard English.[39]

Where has this discussion of the controversy concerning the origins of Black English led? In the light of recent scholarship, the pure Anglicist position has been abandoned, and neither the dialect geographers nor the creolists can offer an airtight argument to support their positions. Perhaps neither position can ever be proved. But no matter which hypothesis one finds most convincing, one can certainly be cognizant of African remnants in sentence structure (see chapter 2) and in vocabulary *(tote* ["carry"], *okra, yam, banana, cooter* ["turtle"], *jazz, banjo, juke, jive, jam, boogie, rap, dig)*.

Basically, the question that remains is whether Black English as spoken by black Americans is an ordinary dialect of English, not directly related to Gullah, or whether it should be regarded as a creole, like Gullah. Robbins Burling, in his intelligent, well-balanced book *English in Black and White,* has suggested one of the more sensible resolutions to the dilemma, and perhaps the only resolution possible considering the present state of the research. Burling posits the idea of a continuum ranging from Non-Standard to Standard English, along which all American dialects can be placed (at least approximately). Along the scale different levels of Black English, ranging from Non-Standard to Standard, would appear beside different levels of white English, ranging from Non-Standard to Standard. Many similarities between the white and black dialects would be evident along with the differences. But certainly the features would overlap and a number of transitional dialects could be identified. Such a continuum would clearly indicate that Black English does not have an identity separate from the English of white speakers. As Burling says, "Once we recognize all these transitional dialects, we can insist upon a sharp separation between black and white English only by indulging in a certain amount of romantic exaggeration."[40] When we eliminate the romance, we can say that today blacks and whites in

America speak the same basic language, English. If so, then there must be English roots to contemporary Black English speech. The unanswerable question is when and how the English influence exerted itself.

But in Black English it is obvious that English roots exist side by side with African roots. Characteristics of Black English as spoken in the urban ghettos can also be traced to the speech of blacks living in the Sea Islands and even in Jamaica. And these points of pronunciation and grammar Burling proceeds to enumerate.[41] To confuse the issue even more, linguists on both sides of the controversy claim that characteristics of Black English such as multiple negation ("I ain't gonna work no more Sundays") and the use of double modals ("I may could go"), are common, both to early British English and to African languages. It is impossible to make a clear choice between linguistic origins to be found on opposite sides of the world. Burling summarizes the situation succinctly:

> Black English is too much like other English dialects to be simply dismissed as a Creole, but at the same time it is too much like the Creoles to be dismissed as a mere dialect. We do not, however, really have to insist that it is only one and not the other. Some elements of creolization have probably gone into the formation of all black dialects, but standard English and other forms of non-Creolized English have had long, persistent influence upon black speech as well. We can see creolization as one influence in the formation of American English dialects, but it is an influence overlaid with a long period of mutual borrowing among all our dialects.[42]

Although to some readers Burling may appear to have perched himself on the dialectal fence, at the present time and given the present state of research, this seems to be the sensible place to be. After more research in the field is completed, he and others like him may descend on one side of the fence or the other. At the moment, however, that is probably not very wise.

NOTES

1. Alex Haley, *Roots* (New York: Doubleday, 1976).

2. *Standard English* is another difficult term for linguists to define, since language that is regarded as "standard" varies to some extent with the region of the country. Certainly, New England Standard is different from Southern or Midwestern Standard English in vocabulary and phonology, although in grammar, educated American dialects are in basic agreement. For the purposes of this book I shall define Standard American English, admittedly rather vaguely, as the variety of English taught in American schools, and spoken and written by educated Americans.

3. During the 1960s the word *dialect,* when applied to the speech of black people, acquired in the minds of a number of black people pejorative connotations of weakness and inferiority in connection with black speech. One who speaks a dialect, Black English speakers feared, was in danger of being controlled politically as well as culturally by those who speak the standard

language. In the more open atmosphere of the late 1970s, and certainly in the context of this book, the word is used descriptively and not judgmentally.

4. The phrase was coined by William Labov in *Language in the Inner City: Studies in the Black English Vernacular* (Philadelphia: University of Pennsylvania Press, 1972).

5. See Joan Fickett, *Aspects of Morphemics, Syntax, and Semology of an Inner-City Dialect (Merican)* (New York: Meadowood Publishers, 1972).

6. See Robert D. Twiggs, *Pan-African Language in the Western Hemisphere* (North Quincy, Mass.: The Christopher Publishing House, 1973).

7. See Robert Williams, *Ebonics: The True Language of Black Folks* (St. Louis: The Institute of Black Studies, 1975).

8. In his widely distributed book *Black English* (New York: Random House, 1973), J. L. Dillard brought the term to the American public.

9. Guy B. Johnson, "St. Helena Songs and Stories," in *Black Yeomanry,* ed. T. J. Woofter, Jr. (New York: Henry Holt, 1930), p. 49.

10. John Bennett, "Gullah: A Negro Patois," *South Atlantic Quarterly* 7 (1908): 339. Part 1 appears on pp. 332–47, part 2 in 8 (1909): 39–52.

11. Ambrose Gonzales, *The Black Border* (Columbia, S.C.: The State College, 1922), p. 17.

12. George Philip Krapp, "The English of the Negro," *American Mercury* 2 (June 1924): 190.

13. Ibid.

14. Reed Smith, *Gullah* (Columbia, S.C.: Bureau of Publications, University of South Carolina, 1926), Foreword.

15. Ibid.

16. Ibid., p. 22

17. Cleanth Brooks, *The Relation of the Alabama-Georgia Dialect to the Provincial Dialects of Great Britain* (Baton Rouge: Louisiana State University Press, 1935).

18. Mason Crum, *Gullah* (Durham, N.C.: Duke University Press, 1940), p. x.

19. Ibid., p. 101.

20. Ibid., p. 111.

21. Melville J. Herskovits, *The Myth of the Negro Past* (New York: Harper and Brothers, 1941), p. 279.

22. Turner consulted Elizabeth Donnan, *Documents Illustrative of the History of the Slave Trade to America* (1935), vol. 4; W. E. Burghardt DuBois, *The Suppression of the African Slave Trade to the United States of America* (1896); and Frederic Bancroft, *Slave-trading in the Old South* (1931).

23. Lorenzo Dow Turner, *Africanisms in the Gullah Dialect* (Ann Arbor: University of Michigan Press, 1949, 1973), p. 1.

24. Ibid., p. 2.

25. David Ramsey, *History of South Carolina, from Its First Settlement in 1670 to the year 1808, 2 vols. (Newberry, S.C. 1858).* Quoted in Crum, *Gullah,* p. 116.

26. Turner, *Africanisms,* p. 5.

27. Raven I. McDavid, Jr., "New Directions in American Dialectology," *Studia Anglica, Poznaniensia* 5 (1973): 9–25.

28. Juanita V. Williamson, "Selected Features of Speech: Black and White," in *A Various Language,* ed. Juanita V. Williamson and Virginia M. Burke (New York: Holt, Rinehart and Winston, 1971), pp. 496–507.

29. Others, such as Robert A. Hall, Jr., in *Pidgin and Creole Languages* (Ithaca: Cornell University Press, 1966); Dell Hymes, in *Pidginization and Creolization of Languages* (Cambridge: Cambridge University Press, 1971); and recently, Derek Bickerton, in *Dynamics of a Creole System* (Cambridge: Cambridge University Press, 1975), have done basic theoretical research.

30. David Dalby, "Black Through White: Patterns of Communication in Africa and the New World," in *Black-White Speech Relationships,* ed. Walt Wolfram and Nona H. Clarke (Washington, D.C.: Center for Applied Linguistics, 1971), pp. 99–138.

31. Much of the discussion of pidginization and creolization is derived from Lorenzo Todd, *Pidgins and Creoles* (London: Routledge and Kegan Paul, 1974).

32. Derek Bickerton, "Priorities in Creole Studies," in David De Camp and Ian F. Hancock, *Pidgins and Creoles: Current Trends and Prospects* (Washington, D.C.: Georgetown, 1974).

33. Frederick Douglass, *My Bondage and My Freedom* (New York: Miller, Orton, and Mulligan, 1853), pp. 76–77.

34. John W. Blassingame, *The Slave Community* (New York: Oxford University Press, 1972), p. 24.

35. Ralph W. Fasold, "Decreolization and Autonomous Language Change," *Florida Foreign Language Reporter* 10 (1972): 9–12, 51.

36. Ibid. In this article, Fasold itemizes seven specific stages of decreolization.

37. J. L. Dillard, *Black English* (New York: Random House, 1973), p. 26.

38. J. L. Dillard, *Black Names* (The Hague: Mouton, 1976), p. 10.

39. The decision in *Martin Luther King Junior Elementary School Children* v. *Ann Arbor School District Board* may help to correct this situation. *United States Law Week* (U.S.L.W.) 48 (July 24, 1979): 2058, reports that

this case is not an effort to require that these black elementary school students be taught "black English," that their instruction throughout their schooling be in "black English," or that a dual language program be provided. Rather, it is an effort to require the court to intervene on the children's behalf to require that the school board take appropriate action to teach them to read in standard English. The claim is founded upon 20 U.S.C.§1703(f), which states "no state shall deny equal educational opportunity to any individual on account of . . . race . . . by the failure of an educational agency to take appropriate action to overcome language barriers that impede equal participation by its students in its instructional programs."

40. Robbins Burling, *English in Black and White* (New York: Holt, Rinehart, and Winston, 1973), p. 115.

41. Ibid. See pp. 116–20.

42. Ibid., p. 121.

2
Black English: Linguists and Speakers Today

ALMOST every aspect of Black English—whether its historical origins, its distinctive linguistic features, or its significance as a literary language—is a potential source of heated controversy. Much of the controversy, which directly concerns both the public image of black people in America and how black people see themselves, often assumes political overtones. Certainly the dispute concerning whether English or creole origins underlie Black English was well heated. And the following discussions of the sociolinguistic origins of the speakers of Black English and of the logical nature of the dialect as well as a description of the distinctive linguistic characteristics of the dialect black people speak, are equally warm.

During the 1960s the sociolinguistic study of Black English and its speakers became big business. The major purpose of these studies was twofold: to describe the actual linguistic features of the dialect spoken by black people and to identify the sociological background of the speakers themselves. New York City, Detroit, and Washington, D.C., three cities with concentrated black populations, were the locations for these studies. William Labov worked in New York City, particularly in Harlem; Roger Shuy, Walter Wolfram, and William Riley worked in Detroit; and Ralph Fasold worked in Washington, D.C. Some of the linguists made a conscious effort to present a broad picture of the speech of a large, densely populated city and to place Black English speech within that context. Others examined the speech heard in inner city ghettos, and described it in isolation from the larger speech community.

In his first book, *The Social Stratification of English in New York City* (1966), William Labov attempted to identify and isolate the linguistic characteristics of the speech of individual New Yorkers. By doing so, he hoped to clarify the relationships among the dialects to be found in the complex speech community of a large city. As he says,

> The work which is reported in this study is an investigation of language within the social context of the community in which it is spoken. It is a study of a linguistic structure which is unusually complex, but no more so than the social structure of the city in which it functions. Within the linguistic structure, change has occurred on a large scale, and at a rapid pace which is even more characteristic of the changing structure of the city itself. Variability is an integral part of the linguistic system, and no less a part of the behavior of the city.[1]

In this study the Black English speaker is but one of the New Yorkers represented; instead of being studied in isolation from the larger speech community, his speech is placed within the context of the city as a whole.

The first study of Detroit speech undertaken by Roger W. Shuy, Walter A. Wolfram, and William K. Riley in 1968, *Field Techniques in an Urban Language Study,*was similar to Labov's first study, in that it also examined the speech of a cross-section of speakers, including Black English speakers, of a single city. In their study the authors stated that their purpose was "to contrast the speech of the so-called 'disadvantaged' with that of the more socio-economically successful."[2] In the study approximately 700 Detroit residents of four major age groups were randomly selected and interviewed. Each was given a questionnaire that elicited three types of speech: conversation, short answers to questions, and oral reading style. In addition the interviewers compiled background information about each speaker that would enable them to correlate speech characteristics with sociological identity. As in Labov's work with New York City speech, Black English was but one of the Detroit dialects analyzed.

For both Labov and Wolfram, their first books, descriptions of the dialects of a variety of speakers in a single city, served as the foundation for later studies of a more specific nature—the full description of the Black English dialect within their chosen city. In his study *A Sociolinguistic Description of Detroit Negro Speech* (1968), Wolfram's intention was to examine the speech characteristics of Black English speakers from a variety of socioeconomic backgrounds in Detroit and to determine the relationships among the various speech levels. As he says,

> To determine if speech is an indicator of social status in the Negro community it is necessary to study the speech of Negroes from several different socio-economic levels. A realistic approach to the speech of Negroes cannot be satisfied with describing one restricted subset of that community. Also, in order to understand the role of linguistic behavior in social mobility it is necessary to determine how different linguistic variables correlate with certain social characteristics.[3]

In narrowing the subject to which he has devoted most of his professional life, Labov undertook two studies. In 1968 he and three colleagues produced a report for the Office of Education at the U.S. Department of

Health, Education, and Welfare entitled *A Study of the Non-Standard English of Negro and Puerto Rican Speakers in New York City*. The title, although ungainly, is self-explanatory, and the study was clearly preliminary to Labov's next book, *Language in the Inner City* (1972), in which he concentrated his linguistic investigation on the speech of black adolescents in South Central Harlem. He labels the speech of these informants "Black English Vernacular," and defines it as "that relatively uniform grammar found in its most consistent form in the speech of black youth from 8 to 19 years old who participate fully in the street culture of the inner cities."[4] The vernacular speech Labov investigated in New York City is typical, he says, of the speech of black youth in all cosmopolitan cities of America, whether they be in the West, the East, the North, or the South.[5]

The narrowest study of all, entitled *Tense Marking in Black English* (1972), was undertaken by Ralph Fasold in Washington, D.C. As the title of his study indicates, Fasold focused his research on a single aspect of the Black English use of the verb. Fasold thoroughly analyzed the Black English use of past and present tenses and distributive *be*. He also discussed the relationship between grammatical and phonological variation and the relevance of sociological factors, such as the social class, age, and sex of the person interviewed, to the linguistic material. The study, detailed and comprehensive, in general supports the earlier conclusions of Labov and Wolfram.

The intention behind all these linguistic descriptions of Black English has been to disprove the notion that Black English is a result of an illogical, unsystematic, almost random, even careless attempt on the part of its speakers to approximate the structured patterns of Standard English. Such a notion has served as justification for a number of theories—the cultural deprivation or deficit theory and the genetic inferiority theory in particular—that in some way suggest black linguistic inferiority. The first theory assumes black culture to be "deficient" and the second, more insidiously, regards black people themselves as genetically inferior to whites. Supporters of these theories thus explain black people's difficulty in mastering Standard English as the consequence of their genetic makeup and cultural environment. These explanations are, of course, unacceptable, not only to black people but also to most modern linguists, trained as they are in the assumptions of the cultural relativism of the last hundred years.

Labov's research in South Central Harlem, which found black culture verbally sophisticated and the children of the area remarkably capable of verbal communication, has, at the cost of romanticizing ghetto speech, helped to overturn the deprivation myths. As Labov says in his most significant article, "The Logic of Nonstandard English":

> We see a child bathed in verbal stimulation from morning to night. We
> see many speech events which depend upon the competitive exhibition

of verbal skills: sounding, singing, toasts, rifting, louding—a whole range of activities in which the individual gains status through his use of language. We see the younger child trying to acquire these skills from older children—hanging around on the outskirts of the older peer groups, and imitating this behavior to the best of his ability. We see no connection between verbal skill at the speech events characteristic of the street culture and success in the schoolroom.[6]

Not only did Labov find the street culture linguistically sophisticated, he also found that the variation of English spoken by the native Harlemites was as structured as Standard English. The variations by which the speech patterns differed from Standard English were far from random utterances; they followed standard rules. Labov's research indicated that the majority of all verbal utterances were complete sentences, and, contrary to public opinion, working-class speakers used more complete sentences than middle-class speakers.

The proportions of grammatical sentences vary with class backgrounds and styles. The highest percentage of well-formed sentences are found in casual speech, and working-class speakers use more well-formed sentences than middle-class speakers. The widespread myth that most speech is ungrammatical is no doubt based upon tapes made at learned conferences, where we obtain the maximum number of irreducibly ungrammatical sequences.[7]

Labov also stated his belief that much Standard English, which at its best is direct and forthright, is all too often full of empty verbiage, of "I think" and of passive voice, of vague and abstract jargon and fillers. For Labov, however, Black English is direct and meaningful more frequently than is Standard English. In many cases its speakers have simplified Standard English diction and are often able to make their points more vividly than Standard English speakers can. At the same time, Labov states emphatically that Black English is a precisely definable language system.

All linguists agree that nonstandard dialects are highly structured systems; they do not see these dialects as accumulations of errors caused by the failure of their speakers to master standard English. When linguists hear Negro children saying *He crazy* or *Her my friend* they do not hear a "primitive language." Nor do they believe that the speech of working-class people is merely a form of emotional expression, incapable of expressing logical thought.

All linguists who work with nonstandard Negro English recognized that it is a separate system, closely related to standard English, but set apart from the surrounding white dialects by a number of persistent and systematic differences.[8]

Perhaps Labov is a bit imperious when he ascribes his ideas to *all* linguists. It would be difficult, if not impossible, for *all* linguists to agree about a subject as controversial as language structure. But certainly the majority of linguists who have written about Black English in the last few years would agree with Labov that Black English is a structured system that differs from Standard English in discernible ways.

Those who do not accept the idea that Black English is a "separate system, closely related to Standard English, but set apart from the surrounding white dialects by a number of persistent and systematic differences" are primarily those closely associated with the compilation of the *Linguistic Atlas of the United States,* which describes and defines American speech according to regional dialects. These dialectologists have generally taken the position that Black English and white English are similar within a particular geographical region. They do not accept any single characterization of Black English that ignores the geographical location or regional origin of the speaker; for them, Black English as a single dialect simply does not exist.

The leading spokesman of the dialectologists is Raven McDavid, whose views on the creolization question have already been discussed. McDavid states his point of view succinctly:

> With our current knowledge it is safest to assume that in general the range of variants is the same in Negro and in white speech, though the statistical distribution of variants has been skewed by the American caste system.[9]

The one exception McDavid makes is Gullah, which he considers an anomaly, and which he cannot fit into any logical system. McDavid coolly rejects Labov's insistence that Black English is a dialect that transcends region and to some extent social class; instead, he asserts that region is the dominant characteristic that determines dialect.

McDavid adamantly disapproves of any discussion that treats the speech of black people apart from the context of their geographical area and social class. For him the speech characteristics of a black speaker from Charleston, South Carolina, are influenced by speakers of other ethnic and class origins in Charleston; as a result, his speech is distinguishable from the speech of a black speaker from Chicago or San Francisco.

Juanita V. Williamson, who has written several articles comparing the speech characteristics of blacks with those of whites from the same region and social class, agrees with McDavid's assertion that there are no significant differences.[10] In one article she examines the distinctive characteristics of the speech of one black character from a novel and one white author of an article. She compares the speech of Dude, the black narrator in Warren Miller's *The Cool World* (1959) with that of Paul Valentine, a klansman and author of an article, "Look Out Liberals: Wallace Power Gonna Get You."[11] Williamson concludes that the speech of both characters is similar and that both characters' speech reflects the characteristics of regional southern speech, not their racial identity. The problem with Williamson's examples is that they are literary, not transcriptions of actual speech, and are therefore subject to idiosyncrasies of style and representation by their respective authors. Since Williamson does not distinguish between speech transcribed and that imagined for literary purposes, her attempt to draw conclusions concerning the authenticity of represented speech is not convincing.

Labov, Dillard, Fasold, Wolfram, and many other linguists strongly disagree with the position of the dialectologists. For them Black English is a variety of American English that differs from Standard English according to the phonological, grammatical, and rhetorical characteristics to be discussed in the latter part of this chapter. For them Black English, unlike other American dialects that clearly reflect regional distinctions, cuts through regional idiosyncrasies. Labov, it is clear, believes that black adolescents from Harlem speak the same way as black adolescents in any large American city.[12] But they speak quite differently from white adolescents of a similar age and class. J. L. Dillard claims that eighty percent of the black population of the United States speaks Black English[13] and that social factors are more important than racial or geographic ones in determining dialect patterns.

According to the "Labov School," a working-class black from Detroit or Chicago will probably speak very much like a working-class black from Macon, Georgia, or Asheville, North Carolina. But his speech will differ in some respects from that of the white speakers of his native region. One reason for relative uniformity in the speech of blacks with similar social backgrounds and different geographical origins is that many of the working-class blacks living in the North maintain connections with their southern relatives. In the North they live in communities with others from similar southern backgrounds and have little contact with people from other regions or ethnic origins. Their isolation, for better or worse, has helped them preserve the linguistic patterns of their southern speech. Despite the extreme positions that recent linguists have assumed on this subject, the importance of regional and class distinctions among Black English speakers is still largely undetermined.

Perhaps as a result of historical dialectal changes, in linguistic circles today the position of the dialectologists is weakening. Although it is possible to identify in other nonstandard American English dialects many of the linguistic characteristics considered inherent in Black English, the combination of Black English linguistic features would be difficult to find in any other than Black American speech. Certain features, such as the use of *be* and the deletion of the helping verb (zero copula), are very rare outside of Black English. Thus the *combination* of features, and the frequency with which these features are used, distinguish Black English from other American English dialects.

Both the dialectologists and the Labov School linguists are, of course, discussing the reality (or realities) of the speech of black Americans in their own time—in America of the 1960s and 1970s. But this study will be focused on another American culture, not real but fictional, and of different times and places. It will be concerned, not with *description* of Black English speech by linguists, but with the *representation* of it by imaginative writers. Literary examples selected from nineteenth-century American fiction will clearly illustrate that regional differences in the representation of Black English speech are very apparent. Perhaps this is the result of the fact that the writers recognized these differences more clearly in a more provincialized America and before a majority of black Americans, having migrated to northern cities during two world wars, shared a more unified culture. Perhaps the recorded regionalisms are also the result of a keener sensitivity to regionalisms, linguistic and otherwise, on the part of more "local color" oriented writers. Yet, although the dialects represented by American writers have varied from region to region and over time, it is undeniable that their undertaking has consistently been to represent a variety of speech that they perceived as in some way "special" because it was spoken by blacks. And since the linguists of today are attempting to describe the dialect that is that "special speech" in its present state of development, it may be useful to take a look at the "special speech" today, as described by the linguists, to see how it relates to and differs from what is usually identified as Standard English.

Actually, the relationship between Standard English and Black English is the relationship, in linguistic terms, between two dialects, or varieties, of English. In a linguistic sense a dialect is a variety of a language. Dialects can be of three types. They can be regional, identifying the speech of a geographical region of the country, as in New England, Southern, or Midwestern dialects. They can be social, identifying the social class of the speaker, as in white working-class or upper-class educated dialect. Or they can identify the ethnic origin of a speaker, as with Black English or Chinese-American or Italian-American dialect. Actually, Black English can be used in any one, or a combination, of these three ways. Standard English, on the other hand, is a variety of English that is spoken in formal and business contexts and is the usual written medium for expository prose and for literature that does not use regional or social or ethnic dialects.

In order to understand how the Black English dialect differs from that of Standard English, it is necessary to examine distinguishing characteristics. The discussion that follows, then, assumes that there is a logical pattern controlling the use of pronunciation and grammatical features in Black English; as Black English differs from Standard English, it does so according to a systematic and predictable pattern. It should be remembered, however, that no Black English speaker uses all of the characteristics identified all of the time. Situation and context will always determine the extent of the use of Black English linguistic features.

Ralph W. Fasold and Walter A. Wolfram, the authors of the definitive article identifying the linguistic features of Black English, "Some Linguistic Features of Negro Dialect,"[14] divide their description of Black English into two sections: pronunciation and grammar. It is very difficult to separate entirely these two aspects of language; they overlap in many ways. Hence, although pronunciation features will be described separately at the beginning, the discussion that follows will suggest how these characteristics influence related grammatical forms.[15]

PRONUNCIATION FEATURES OF BLACK ENGLISH
Reduction of Consonant Clusters

When two or more consonants end a word, Black English speakers, according to Fasold and Wolfram, will generally not pronounce the final consonant. Words such as *test, desk, hand,* or *cold,* in which the final consonant is pronounced in Standard English, are pronounced *tes', des', han',* and *col'* in Black English. But reduction also occurs in words that end in consonant clusters caused by the addition of a final *-ed* suffix. In Standard English the *-ed* suffix that forms the past tense of regular verbs can be pronounced either as *d* or as *t: moved* is pronounced *movd,* while *walked* is pronounced *walkt.* If the sounds in a final consonant cluster are either voiced* or voiceless,** then in Black English the final consonant in the consonant cluster will be lost in pronunciation: *moved* (*v* and *d* are both voiced) will be pronounced *mov'* (*Jerry mov' yesterday*) and *walked* (*k* and *t* are both voiceless) as *walk'* (*Jerry walk' home*). Reduction of the final consonant cluster will affect three different situations in which *-ed* is used: the past tense marker in the examples discussed above, the past participle (*The boy was scratch' by his brother*) and past participial adjectives (*She had a slash' finger*).

Pronunciation of -s in the formation of the plural

In Standard English the plural for nouns is formed by adding either *-s* or *-es* to the base noun. Although the spelling has regularly only these two variations, the pronunciation of the plural noun ending has several possibilities. First, if, in the singular, a word does not end in an *s*-like sound (*s, sh,* or *z*) *-s* is added; however, there are two possibilities for its pronunciation. After voiceless sounds it is pronounced as *s* (*pots*); after voiced sounds it is pronounced as *z* (*pans: panz*). Second, if the base word already ends in an *s*-sound, the plural suffix will be *-es.* Pronunciation will approximate *-iz: kiss > kisses (kissiz); grace > graces (graciz).* But there is a third possibility in Black English. According to Fasold and Wolfram, words that end in *-s +* *p, t,* or *k,* which in Standard English would form their plural by adding

---

*Voiced sounds occur when the pronunciation of all final consonants makes the vocal cords vibrate, as with *b, d, g, z.*

**Voiceless sounds occur when the pronunciation of all final consonants does not make the vocal cords vibrate, as with *t, p, k, s.*

simple -s, use the -es plural instead. Words like *wasp, test,* and *desk* lose their final consonants in pronunciation as a result of the final consonant cluster rule. We are then left with *was', tes',* and *des'.* To make these words plural, the black speaker will add the -es suffix, which in Standard English is normally used to form the plural for words that end in final -s. Thus the plural for such words in Black English is *wasses, tesses, desses.*

th

In Standard English, *th* has two pronunciations, either voiced as in *the* or unvoiced as in *think.* Fasold and Wolfram observe that in Black English, pronunciation of *th* depends upon its position within a particular word.

a. At the beginning of a word in which *th* is voiced, as in *the, they, that,* Black English speakers will pronounce *th* as *d: de, dey, dat.* In words beginning with unvoiced *th,* as in *think* and *thought,* Black English speakers may pronounce *th* as *t: tink* or *tought.* And third, if inital *th* is followed by *r,* as in *throat* or *three,* the Black English speaker may pronounce *th* as *f: froat* or *free.*

b. When voiceless *th* occurs in the middle of a word, it may be pronounced by Black English speakers as *f: nothing > nufin'.* Voiced *th* may be pronounced as *v* in some varieties of Black English: *brother > bruvah.*

Loss of r and l

According to Fasold and Wolfram, in Black English both *r* and *l* are pronounced when they occur at the beginning of a word. However, when they occur after a vowel (in postvocalic position), either between a vowel and a consonant, as in *help,* or between two vowels, as in *Carol,* or at the end of a word, as in *sister* and *toll, r* and *l* may disappear: *hep; Ca'ol; sistuh; toe.* The pragmatic result of the loss of *r* and *l* is the creation of a number of homophones not characteristic of other English speakers: *he(l)p: hep; Ca(r)ol: Cal; to(ll): toe; fo(ur): foe.*

Final d

In final position, Fasold and Wolfram observe, *d* may either be devoiced, so that it is pronounced as *t* in Black English, or be lost. Examples of devoicing include: *mud > mut; good > goot.* For some black speakers, the final *d* of *good* may be completely lost—either before a consonant *(goo' man)* or before a vowel *(goo' egg).* Final *d* can also be lost when it occurs as the *-ed* suffix on a verb whose stem ends with a long vowel: *played (Yesterday he play baseball).*

Nasalization

a. Fasold and Wolfram assert that in the pronunciation of the *-ing* suffix *(singing, raining),* the final [ŋ] of Standard English is reduced to [n] (singin', rainin'). Although this characteristic is associated with most nonstandard varieties of English, it occurs perhaps with more frequency in Black English and is a clearly accepted characteristic of Black English speech.

b. In final position [*n*] is often lost as a clearly pronounced sound and the vowel that precedes it is nasalized instead: *rum > rū; run > rū*. These words may thus be found as homophones in Black English.

Loss of initial unstressed syllable

When the first syllable of a word is unstressed, the Black English speaker may omit it altogether: *complain > plain; about > bout*.

Vowels

In some black speech, usually that found in the South or in the speech of blacks recently come North, vowels may be pronounced differently from Standard English. Words with vowel glides, as *like* or *my* may be pronounced without the glide, as in *lak* or *mah*. Back or mid-vowels may be pronounced as more fronted sounds: *get > git; again > agin*. Still other vowels may have a tendency to diphthongize, as in *caint* for *can't* or *laig* for *leg*.

Ask

One final pronunciation feature, according to Fasold and Wolfram, that can be widely observed as characteristic of Black English speech (although it also occurs in other nonstandard varieties of English) is the pronunciation of *ask*. Black English speakers often reverse the *-sk* pronunciation to *-ks* so that *ask (aks)* becomes homophonous with *axe*.

GRAMMATICAL FEATURES OF BLACK ENGLISH

In the discussion that follows it will be clear that it is frequently impossible to distinguish between the pronunciation and the grammatical features of Black English in a precise way; the two categories overlap in many situations. When a pronunciation rule applies in a grammatical context, it becomes a rule of grammar; more precisely, the pronunciation rule and the grammar rule operate concurrently.

THE VERB SYSTEM

According to Fasold and Wolfram, many of the most significant features of Black English can be found in the verb system.

Third person singular present tense

Instead of pronouncing (or writing) the final *-s* of the third person singular present tense verb of Standard English *(he walks)*, Black English speakers regularize it so that it conforms to the other forms in the Standard English present tense conjugation:

Standard English		Black English	
I walk	We walk	I walk	We walk
You walk	You walk	You walk	You walk
He, she, it walks	They walk	He, she, it walk	They walk

Some Black English speakers may also regularize the past tense, using *was*: *You was there; we was there; they was there.*

-ed *suffix to mark the past tense*

The frequent loss of *-ed* suffix in Black English illustrates clearly the confusion between pronunciation and grammar rules, for what has earlier been identified as a pronunciation rule explains the absence of many past tense and past participial *-ed* markers in spoken and written Black English. Final *-ed* on past tense regular verbs can be lost either because of the consonant cluster rule (which explains *missed > miss'*) or because of the *d*-deletion rule after a long vowel, as in *played > play*. Its loss can also be explained as a grammar rule.

Contraction (zero copula)

In cases in Standard English in which contraction of a "helping verb" (usually *to be* in present or future tenses or *to have*) can occur, Black English speakers often delete the helping verb or its contraction. The end result is a statement that seems to be missing a verb.

Standard English, Full Form	Contracted Form	Deleted[16]
You are in the store.	You're in the store.	You in the store.
He is going.	He's going.	He going.
We are hungry.	We're hungry.	We hungry.
He will be here tonight.	He'll be here tonight.	He be here tonight.
He would go.	He'd go.	He go.
He has gone home.	He's gone home.	He gone home.
They have walked seven miles.	They've walked seven miles.	They walk seven miles.*

Be

Although Black English speakers often use inflected forms of the verb *to be—am, is, are, was, were—*many of them also use uninflected *be* in a position for which a Standard English speaker would use an inflected form.

> Usually I be the one that have to go find everybody.
> Most of the problems always be wrong.
> Most of the time they be up on the playground.
> Sometimes we just be joking.
> When he turns it, one be going this way and the other one be going all around.[17]

Be, as used in these examples, is never used in Standard English. Robbins Burling explains its Black English use clearly:

*-ed marker of the past participle is lost because of the *d*-deletion rule.

be often implies a general state, or a habitual or intermittent action, rather than a single event. Thus *he be tired* might mean *he is tired often* or *he is tired most of the time,* while *he is tired* could suggest instead *he is tired right now.* This use of *be* provides a concise way to indicate a meaning that can be communicated only by several varied and larger constructions in standard English.[18]

NEGATION

Fasold and Wolfram observe that *ain't* occurs in Black English either as a substitute for *didn't (He ain't hit me)* or, as with other nonstandard English dialects, as a negative form of *is, are, am,* as well as of *have* and *has (He ain't going; She ain't got a button).*

But Black English has another type of negation that differs from Standard English: multiple negation. Ever since their elementary school grammar classes, children have been warned that "two negatives make a positive." The statement codifies an unnatural rule that has been imposed upon English grammar since the eighteenth century. Unfortunately, the rule is still alive and well. In Old English and in Middle English, however, and even in Shakespeare's time, two negatives or more served to *intensify* the negative quality of a sentence, not to delete it.[19] The schoolmarmish insistence that Standard English speakers use only one negative to a sentence reduces the forcefulness with which a Standard English speaker is able to make a negative statement. Fortunately for them, Black English speakers do not have this problem. Two, or even three, negatives to a sentence are permissible in Black English, although they must be used according to clearly defined rules.[20]

The Standard English sentence, *Nobody knows it* appears in Black English as *Nobody don't know it* or *Don't nobody know it;* both the subject-pronoun *(nobody)* and the helping verb *(don't)* are negativized (in addition, the subject and verb do not agree). Standard English *Nobody knows anything* occurs in Black English as *Nobody don't know nothing;* in this case both pronouns and the verbs are negativized (and again the subject and verb do not agree). In all negative statements, the Black English speaker will convert the *any, anything,* or *anyone* of Standard English into their negative equivalents *(none, nothing, nobody)* every time they occur. At the same time he will preserve the negative accompanying the verb: *He don't want none; He don't want nothing.* In other words, in Black English only the negative form of *any* can appear in a negative sentence. Furthermore, the verb in a negative sentence must always be negativized, even though the "any" pronouns already appear in negative form.

Black English also allows multiple negation in sentences in which *never* and *neither* are used: *She don't never go nowhere; He ain't going neither.*

NOUN AND PRONOUN ENDINGS (suffixes)

The omission of final *-s* either from the possessive or from plural nouns is another characteristic of Black English. In the possessive the omission can occur from either the nouns or proper nouns in which possession should be indicated: *the boy hat; Jack Johnson car; That Mary coat.*

Fasold and Wolfram note that occasionally the Black English speaker will also omit final *-s* from plural nouns *(She is five year old)*. And when selected nouns form their plurals irregularly, without adding final *-s (foot, feet; deer, deer; child, children)*, the Black English speaker will regularize the plural (actually forming a double plural) by adding final *-s: foot > feets; deer > deers; child > childrens*.

PRONOUNS

Pronominal apposition to the subject, or what is sometimes referred to as double subjects, is yet another feature of Black English: *My English teacher, she mean; My dog, he bark too much.* Black English speakers do not use this form exclusively, but rather alternate it with the simple subject-verb progression of Standard English: *My English teacher mean; My dog bark too much.*

Southern, more often than northern speakers, may not use the possessive pronoun in possessive position, but will use either the nominative or the objective form instead *(he shirt; me shirt)*.

Finally, the pronoun *it* in Black English is sometimes substituted for *there* at the beginning of a sentence: *It's a boy in my class name Robert* and *Isn't it a main street in this town?*

QUESTIONS

Although many Black English speakers compose questions the same way Standard English speakers do, by inverting the order of subject followed by verb in declarative sentences, others, instead of putting the verb before the subject in questions *(John threw the ball > Did John throw the ball?)*, ask the question without inverting the subject-verb word order. Fasold and Wolfram note that the Black English speaker would more likely ask, *John threw the ball?* Sometimes Black English speakers omit the verb auxiliary used to designate a question in Standard English. Compare Standard English: *Is he coming with us?* with Black English: *He coming with us?* in which the question signal, initial *is*, is omitted.

Although all of the speech characteristics described above are, according to Fasold and Wolfram, directly associated with the speech used by Black English speakers, not every Black English speaker will use all of the Black English speech characteristics all the time. He may well use a particular feature in one context and then, probably unconsciously, slip into the Standard English version in another context. This process can be observed in the wide range of examples of Black English speech representations from nineteenth- and twentieth-century American fiction in the next three chapters. In these examples the variety of literary effects possible will be made evident.

HYPERCORRECTION

Some speakers, particularly those in transition from a lower to a higher social status, and therefore increasingly conscious of the implications of their speech, have a tendency to use a phenomenon that Fasold and Wolfram call "hypercorrection." Hypercorrection occurs when a speaker caught between two language varieties, in this case Black English and Standard English, is aware that he is making an error according to the rules of Standard English, and then attempts to correct himself. He may, for instance, omit the final -*s* on the Standard English third person singular present tense form *(he walk)*. Then he will correct that form *(he walks)* and in the process will add final -*s* to some or all of the other present tense forms of that verb *(I walks, you walks, we walks, they walks)*. An interesting literary example of hypercorrection appears in Alice Walker's novel, *The Third Life of Grange Copeland*. In the following passage, Mem, a schoolteacher, gives a lesson in grammar to her future husband, Brownfield. Her eager student, certain he has learned his lesson well, happily repeats the hypercorrect form, "we haves a friendship."

> "In the first place," she would begin, in an intense prim way Lorene and Josie scoffed at, "if you have two or three words to say and don't know which word means two or more, it is better to just not use 's' on the end of any of the words. This is so because the verb takes on the same number as the subject. You understand? Well, all I'm saying is 'I *have* some cake,' *sounds* better than 'I *haves* some cake.' Or, 'We have a friendship,' is better than 'We *haves* a friendship.' Now is that clear?" And she would look at him, properly doubtful, wrinkling her brow. And he would nod, yes, and say over and over happily in his mind, We haves a friendship! *We,* Mem and me, haves us a friendship! and he would smile so that she would stop her frowning and smile too.[21]

LEXICAL FEATURES OF BLACK ENGLISH

In describing a language or a dialect, linguists often organize their discussions by attending to three elemental characteristics: pronunciation, grammar, and lexical features. Fasold and Wolfram consider only the pronunciation and grammatical features of Black English, not its vocabulary. Although one might anticipate that the lexical features of Black English should be distinctive enough for full linguistic consideration, this is not the case.

In spite of the fact that a number of African words like *hoodoo, voodoo, goober, yam, juke* (as in *jukebox*), *jazz, gumbo, tote, jambalaya,* and *banjo* entered English from African languages, they have been in common use for several generations and are hence associated with black speakers primarily because of their origin. In what he calls "an initial, tentative survey of the African influence on black American (and hence also on general American) speech,"[22] David Dalby has identified eighty words associated with American speech that he has traced to African languages, primarily Mandingo and

Wolof. If African culinary, zoological, botanical, and musical terms now missing from the list were to be included, Dalby conjectures that the total number of words would be approximately one hundred, and many of these one hundred words have been adapted into general American English through Black English.

Thus the vocabulary of Black English is not distinctive because of its connection with African languages. Neither is there a tendency to invent new words or even to create unusual compoundings. Its distinction is much more subtle and often involves manipulation of existing English words for ironic effect. The possibilities for irony contribute to the creative manipulation of language by many black speakers—frequently urban male teenagers[23]—and offer infinite possibilities for the literary imagination.

CODING AND MANIPULATION OF MEANING

Not a great deal has been written about the variety of ways in which Black English speakers create new meanings for existing English words. In an interesting discussion of what she calls "Black Semantics," Geneva Smitherman identifies four traditions that have shaped black speech in America: "West African language background," "servitude and oppression," "music and 'cool talk,'" and "the traditional black church."[24]

According to Smitherman, these four "traditions" contributed to the formation of Black English from the early days of slavery, when the influence of West African languages was strongest, through the period of the Civil War and its aftermath, to the twentieth century, when black urban culture became established in the northern cities as the phenomenon of "hip" street culture began to assert itself.

For a literary study, the manipulation of alternative meaning is an important characteristic of Black English. And this manipulation allegedly has its origins in the special historical experience of the black speaker and in his linguistic adjustment to that history. According to the tradition, ever since the early days of slavery, first as a protective maneuver, later as a means of preserving a sense of separate identity, black people in America have chosen to communicate with one another in a coded language, a language white people could not understand.

It is generally assumed that in the early days of slavery a slave could not speak fluently with another slave unless he found his companion to be of his own home community in Africa. In order to guard against plotting and rebellion, slave owners, it is said, usually did not allow slaves who spoke the same language to work or to live together; as a result, communication among them was difficult. As new generations of children were born who learned English and did not know African languages, coding tended to occur among blacks speaking English. At this stage the slaves used the existing framework of the English language as they knew it, but they imposed secondary meanings on it, sometimes to disguise the "real" meaning and sometimes for ironic effect. The result was a duality of meaning, a kind of double-talk. One of the most convenient examples of such communication was the Negro Spiritual. When whites heard the Negroes singing religious songs, they were pleased that the slaves were absorbing the message of Christianity they were being taught. There was no suspicion that the slaves could be plotting to escape to the North when they sang "Steal Away to Jesus," or to board the "freedom train" when they sang "Bound for Glory," or were considering the possibility of returning to Africa when they sang "Deep River, My Home is Over Jordan."[25]

After the abolition of slavery, the use of coded communication with its attendant ironies continued among blacks; indeed, it has become a significant linguistic characteristic of Black English in our time. The most satisfactory way to control understanding in conversation is to speak a language an outsider cannot understand. Pig Latin—a primitive technique for coding in English—was adapted to black usage in the 1920s and 1930s. In Pig Latin, the first letter of a word is moved to the end and *ay* is added; according to popular conjecture it produced *ofay,* meaning "white man," from *foe.*[26] *Ofay* is a word that gained rather widespread usage, even in the middle of a sentence that did not contain another Pig Latin word. The word is represented in *Dutchman,* a play written by Amiri Baraka. Here Clay, the protagonist, says, "Old bald-headed four-eyed ofays popping their fingers . . . and don't know yet what they're doing."[27]

A more recent phenomenon of this century, the "fancy talk" or "cool talk" associated with young males in the urban ghettos is characterized by an extraordinary manipulation of meaning. Still working within the framework of English vocabulary, these speakers assign secondary and tertiary levels of meaning to words and phrases. The tradition of double-talk is still very much in evidence. One of the narratives Bruce Jackson has collected, "Junkies' Heaven," vividly illustrates typical street language and its manipulation of meaning.

> It was the night before Christmas and all through the pad
> cocaine and heroin was all the cats had.
> Stuffed in the icebox, stacked real high,
> they had cocaine cookies and morphine pie.
> Now me and my pal Hookamonie and my pal Doc
> had all settled down for a heroin shot,
> while the rest of the cats was knocked out and snuggled in bed,
> visions of opium just danced in their head.
> The stockings was hung by the foot of the bunk,
> hoping that St. Nick would soon fill 'em with junk.[28]

A particularly skilled manipulator of Black English is H. Rap Brown. True to his name, Brown prides himself on his ability to "rap" and to "signify," to engage in an elaborate form of verbal insult, of which the following is an example:

Man, you must don't know who I am
I'm sweet peeter jeeter the womb beater
The baby maker the cradle shaker
The deerslayer the buckbinder the women finder
Known from the Gold Coast to the rocky shores of Maine
Rap is my name and love is my game.
I'm the bed tucker the cock plucker the motherfucker
The milkshaker the record breaker the population maker
The gun-slinger the baby bringer
The hum-dinger the pussy ringer
The man with the terrible middle finger.
The hard hitter the bullshitter the poly-nussy getter
The beast from the East the Judge the sludge
The women's pet the men's fret and the punks' pin-up boy.
They call me Rap the dicker the ass kicker
The cherry picker the city slicker the titty licker
And I ain't giving up nothing but bubble gum and hard times and I'm
    fresh out of bubble gum.
. . . .
I'm a bad motherfucker. Rap the rip-saw the devil's brother'n law.
I roam the world I'm known to wander and this .45 is where I get my
    thunder.
I'm the only man in the world who knows why white milk makes
    yellow butter.
I know where the lights go when you cut the switch off.
I might not be the best in the world, but I'm in the top two and my
    brother's getting old.
And ain't nothing bad 'bout you but your breath.[29]

Such an active manipulation of language offers great potential for literary treatment and has been imitated and reproduced by American writers.

One of the ways of achieving complexity of meaning is linguistic reversal, a technique David Dalby traces to West African languages.[30] In linguistic reversal a word like *bad* or *mean* assumes a meaning opposite to that denoted: a *bad momma* or a *mean dude* means "a good woman" or "a good man." In a poem entitled "All in the Street," from *In Our Terribleness* (1970), Amiri Baraka reverses the meaning of *terrible:*

> Terribleness is a definition. It is a description. Muhammad Ali is a terrible dude. You member when he beat Chuvalo's ass. Kept stickin his hand in the sucker's face. Yeh. Man thass a terrible dude. For real.[31]

Complexity of meaning is also achieved through the manipulation of conventional figures of speech. Metonymy, or the use of the part for the whole, is a figure of speech that can often be used ironically in Black English—for example, *threads* can be used to refer to *clothes*. By its very nature and by its tendency to reduce an object to something of lesser consequence or from a serious to a nonserious level, metonymy is intimately associated with irony.

Black English speakers also derive multiple and ironic meanings from speech by punning. *Fox,* widely used as a term for a woman *(foxy lady),* is an obvious sexual metonymy as well as a sexual pun. In the title of her poem "The Great Pax Whitie," Nikki Giovanni puns on the Latin term for peace, *pax-pox,* while Amiri Baraka titles a book of essays *Raise, Race, Rays, Raze.* Some of the most humorous punning is on names, as in "I want my Fanny Brown." In the name of a rock concert in Washington, D.C., in July 1978, "Chocolate Jam," there is at least a triple pun.

At the end of her novel *Song of Solomon,* Toni Morrison, in recognition of the lively imagination associated with the naming of black people, has her main character, Milkman, whose own name is a pun, review the names of the people in his life. Many of the names—names their owners "got from yearnings, gestures, flaws, events, mistakes, weaknesses"—are puns.

> Macon Dead, Sing Byrd, Crowell Byrd, Pilate, Reba, Hagar, Magdalene, First Corinthians, Milkman, Guitar, Railroad Tommy, Hospital Tommy, Empire State (he just stood around and swayed), Small Boy, Sweet, Circe, Moon, Nero, Humpty-Dumpty, Blue Boy, Scandinavia, Quack-Quack, Jericho, Spoonbread, Ice Man, Dough Belly, Rocky River, Gray Eye, Cock-a-Doodle-Doo, Cool Breeze, Muddy Waters, Pinetop, Jelly Roll, Fats, Leadbelly, Bo Diddley, Cat-Iron, Peg-Leg, Son, Shortstuff, Smoky Babe, Funny Papa, Bukka, Pink, Bull Moose, B.B., T-Bone, Black Ace, Lemon, Washboard, Gatemouth, Cleanhead, Tampa Red, Juke Boy, Shine, Staggerlee, Jim the Devil, Fuck-Up, and *Dat* Nigger.[32]

Perhaps the figure of speech most widely used in the English language is metaphor. In Black English, terms of address like "Brother" and "Sister," taken from the language of the Black Church to address a member of the "family" of the faithful, are now terms of address used by one black person to address a member of the "family" of all black people. "Baby" and "Momma," other words that suggest familial relationships, are used either in a sexual context, to reflect something of the speaker's desired, if not actual, relationship with the person he addresses, or as a term of affectionate collegiality or community by people of the same as well as of opposite sexes.

Much of the language of seduction is metaphoric, as, for instance, in the proposition, "Say, baby, give me the key to your pad. I want to play with your cat."[33] *Cat* here is substituted for the expected sexual metaphor, *pussy.* The metaphoric dimension is still present, but the substitution suggests a double intention by the speaker. Traditionally, the use of metaphor is associated with language describing excretory and sexual anatomy and function, identified as "obscene" in English. Although "obscene" language is not used exclusively by blacks, and did not originate with black speakers, it appears with a high degree of frequency in contemporary Black English, uttered by both male and female speakers; obscenity is used to communicate a variety of meanings. Sometimes it is simply a device to attract attention.

Most often it is used to express disapproval or disgust, as it is with white speakers who use it. But obscenity in Black English can also be used to express a positive idea.[34] Amiri Baraka, for instance, concludes his poem "In Our Terribleness" with the following obscene lines, which convey positive meaning.

> Since there is a "good" we know is bullshit, corny as
> Lawrence Welk On Venus, we will not be that hominy shit.
> We will be, definitely, bad, bad, as a mother-fucker.[35]

And there are other manipulations of meaning. An obvious example is the noun *shit,* of Anglo-Saxon origin and once of a clear and specific meaning. Overused in English, it has long been an expletive (as its equivalent, *merde,* is in French). But black speakers have extended its use; for many Black English speakers under forty, *shit* is an almost ubiquitous noun. It can show traces of its original meaning: "Don't give me none of that shit," or function simply as an unspecific noun, as in "Some shit!" a term of awesome approval. It can even, as it does in Claude Brown's *Manchild in the Promised Land* or in Sonia Sanchez's poem "Why I don't get high on shit," serve as a code word for heroin. Yet *shit* can still function in metaphoric figures with full denotative intensity, as in "shit-filled bastard."

The more usual, and perhaps more distinctively black obscenity is *motherfucker,* sometimes spelled (in phoneticized Black English) *muthafucka.* This word originated as a metaphoric expression of extreme and serious disapprobation. The Black English speaker has manipulated its meaning to an ironic purpose. In Black English the word in its adjectival form is used as a simple intensifier, and it can intensify either approval or disapproval. This usage perhaps communicates a subtle and ironic awareness that the word has become so overused in Black English as to become devoid of meaning; perhaps the awareness also includes a sense that the original metaphor has been killed by the ubiquity of black anger.

Because any full description of a language or dialect is a detailed and complex undertaking, there is space here for only a few examples of what makes Black English linguistically distinctive. In spite of all the attention that has been focused on Black English in an attempt to describe and decode it, the linguists have not yet completed their work. Much information is still lacking concerning Black English rhythm, intonation, inflection, and accent. In various ways linguists, critics, and ethnicists have drawn analogies between the rhythms, pitch changes, and intonations in Black English and those in the music of African, North American, and Caribbean blacks. But no clear verdict is in, and in a brief account such as this it is impossible to do more than to note the widespread recognition of these distinctive features of Black English and the use made of them by American writers.

Of course, the Black English that a number of linguists have described—or for that matter, the Black English characterized by figurations, rhythms, and-or intonations—can hardly be assumed to be identical to that heard and represented in the nineteenth century by Hugh Henry Brackenridge or Edgar Allan Poe or Charles W. Chesnutt, or, for that matter, by Thomas Dixon, or Margaret Mitchell, or even Ralph Ellison in the twentieth century. If the dialectal speech of black North Americans is characterized by any single feature, it is that of rapid change. Yet it is interesting to note how many of the features of Black English identified by the commentators have been represented in American fiction by imaginative writers over the whole space of the country and over the past two hundred years. So, although it is not possible to assume that the above summary description is definitive, it is possible to allow it at least to be directive and to serve as a guide to the problem of central concern in this study—the representation of Black English in American fiction, its history, and its development.[36]

NOTES

1. William Labov, *The Social Stratification of English in New York City* (Washington, D.C.: Center for Applied Linguistics, 1966), p. 3.

2. Roger W. Shuy, Walter A. Wolfram, and William K. Riley, *Field Techniques in an Urban Language Study* (Washington, D.C.: Center for Applied Linguistics, 1968), p. 3.

3. Walter A. Wolfram, *A Sociolinguistic Description of Detroit Negro Speech* (Washington, D.C.: Center for Applied Linguistics, 1968), p. 2.

4. William Labov, Introduction, *Language in the Inner City: Studies in the Black English Vernacular* (Philadelphia: University of Pennsylvania Press, 1972), p. xiii.

5. Ibid.

6. William Labov, "The Logic of Nonstandard English," *Language in the Inner City: Studies in the Black English Vernacular* (Philadelphia: University of Pennsylvania Press, 1972), p. 212.

7. Ibid., p. 222.

8. Ibid., p. 237.

9. Raven I. McDavid, Jr., "American Social Dialects," *College English* 26 (January 1965): 258.

10. See Juanita V. Williamson, *A Phonological and Morphological Study of the Speech of the Negro of Memphis, Tennessee.* Publications of the American Dialect Society 50 (1968).

11. Juanita V. Williamson, "Selected Features of Speech: Black and White," in Juanita V. Williamson and Virginia M. Burke, eds., *A Various Language: Perspectives in American Dialects* (New York: Holt, Rinehart, and Winston, 1971), pp. 496–507.

12. See n. 4 above.

13. J. L. Dillard, *Black English* (New York: Random House, 1972), p. 229.

14. In R. W. Fasold and R. W. Shuy, *Teaching Standard English in the Inner City* (Washington, D.C.: Center for Applied Linguistics, 1970). The following discussion relies heavily on this very important article.

15. In the following presentation I have purposely simplified as much as possible. Anyone interested in a more detailed discussion is invited to consult Fasold and Wolfram's article or Robbins Burling's *English in Black and White* (New York: Holt, Rinehart, and Winston, 1973).

16. The first three examples in the table are taken from Robbins Burling, *English in Black and White*, p. 53.

17. Ibid., p. 69.

18. Ibid.

19. The following examples are taken from H. L. Mencken, *The American Language* (New York: Alfred A. Knopf, 1937), pp. 469–70.

Old English: *Nan ne dorste nan thing ascian,* which translates literally to *No one dares not ask nothing.* Middle English: *He never hadde nothing.* Shakespeare: *Richard III:* "I never was nor never will be." *Romeo and Juliet:* "I will not budge for no man's pleasure."

20. Both Fasold and Wolfram in "Some Linguistic Features of Negro Dialect," and Robbins Burling in *English in Black and White,* chapter 4, describe the rules for multiple negation in elaborate detail.

21. Alice Walker, *The Third Life of Grange Copeland* (New York: Harcourt, Brace, Jovanovich, 1970), p. 46.

22. David Dalby, "The African Element in American English," in Thomas Kochman, *Rappin' and Stylin' Out* (Urbana: University of Illinois Press, 1972), p. 175.

23. See Labov, *Language in the Inner City.*

24. Geneva Smitherman, *Talkin and Testifyin* (Boston: Houghton Mifflin, 1977), p. 43.

25. Miles Mark Fisher, in *Negro Slave Songs in the United States* (New York: Citadel Press, 1953), discusses the social significance of the spirituals in detail.

26. David Dalby disputes this widespread popular origin. He believes that *ofay* is more likely derived from an African word for "white man." See Dalby, "The African Element."

27. LeRoi Jones, *Dutchman,* in Clinton F. Oliver and Stephanie Sills, *Contemporary Black Drama* (New York: Charles Scribner's Sons, 1971), p. 229. Werner Sollors, in *Amiri Baraka/LeRoi Jones: The Quest for a "Populist Modernism"* (New York: Columbia University Press, 1978), p. 268, n. 2, traces the evolution of this current name. Although Baraka wrote some of the work I shall discuss in this and the following chapters under the name of LeRoi Jones, I have chosen, following Sollors's example, to refer to him by his most recent African name.

28. Bruce Jackson, *"Get Your Ass in the Water and Swim Like Me"* (Cambridge, Mass.: Harvard University Press, 1974), p. 206.

29. H. Rap Brown, "Street Talk," in Thomas Kochman, *Rappin' and Stylin' Out* (Urbana: University of Illinois Press, 1972), pp. 206–7.

30. Dalby, "The African Element," p. 177.

31. Imamu Amiri Baraka and Fundi (Billy Abernathy), *In Our Terribleness* (Indianapolis: Bobbs-Merrill, 1970), n.p.

32. Toni Morrison, *Song of Solomon* (New York: Knopf, 1977), p. 330.

33. Thomas Kochman, "Toward an Ethnography of Black American Speech Behavior," in *Rappin' and Stylin' Out* (Urbana: University of Illinois Press, 1972), p. 244.

34. Smitherman, *Talkin and Testifyin,* pp. 50–62.

35. Baraka and Fundi, *In Our Terribleness,* n.p.

36. In *Black English and the Mass Media* (Amherst: University of Massachusetts Press, 1981), Walter M. Brasch, discusses the representation of Black English in a broad spectrum of literary forms—fiction, nonfiction, journalism, folk song, drama, radio shows, advertisements— and sees the use of Black English as falling within five distinct cycles, each determined by frequency of use. Brasch says that each cycle lasts from 25 to 40 years, and is separated by an "inter-cycle" of between 10 and 20 years, characterized by reduced frequency of use. Brasch's cycles are the Colonial-Revolutionary Cycle (ca. 1765–ca. 1800), the Antebellum Cycle (ca. 1820–ca. 1860), the Reconstruction Cycle (ca. 1867–ca. 1902), the Negro Renaissance Cycle (ca. 1915–ca. 1940), and the Civil Rights Cycle (ca. 1958–ca. mid-1980s). His book, an interesting cultural history of the use of Black English, serves as important background for this study.

3
Black English in Fiction, 1790–1900: The Identification of an American Dialect

Any imaginative writer must consciously determine the written form that the speech of his characters will assume. He must decide whether he will record their speech in Standard English or whether he will use dialectal features to represent their speech. A writer who chooses to use dialectal features will usually do so either because he expects to impose an atmosphere of "realism" on his material or because he wants to emphasize the linguistic idiosyncracies of a character's speech for humorous or ironic effect.

Whatever decisions about the representation of dialect a writer makes will generate various literary consequences. For instance, if a black high school dropout from Harlem is represented as speaking Standard English to his friends, his characterization is not likely to be convincing. A boy with such a background clearly would not be expected to speak Standard English. If the author, however, records some of the more distinct dialectal features of the boy's speech, his characterization will probably be more realistic, and hence more believable. In many situations, much about a character's origins, his social class, and even his race can be established by the recording of his speech in dialect. Dialectally recorded speech often contributes an atmosphere of authenticity of characterization, and it can support the author's sense of "local color," his descriptive recreation of a particular time and place.

Humor or irony in characterization can also be communicated by an author who records dialectal features. Speakers of dialect are funny, at least in part, because in most cases they speak differently from the speech that is assumed for the reader, or because the reader confronts unexpected (or "incorrect") orthography or syntax in print. Thus the reader's amusement may be partly motivated by surprise, partly by a patronizing attitude. Juxtaposition of different dialects, or the intrusion of a dialect speaker in an incongruous environment, one in which another dialect is expected, offers other opportunities for humor; we are amused by the incongruity. A speaker from Brooklyn at a rodeo in Wyoming, a rancher in Paris, an English gentleman at a Texas barbecue, or an American tourist at a May Day parade in Moscow, are all potential subjects for humor. And their speech is clearly a rich source for such humor.

An author's literary purpose in using dialect is, of course, important in the ultimate effect of his work. But the way he chooses to record the dialect also contributes to the literary impact of his work. If he uses dialect in a literary context, a writer has a choice of dialectal features from which to draw: phonological recording, syntactic variations, manipulation of word meanings and figures of speech, representation of rhythm. He can use all of these features together, a combination of two or three of them, or even only one of them. His choice of features will, however, be linked to his decision as to how complete, and hence how accurate, his representation of dialect will be. He may attempt to record as fully as he can the dialect of a particular group of speakers within a particular geographical region; then he will call attention to the "specialness" of his character's speech. Or he may wish to record only the most obvious features, features most popularly associated with a geographically broad dialect; then his character will be more available to the reader's empathy. Whatever his decision, it will generate a variety of consequences.

If a writer of English decides to record pronunciation features, either alone or in combination with other dialectal features, he will face a number of problems. First, he will have to adapt the sounds of the dialect speech he wishes to record to the Roman alphabet. Linguists today agree that the only way to record dialect accurately is to use the International Phonetic Alphabet, but this certainly would have no place in a work of fiction. However, each author's idea of how to adapt the dialect sounds to the Roman alphabet will vary. The absence of an accepted system makes idiosyncratic systems possible, although it will soon become clear that all are not equally successful.

It is obvious that any writer records the sounds of dialect speech according to a highly individualized phoneme-letter system—a system shaped in part at least by the dialectal characteristics the writer himself uses. But when an imaginative writer undertakes to create direct dialect speech—not simply to record it—he must depend upon the accumulation of dialect pronunciations of particular words, or unusual syntactic combinations he has previously heard; he must draw features from this mnemonic accumulation and imagine these features in new combinations. Thus by a combination of memory and imagination he will "represent" imagined speech appropriate for his characters. Still, no matter how conscientiously he tries to recreate the remembered sounds, no matter how many significant dialectal features he has used, the best he can do is to approximate speech production in the dialect in question. And no matter how "technical" his approach to this problem, he is still dependent upon his memory and his imagination for the reproduction of the dialect.

And, of course, the writer is dependent on the reader, who must reconvert his "representation" back into the imagined sounds of dialectal speech. If the reader's phoneme-letter system differs from that of the writer (as in the majority of cases it must be assumed to do), and if the recorded dialect is unfamiliar to him, this imaginative reconversion may be so distorted as to make the dialect unrecognizable to the reader.

The process of the representation of dialect in literature, then, is far from scientific; the process that every author must follow is not one that can often result in precision. Any literary writing of dialect must be regarded as suggestion rather than as authentic representation of the speech of a particular group of speakers.

Yet a reader, even if he recognizes a dialect, may find himself completely overwhelmed by the "foreign" look of a dialect passage in print. The following passage from Joel Chandler Harris's *Uncle Remus: His Songs and His Sayings* (1880) presents such a problem for the reader:

> "Las' he year Brer B'ar comin' sho nuff, but 'twuz de same ole chune—'One 'simmon mo' en den I'll go'—en des 'bout dat time Brer B'ar busted inter de patch, en gin de tree a shake, en Brer Possum, he drapt out longer de yuther ripe 'simmons, but time he totch de groun' he got his foots tergedder, en he lit out fer de fence same ez a race hoss, en 'cross dat patch him en Brer B'ar had it, en Brer B'ar gain' eve'y jump, twel time Brer Possum make de fence Brer B'ar grab 'im by de tail, en Brer Possum, he went out 'tween de rails en gin a powerful juk en pull his tail out 'twixt Brer B'ar tushes; en, lo en beholes, Brer B'ar hole so tight en Brer Possum pull so hard dat all de ha'r come off in Brer B'ar's mouf, w'ich, ef Brer Rabbit hadnt' happen up wid a go'd er water, Brer B'ar 'der got strankle."[1]

When confronted with this passage, almost any reader will find that his reading speed is much slower than it is when he is reading Standard English. Considerable effort is involved, first in "translating" the passage into Standard English so that words and meaning are intelligible, then in "reconverting" the dialect representation into imagined sound, so that the dialect can be recognized. If passages written in dialect are long and frequent, such an effort of concentration may well reduce the pleasure the reader gains from the literary work before him; it will certainly disturb the rhythm of his reading speed.

In order to avoid these and other difficulties, a writer who wishes to record pronunciation features may reduce the number of variations he includes and allow a few significant features to suggest symbolically the speech characteristics of a dialect. A passage from Zora Neale Hurston's *Their Eyes Were Watching God* (1937), a book whose dialect representation will be considered more fully later, is an example. Whatever else may be true of it, certainly the choice of distinctive pronunciation features makes it easier to read than the passage from Harris.

> "De way you looked at me when Ah said whut Ah did. Yo' face skeered me so bad till mah whiskers drawed up."
> "Ah ain't got no business bein' mad at nothin' you do and say. You got it all wrong. Ah ain't mad atall."
> "Ah know it and dat's what puts de shamery on me. You'se jus' disgusted wid me. Yo' face jus' left here and went off somewhere else. Naw, you ain't mad wid me. Ah be glad if you was, 'cause then Ah might do somethin' tuh please yuh. But lak it is—"[2]

There is another difficulty created by the representation of spoken dialect, and that is the problem of "eye dialect." The writer who represents dialectal speech is obviously engaged in setting down, by whatever means, those characteristics of a dialect which are real pronunciation features. But in this process he may also introduce variations from normal spelling that do not indicate significant dialectal differences in pronunciation. Such variations are dialect in the written language, and appear to be dialect to the reader, but upon examination it can be seen that they do not represent significant dialectal pronunciation features. Such variations are called "eye dialect" features. *What,* for example, can be spelled *whut* in eye dialect; *says* becomes *sez; was* becomes *wuz; love* becomes *luv.* These features are somewhat decorative, but they do not represent real dialectal features. Eye dialect calls the reader's attention to the "difference" of the speech without really contributing to its "realism." And excessive use of eye dialect is frequently distracting for the reader. Its use often results from an author's lack of linguistic knowledge and his over-attention to what he regards as dialect features. Often eye dialect is added in the represented speech of a character who is to be patronized by the reader. The effect of eye dialect is often a spurious one, and it is an effect cheaply gained.

Usually, pronunciation features are not used alone in literature to signify dialect speech. They are often combined with the representation of grammatical features. And, as was evident from the discussion of the dialectal features of Black English in chapter 2, the distinction between these categories is frequently confused.

Grammatical characteristics, which record the actual syntactical features of a dialect, either in conjunction with pronunciation features or alone, offer the writer of fiction and his reader a number of advantages. In the first place, grammatical characteristics, because they record the distinctive syntactical features of a speech variety, are often regarded as the most significant of the dialect features. Moreover, while they indicate distinctive dialect features, they are usually not difficult to read. Therefore, the reader's pace in reading such dialect writing is not significantly disturbed. Many grammatical characteristics, however, are associated with a number of nonstandard dialects, not with one alone. However, a specific dialect, such as

Black English, is characterized by a particular set of grammatical features. Usually the writer who transcribes Black English speech selects from these features and uses them, either alone or in combination with phonological and lexical features, to identify and individuate his character's speech.

Of course, speech is not the only feature that individualizes a literary character. A writer can describe physiognomy, body shape, dress, habits, movements, and can directly identify ethnic origins, personal history, even thoughts (although these are usually represented through a kind of indirect speech). Yet when all is said and done, literature is made of words, not pictures. What a character says and how he says it—not how he looks—are his most prominent characteristics. In fiction particularly, by his speech shall ye know him.

Throughout the development of American fiction, writers have used different combinations of pronunciation, grammatical, lexical, and rhythmic features to suggest the dialect a character speaks. Although many dialects have been used, Black English has been one of the dialects most frequently and consistently recorded. By a chronological consideration of some literary examples of Black English, it will be possible to indicate how and why ways of representing Black English in a literary context have changed over the years. In this and the following two chapters, selections from American fiction will be analyzed according to their use of pronunciation features, eye dialect, grammatical features, unusual vocabulary, manipulation of word meanings, figurative language, and rhythmical features.

Yet the representation of dialect does not exist and therefore cannot be discussed in isolation. It is important for the contribution it makes to the overall literary effect of a passage and of a work; but equally important is the author's attitude toward black people and his identification and choice of black characters in his work. As the cultural attitude toward blacks changes from the beginning of the nineteenth century to the present, the literary representation of Black English speech also changes. And there is always a correlation between the type of literary character portrayed and the way in which his speech is rendered.

Much of the portrayal of black characters in fiction has been achieved through the use of stereotypes. In an article originally published in 1933, "Negro Characters as Seen by White Authors," Sterling Brown identifies seven stereotypes of black characters in literature: "(1) The Contented Slave, (2) The Wretched Freeman, (3) The Comic Negro, (4) The Brute, (5) The Tragic Mulatto, (6) The Local Color Negro, and (7) The Exotic Primitive."[3] Black as well as white writers, Brown tells us, have made use of these stereotypes in their fiction. For example, Charles W. Chesnutt in *The House Behind the Cedars* and Nella Larsen in *Passing* and *Quicksand* use "The Tragic Mulatto," and Claude McKay's Jake in *Home to Harlem* can be seen as an example of "The Exotic Primitive." After the Harlem Renaissance, however, the tendency to stereotype black characters by either black or white writers begins to disappear, and the characterization of blacks in American fiction becomes increasingly complex.

Closely associated with the literary stereotype of the black is an elaborate and somewhat conventionalized system of dialect representation. As we shall see in the examples from nineteenth-century fiction that immediately follow, the representation of the speech of stereotyped black characters, except for "The Tragic Mulatto" (who usually speaks Standard English), is usually heavily laced with pronunciation and grammatical features. The more exaggerated the stereotype, the more ornate the representation of the black character's dialect speech. Once the stereotypes disappear, however, the nineteenth-century methods of recording dialect become simplified. Such simplification will coincide with a fuller and more complex awareness of dialect-speaking black characters.

This chapter will consider the representation of Black English in nineteenth-century fiction, fiction written by both black and white Americans. Although presented chronologically, the passages are of necessity highly selective. In this brief survey of nineteenth-century American dialect writing one can make no claim to be comprehensive. Still, perhaps, in such a rapid survey, the principal directions in the representation of Black English in American fiction can be identified.

A good place to begin is with Hugh Henry Brackenridge, one of the earliest American novelists to employ Black English-speaking characters. Brackenridge himself was born in Scotland in 1748; his family migrated to America five years later, and settled in York County, Pennsylvania, in a Scots-Irish community. His only fictional work is a picaresque novel, *Modern Chivalry,* written in installments between 1792 and 1815, and still unfinished at its author's death. The novel—with a clearly satiric purpose—depicts the adventures of a quixotic Captain Farrago and his Irish Sancho Panza, Teague O'Regan. The object of Brackenridge's rather broad and humorous satire is the burgeoning democratic American society—its lawyers, doctors, politicians, clergymen. In the passage that follows, a black slave incongruously speaks before members of a Philosophical Society. If we are to use Sterling Brown's classification, Cuff, the slave, is a stereotyped combination of "The Contented Slave" and "The Comic Negro."

Cuff has been invited to speak before the Society because he has discovered an oddly shaped stone that the Philosophical Society has determined to be a petrified Indian moccasin. He does not know what to say, and his master, Colonel Gorum, having heard that an oration expounding the theory that black people are descended from whites had been delivered before the Society in a previous year, suggests that Cuff do justice to his race and argue that blacks were the original inhabitants of the earth and thus the ancestors of the whites, not the descendants. The Colonel explains the theory beforehand, so Cuff is not given an opportunity for originality. Cuff is told what to say, and hence has only to reiterate the argument before the Society. So Cuff is, in effect, being set up by the Colonel as an object of ridicule. In order to make its meaning clear, the Colonel summarizes Cuff's speech in Standard English before Cuff delivers it. Thus the reader, as he reads the speech, attends, not to the substance of what Cuff is saying, but to the way he says it. The pompous Philosophical Society, which considers such absurd questions in its deliberations, is, of course, as much the object of Brackenridge's satire as is Cuff. In a democratic society, no one escapes Brackenridge's ridicule.

"Massa shentiman; I be cash crab in de Wye riva: found ting in de mud; tone, big a man's foot; hols like to he; fetch Massa: Massa say, it be de Indian maccason.—O! fat de call it; all tone. He say, you be a filasafa, Cuff: I say, O no, Massa; you be de filasafa. Wel; two tree monts afta. Massa call me, and say, You be a filasfa, Cuff, fo' sartan: Getta ready, and go dis city, and make grate peech for shentima filasafa. I say, Fat say? Massa: Massa say, somebody say, dat de first man was de fite man; but you say, dat de first man was de black a-man. Vel, I set out: come along: Massa gi me pass. Some say, where you go, Cuff? I say, dis city, be a filasafa. O no, Cuff, you be no filasafa: call me fool, gi me kick i'de backside; fall down, get up again, and come to dis city.

"Now, shentima, I say, dat de first man was de black a man, and de first woman de black a woman; an get two tree children; de rain vasha dese, and de snow pleach, an de coula come brown, yella, coppa coula, and, at de last, quite fite; and de hair long; and da fal out vid van anoda; and van cash by de nose, and pull; so de nose come lang, sharp nose.

"Now I go home, Massa shentima; an tel grate Massa, dat make peech, an ibedy body vas da; an den Cuff fin a more tings—cabs, oysta, cat-fish, bones, tones, ibedy ting; sen to you, shentima."*⁴

*The notation that appears at the bottom of this page and subsequent pages on which a literary passage is quoted will list more fully than textual discussion allows the phonological and grammatical dialect features of the passage. The pronunciation and-or grammatical characteristics here listed are primarily those identified by Fasold and Wolfram and set forth in chapter 2. However, since texts exemplifying the early stages of Black English are included in the discussion, when appropriate, features other than those Fasold and Wolfram describe are also noted. These notations are not intended to be comprehensive; they are included only to inform more fully the more linguistically oriented reader.

Of course, "Regularization of the third person singular present tense" is, logically, a subcategory of "Lack of subject-verb agreement." I have discussed the former as a separate category because this regularization is such an important and distinguishing feature of Black English.

Pronunciation Features

1. Reduction of consonant clusters: *catch* > *cash* (but *fetch* remains); *old* > *ol; and* > *an; send* > *sen; find* > *fin.* Reduction combined with loss of *r: Master* > *Massa.*

2. Changes in *th:*

   a. *th* (voiced) > *d: the* > *de; that* > *dat; this* > *dis; then* > *den; there* > *da; with* > *vid; another* > *anoda.*

   b. *th* (unvoiced) > *t: thing, things* >*ting, tings; months* > *monts; three* > *tree.*

3. Loss of *r: river* > *riva; color* > *coula; oyster* > *oysta; copper* > *coppa; after* > *afta.*

Given his Scottish origin and his long experience of living in Western Pennsylvania, Brackenridge probably had very little opportunity to hear black people speak. The dialect Brackenridge undoubtedly knew best was the Scots dialect of his widely read contemporary, Robert Burns, whose collection of dialect poetry *(Poems: Chiefly in the Scottish Dialect)*, had been published in 1786. To vitalize his own satire, Brackenridge included occasional dialect speakers that could be found in America. At the end of the eighteenth century in western Pennsylvania, the speech of the black man was certainly somewhat exotic. Thus, it is not surprising that Brackenridge's representation of Black English dialect is grossly exaggerated. Pronunciation features, some of which are clearly Black English and some of which are not, dominate the passage; the method of representation is not dissimilar to that of Burns in his emphasis on pronunciation features. As can be seen more comprehensively in the analysis that follows the passage, Brackenridge records two changes in *th:* Standard English voiced *th* becomes *d* and Standard English unvoiced *th* becomes *t* in Cuff's speech. There are also examples of Standard English *v* appearing as Black English *b* (a feature that Fasold and Wolfram do not list, but one associated with literary Black English of the nineteenth century), the loss of final *r* and considerable reduction of consonant clusters.

In representing Cuff's speech, Brackenridge uses a number of phonological features that seem to have no relation to the Black English of our own time. Standard English *w* is recorded as *v* in his dialect, a sound that is often associated with northern European immigrant pronunciation in English, as in *vel* and *vas* for *well* and *was,* respectively. Perhaps Brackenridge is unconsciously recalling the speech of German immigrants in Western Pennsylvania. In other situations he records *w* as *f*, *b* as *p*, and he drops the *v* sound in *give* to form *gi*, a form that he takes from Burns. Eye dialect is frequent in the passage; for example, *philosopher* is spelled *filasafa; great* is spelled *grate;* and *tell* is spelled *tel.* The pronunciation represented by these

4. *v > b: everybody > ibedy body.*Although Fasold and Wolfram do not include the transformation of *v* to *b* as a Black English feature, it occurs frequently in literary Black English dialect of the nineteenth century.)

(In addition to the features listed above, Breckenridge includes some pronunciation features that are not today generally associated with Black English.

1. *w > v: well > vel; was > vas; washes > vasha; with > vid; one* (pronounced *won*) *> van.*

2. *w > f: what > fat; white > fite.*

3. *b > p: bleach > pleach.*

4. Loss of final *v: give > gi.*)

Eye Dialect: *philosopher > filasafa; great > grate; tell > tel; fall > fal.*

Grammatical Features
Verbs

1. Regularization of third person singular present tense: *de coula come brown; de nose come lang; Massa say; Massa gi.*

2. Zero copula: *Cuff fin; where you go.*

3. *Be: I be; you be; it be.*

transcriptions is no different from that of the Standard English speaker—except perhaps for the final *a* in *filasafa.*

Yet, in comparison with the pronunciation features transcribed here, the grammatical features in the passage are somewhat sparse. Brackenridge uses three verb formations that are today associated with Black English; he regularizes the conjugation of the verb *to be* in the present tense of all persons, so that Cuff says *I be, You be,* and *it be.* There are also several examples of the regularization of the third person singular present tense form, as in *Massa say, Massa gi,* and of zero copula, as in *Cuff fin* and *Where you go.*

The Black English dialect Brackenridge records is presumably not to be associated with any particular region. But, more important, his exaggeration of pronunciation features is a form of phonological caricature; by calling attention to the "specialness" of Cuff's speech and the incongruity of that "specialness" with his subject and his situation, Brackenridge subjects the black character to the ridicule of his presumably Standard English reader.

Although the connotation may be irrational, there is very likely an association within the reader's mind between Cuff's speech and his illiteracy and implied limited intelligence. The odd orthography, used to suggest his pronunciation, is associated with the assumption that the black is unable to read and write and spell—and is therefore someone over whom the literate reader can feel superior and at whom he can laugh. Brackenridge got none of this from Burns.

Edgar Allan Poe was from quite a different tradition than Brackenridge. Although he was not generally known as a satirist, Poe also occasionally used black characters and represented their dialectal speech. Poe identified himself as a southerner; he grew up in ante-bellum Richmond and later supported slavery on "moral" grounds. In a review of two books on slavery that he wrote for *The Southern Literary Messenger* in April 1836, Poe describes what he calls the "peculiar nature" of the Negro, particularly his devoted loyalty to his white master:

> we shall take leave to speak, as of things *in esse,* in a degree of loyal devotion on the part of the slave to which the white man's heart is a stranger, and of the master's reciprocal feeling of parental attachment to his humble dependant, equally incomprehensible to him who drives a bargain with the cook who prepares his food, the servant who waits at his table, and the nurse who dozes over his sick bed. That these sentiments in the breast of the negro and his master, are stronger than they would be under like circumstances between individuals of the white race, we believe. That they belong to the class of feelings "by which the heart is made better," we know.[5]

In Poe's short story "The Gold Bug" (1843) occurs one of the rare occasions in Poe's fiction in which a black character speaks. In this story the speech and character of Jupiter exemplify the "peculiar nature" Poe attributes to blacks. Jupiter is a slave who, although he has been freed, continues by choice to serve his "Massa Will" Legrand, and even follows him from New Orleans to very simple accommodations on Sullivan's Island (near Charleston, South Carolina, the setting for the story). The plot revolves around Legrand, an entomologist who finds a rare, golden-colored insect ("the gold bug") on the beach and, with the care of a detective following clues, eventually discovers treasure buried many years before by the pirate Captain Kidd. Early in the story, before the treasure is uncovered, Legrand is obsessional and withdrawn; his behavior is cause for worry by the loyal Jupiter. In the passage that follows, Jupiter reports his Master's strange behavior to the narrator-visitor.

"Well, Jup," said I, "what is the matter now?—how is your master?"

"Why, to speak the troof, massa, him not so berry well as mought be."

"Not well! I am truly sorry to hear it. What does he complain of?"

"Dar! dat's it!—him neber plain of notin—but him berry sick for all dat."

"*Very* sick, Jupiter!—why didn't you say so at once? Is he confined to bed?"

"No, dat he aint!—he aint find nowhar—dat's just whar he shoe pinch—my mind is got to be berry hebby bout poor Massa Will."

"Jupiter, I should like to understand what it is you are talking about. You say your master is sick. Hasn't he told you what ails him?"

"Why, massa, taint worf while for to git mad about de matter—Massa Will say noffin at all aint de matter wid him—but den what make him go about looking dis here way, wid he head down and he soldiers up, and as white as a gose? And den he keep a syphon all de time—"

"Keeps a what, Jupiter?"

"Keeps a syphon wid de figgurs on de slate—de queerest figgurs I ebber did see. Ise gittin to be skeered, I tell you. Hab for to keep mighty tight eye pon him noovers. Todder day he gib me slip fore de sun up and was gone de whole ob de blessed day. I had a big stick ready cut for to gib him deuced good beating when he did come—but Ise sich a fool dat I hadn't de heart arter all—he looked so berry poorly."*[6]

---

*Pronunciation Features

1. Reduction of consonant clusters (combined with loss of *r*): *Master > Massa.*

2. Changes in *th:*

   a. *th* (voiced) > *d: the > de; then > den; this > dis; there > dar; that > dat; with > wid; the other > todder.*

   b. *th* (unvoiced) > *t: nothing > notin* (see also 2c).

   c. *th > f: worth > worf; truth > troof; nothing > noffin* (see also 2b).

3. Nasalization: *nothing > notin* or *noffin; getting > gittin.*

4. *v > b: very > berry; heavy > hebby; never > neber; give > gib; of* (pronounced *ov*) > *ob.*

5. Loss of initial unstressed syllable: *complain > plain; about > bout; before > fore; manoevers > noovers; upon > pon.*

6. Vowel fronting: *get > git; such > sich.*

Poe's reason for using dialect speech in characterizing Jupiter is probably twofold. Although contemporary critics have not responded favorably to his attempt, Poe probably intended that the dialect would help to localize the story in the Charleston area as well as to individualize Jupiter, to indicate his "specialness." Also, Jupiter's unusual speech provides the reader with a certain distance, perhaps even a "comic relief" from the secretive and obsessed activity of Legrand as he attempts to determine where the treasure is located. Jupiter is an important character in the early part of the story, up to the point at which the treasure is found. But in the last part of the story, as Legrand describes how he deciphered the code that led him to the treasure, Jupiter disappears into the background.

A number of critics have pointed out that Jupiter's dialect is not regionally authentic.[7] Certainly his speech is not pure Gullah.[8] Eric Stockton, who has made a thorough study of Jupiter's dialect, concludes that "Jupiter's speech is as much substandard as it is Southern Negro."[9] Serious concern with authenticity in the representation of dialect in literature would not occur until after the Civil War, really not until the more insistently realistic "local color" movement began in the 1880s, forty years after "The Gold Bug." But although Poe's Jupiter may or may not speak accurately the black dialect of his region (and one must remember that Jupiter is not a Gullah speaker; he has come from New Orleans), his speech does include a number of features that would today be recognized as characteristic of Black English. Thus perhaps his use of dialect does contribute adequately to suggest a generalized "southern" locale.

In his representation of Jupiter's dialect, Poe rather evenly balances pronunciation and grammatical features. Jupiter pronounces *th* three different ways; when it is voiced, he pronounces *th* as *d;* when *th* is unvoiced, he pronounces it either as *t,* as in *notin,* or as *f,* as in *noffin.* The inconsistency in the pronunciation of unvoiced *th,* particularly within a very few lines, might suggest careless or naive linguistic observation on Poe's part. Jupiter also pronounces *v* as *b,* as in *berry* for *very,* and as is illustrated by a single example, *Massa,* his speech reflects reduction of consonant clusters and the loss of *r.* There are a few examples of nasalization, as in *notin, noffin,* and

---

Grammatical Features
Verbs
    1. Regularization of third person singular present tense: *he keep; he look; Massa Will say; what make him.*
    2.a. Zero copula: *before de sun up.*
      b. Copula accompanied by object as subject: *him not so berry well; him berry sick.*
Negative
    1. *aint.*
    2. Double Negative: *him neber plain of notin; he aint find nowhar; noffin at all aint de matter.*
Nominative pronoun as possessive: *he head; he soldiers (shoulders).*

gittin, and there are several examples of words that have lost their initial unstressed syllable, as in *plain* for *complain* and *bout* for *about.*

In addition, the passage is filled with nonstandard spellings, that can perhaps only be identified as "southernisms," not specifically as examples of Black English: *whar* for *where, figgurs* for *figures.* One of the more interesting spellings, or at least word substitutions, is *syphon* for *ciphering.* The preservation of *ph* in a simplification of a word Jupiter has difficulty understanding and pronouncing is peculiar, to say the least. But Poe's choice of *ph* instead of *f* achieves a comic effect by the introduction of a malapropism. Still, *syphon* is a word in English; *syfon* is not. Similarly, Poe also records Jupiter's pronunciation of *shoulders* as *soldiers*—a comic word substitution that might be explained by the fact that [s] is commonly pronounced [ʃ] in Gullah. Indeed, the two words might well have been legitimate homonyms at one time.[10]

Poe's representation of Jupiter's speech reflects the most distinctive characteristics of Black English grammar. Poe uses three Black English variations of verb structure: regularization of third person singular present tense, as in *he keep, he look;* zero copula, as in *before de sun up,* and the copula accompanied by the object as subject, as in *him not so berry well,* and *him berry sick.* The most significant grammatical feature in addition to verb variation in Black English is the use of the negative. Poe has Jupiter use *aint* (without the apostrophe) as well as the double negative, in *him neber plain of notin.* He also uses the nominative instead of the possessive pronoun form, in *he head* and *he soldiers (shoulders).*

In the example from Poe's story and in the literary selections from the work of other writers that follow, it will be interesting to observe each author's use of the apostrophe to indicate contraction. Some writers use it compulsively; others try to dispense with it entirely, at least when they write dialect. Poe uses the apostrophe somewhat inconsistently. He does not use it to signify missing letters in *aint, taint, Ise, notin,* or *noffin;* but he uses it for that very reason in Standard English contractions, such as *hadn't* and *dat's,* but again not with sufficient consistency as to suggest deliberation.

Whereas Brackenridge's version of Black English is almost grotesque, Poe's, although exaggerated, is somewhat more intentionally "realistic." Poe's purpose in transcribing Black English dialect is more complex; here the presence of dialect speech establishes a vague authenticity of setting ("realism") and a certain comic "relief" or distancing as well. Poe's purpose here is not purely or even centrally satiric. Still, Poe's "realism" cannot yet be specifically associated with the setting of the story. That kind of dialectal authenticity was to be a concern only of later American writers.

There were other examples of Black English dialect representations in the years before the Civil War, and Black English dialect was represented for purposes different from satire or authentication. Herman Melville is not usually thought of as a dialect writer, and—in spite of his five years at sea, during which he often closely associated with black sailors—he did not frequently introduce black characters into his work. Yet a number of blacks are to be found in Melville's novels and stories—Babu, of course, in "Benito Cereno" of 1856 (who is not a North American and is therefore not a speaker of any English dialect), the protagonist of *The Confidence Man* of 1857 (whose Black English speech may well not be a natural dialect but rather a contrivance that serves his disguise), and several of the Pequod's crew in *Moby-Dick* (1851)—Daggoo (an African, not an American black), Pip (whose speech is sailor's dialect, not Black English), and Fleece, the cook.

One particularly interesting passage appears in chapter 64 of *Moby-Dick*. Fleece, having prepared whale steak for Stubb from the second mate's whale, is instructed by Stubb to preach so as to quiet the sharks, who are also noisily eating whale flesh. Fleece speaks in dialect—in his case, Black English. He is, of course, not the only dialect speaker aboard the *Pequod* (the noble Queequeg speaks his own dialect, and, in fact, Ahab and many others speak a kind of nautical dialect, which becomes almost a Standard English for the purposes of the dialogue of the book). But Fleece's dialect is atypical—"special speech"—(as is Queequeg's). Like Queequeg, because of his "special speech," Fleece is briefly awarded a special status. Fleece, following Stubb's instruction, preaches a brief sermon to the sharks (one of course remembers Father Mapple's earlier sermon).

> "Your woraciousness, fellow-critters, I don't blame ye so much for; dat is natur, and can't be helped; but to gobern dat wicked natur, dat is de pint. You is sharks, sartin; but if you gobern de shark in you, why den you be angel; for all angel is not'ing more dan de shark well goberned. Now, look here, bred'ren, just try wonst to be cibil, a helping yourselbs from dat whale. Don't be tearin' de blubber out your neighbour's mout, I say. Is not one shark dood right as toder to dat whale? And, by Gor, none on you has de right to dat whale; dat whale belong to some one else. I know some o' you has berry brig mout, brigger dan oders; but den de brig mouts sometimes has de small bellies; so dat de brigness ob de mout is not to swallar wid, but to bite off de blubber for de small fry ob sharks, dat can't get into de scrouge to help demselves."*[11]

Pronunciation Features
    1. Changes in *th:*
        a. *th* (voiced) > *d: that* > *dat; the* > *de; then* > *den; than* > *den; brethren* > *bred'ren; the other* > *toder; others* > *oders; themselves* > *demselves; with* > *wid.*
        b. *th* (unvoiced) > *t: mouth* > *mout.*
    2. *v* > *b: govern* > *gobern; civil* > *cibil; yourselves* > *yourselbs; very* > *berry; of* > *ob.*
    3. Nasalization: *tearing* > *tearin'.*
    4. Loss of glide: *point* > *pint.*

Grammatical Features
Verbs
    1. Lack of subject-verb agreement: *You is; mouts has.*
    2. *Be: You be.*

Melville has here used many of the usual techniques of phonological representation of Fleece's speech—*d* for *th*, *b* for *v*, for instance—and many of the usual syntactical features—the absence of subject-verb agreement *(You is sharks)* and the use of *be* as an active verb: *You be angels.* Furthermore, he has added other features—elaborate elisions *(toder* for *the other)*, strange word substitutions *(on* for *of*, and *dood*, which Charles Feidelson in a note identifies as a "misprint" for *good*, but which may as well be a dialect spelling—for *good*, or for *dead)*, and strangely punned sound insertions *(brig* for *big* and *brigger* for *bigger)*. Although it is not possible to comment on all of the features, it is clear that Melville has not stinted himself in his representation of either phonological or syntactical features. At one point *(by Gor)* he even seems to add features from other dialects—here from a Cockney dialect.

What is important is that Fleece's "special speech," far from making him the object of satire or reducing him to a mere item in a system of authentication, actually gives Fleece a kind of moral distance, allows him to comment analogically and ethically on the conduct of the "carnivoracious" sharks and sailors. The "specialness" of Fleece's dialect speech, like that of Queequeg, establishes for him an authority that makes his sermon a window through which the reader can attain a moral perspective on the action of the book.

Melville's humanitarian impulses toward men of all races are well known, but his awareness of the literary possibilities inherent in the representation of dialect speech is perhaps less familiar. It is interesting in this regard to remember the *brig-big* pun, or to note Fleece's final speech in this scene. For here Melville exploits a syntactical feature of Black English to shape a rhetorical pattern, a pattern that underlies the point of Fleece's "sermon."

> "Wish, by gor! whale eat him, 'stead of him eat whale. I'm bressed if he ain't more of shark dan Massa Shark hisself," muttered the old man, limping away; with which sage ejaculation he went to his hammock.[12]

The chiasmus achieved here *(whale eat him, 'stead of him eat whale)* could not have been achieved in Standard English; thus Melville here suggests that Fleece's "special" language not only gives Fleece a certain rhetorical ascendancy over the arrogant, patronizing, but rather perceptually blunted Stubb, but also demonstrates an intrinsic capability for communication that is unavailable to the more Standard English speakers. In this passage—and it is certainly one of the earliest such passages in American literature—the dialect speaker is not simply a "substandard" speaker. Here the "specialness" of speech implies "special" awareness, even "special" verbal capabilities, skills that seem akin to prophetic powers.

Yet there were still other literary uses that American writers found for Black English in the years before the Civil War. The use of dialect in the abolitionist novels is of quite a different nature from that in either earlier or later literature. The abolitionist novel was a peculiar literature, a literature of polemic. And, of course, the black speakers in those novels were the objects of a particular attention.

Harriet Beecher Stowe, a New Englander who was born in Litchfield, Connecticut, lived for a time in Cincinnati, Ohio, but spent much of her adult life in Brunswick, Maine, hardly a significantly black population center. In rebelling against the stringent Calvinist doctrine of her father, Lyman Beecher, Stowe found an outlet for her imaginative energy in the romantic and sentimental novel that was popular during the 1830s and 1840s. Her first novel, *Uncle Tom's Cabin,* written in installments during 1851–52 for the *National Era,* a weekly anti-slavery newspaper, is of this tradition. Stowe's only personal exposure to slavery was brief; while she was in Cincinnati she crossed the Ohio River for one short visit to the border state of Kentucky, a slave state. Most of Stowe's information about slavery came from stories she was told in Cincinnati, from accounts of life on a Louisiana plantation reported by her brother, or from her reading. Yet her New Englander's understanding of the institution of slavery and her intense disapproval of the inhumanity of a system that would countenance the breaking up of families in order that an unjust and unchristian economic system might be perpetuated, was remarkable.

Stowe's portrayal of black characters is hardly comic. Throughout her novel she points out the cruelty and injustice of slavery, and focuses particularly on the suffering of a number of individual blacks as examples. In the following passage, Aunt Chloe, Uncle Tom's wife, expresses her views concerning the inevitable pattern of life a black slave could anticipate.

> "Ay, crow away, poor crittur!" said Aunt Chloe; "ye'll have to come to it, too! ye'll live to see yer husband sold, or mebbe be sold yerself; and these yer boys, they's to be sold, I s'pose, too, jest like as not, when dey gets good for somethin'; an't no use in niggers havin' nothin'!"*[13]

Pronunciation Features
1. *th* > *d: they* > *dey* (but *they's* is also used).
2. Nasalization: *nothing* > *nothin'*; *something* > *somethin'*; *having* > *havin'*.
3. Loss of initial unstressed syllable: *suppose* > *s'pose*.
4. Vowel fronting: *just* > *jest*.
Eye Dialect: *maybe* > *mebbe*; *you'll* > *ye'll*.

Grammatical Features
Verbs
1. Lack of subject-verb agreement: *dey gets; they's to be sold*.
Negative
1. *an't*.
2. Double negative: *an't no use in niggers havin' nothin'*.

As the above brief passage suggests, Stowe relies on a few of the most obvious pronunciation and grammatical features to represent Aunt Chloe's dialect. Only three pronunciation features appear here; in the first place, *th* is recorded as *d,* as in *dey* for *they.* But inconsistently for a dialect speaker, *they's* is used as well. Stowe also uses nasalization, as in *nothin', somethin',* and *havin',* and includes one example of the loss of the unstressed syllable, *s'pose.* Although the real pronunciation features are few, Stowe relies— probably as a substitute for her inadequate knowledge of Black English pronunciation—on what might be regarded as occasional eye dialect, as in *mebbe* and *ye'll.* Her representation of grammatical features is likewise simplified. There are two examples of lack of subject-verb agreement: *dey gits* and *they's to be sold,* and two examples of Black English negatives: *an't,* a peculiar variation of *ain't* and, within the same utterance, a double negative: *an't no use in niggers havin' nothin'!*

In another passage from the same novel, this one representing Uncle Tom's speech, dialectal inconsistencies are even more clearly apparent.

> "I's older, ye know," said Tom, stroking the boy's fine, curly head with his large, strong hand, but speaking in a voice as tender as a woman's, "and I sees all that's bound up in you. O, Mas'r George, you has everything,—l'arnin', privileges, readin', writin',—and you'll grow up to be a great, learned, good man, and all the people on the place and your mother and father'll be so proud on ye! Be a good Mas'r, like yer father; and be a Christian, like yer mother. 'Member yer Creator in the days o' yer youth, Mas'r George."[14]

In this passage, Tom, who is, of course, a very sympathetic and "human" character, begins speaking in dialect, but by the middle of the passage he is speaking what seems to be predominantly Standard English: "and you'll grow up to be a great, learned, good man, and all the people on the place and your mother and father'll be so proud. . . ." The last two sentences of his speech revert once again to dialect. It is almost as if—*contra* Melville—too much Black English dialect is not sufficiently dignified for the communication of "serious" thoughts. But there are some peculiarities even in the sentences written in dialect. The preservation of final *r* in *Mas'r,* for instance, is not considered by Fasold and Wolfram to be a distinctive feature of Black English. Likewise, Stowe represents *your* as *your* and *yer* interchangeably—a hesitant example of eye dialect. Indeed, on the whole, Stowe's commitment to dialect appears uncertain. There are similar inconsistencies within the speech of dialect-speaking characters besides Uncle Tom and Aunt Chloe. And George and Eliza, two mulatto slaves who escape to Canada, speak a pure Standard English throughout the novel.[15]

Stowe's experience in New England did not prepare her to represent southern Black English "realistically" or consistently, and for the purpose of her novel it was not necessary for her to do so. As with Poe, one of Stowe's purposes in using dialect was to impose a southern atmosphere on her novel. Yet—and here she differs both from Poe and from Melville—she seems strangely reluctant in her dialect representation, as if she considered dialect to be "substandard" English; hence too much of it was politely to be ignored, lest too much emphasis betray a lack of empathy for those black slaves whose lives and family ties were destroyed by what was, for Stowe and for many others, an "unchristian" institution. For Stowe, then, dialect was used in a limited way; since she was essentially a polemicist, dialectal accuracy was not of major importance.

The unexpected but overwhelming reception of *Uncle Tom's Cabin* in America, and its even greater reception in England, paved the way for another abolitionist, William Wells Brown, the "father of the American Negro novel." Brown, born into slavery, reputedly the son of a white slaveholder and a slave mother, was himself a fugitive who escaped when he was eighteen and was trained by the abolitionists as a writer and public speaker. Known primarily as an anti-slavery lecturer, a historian and writer of narratives, Brown published his sole novel, *Clotel, or the President's Daughter* in four different versions. The first version, on which the following discussion is based, appeared in London in 1853, on the heels of the furor over *Uncle Tom's Cabin*.[16] Brown's primary intention in the novel was again polemical; it was to communicate to English readers the inhumanity of slavery and to enlist their aid in its abolition. In the 1853 version the novel's plot revolves around a slave, Currer, and her two daughters, allegedly fathered by Thomas Jefferson. It records the separation of mother and daughters from one another and their mistreatment at the hands of a variety of white owners. All three women die early and tragically. The melodramatic climax of the novel occurs when Clotel, one of the daughters, jumps to her death from the bridge across the Potomac River, within sight of Washington and freedom. Although the novel belongs to a sentimental tradition, whatever strength it has lies in a number of realistically described scenes depicting slave life. One of them focuses on the slave market. In the following passage Pompey, himself a slave who works for a slave trader and who, in Brown's view, helps to perpetuate the system because he cooperates with his master in mistreating fellow slaves, prepares two men for the New Orleans slave market.

> Pompey selected five of the old slaves, took them into a room by themselves, and commenced preparing them for the market. "Well," said Pompey, addressing himself to the company, "I is de gentman dat is to get you ready, so dat you will bring marser a good price in de Orleans market. How old is you?" addressing himself to a man who, from appearance, was not less than forty. "If I live to see next corn-planting time I will either be forty-five or fifty-five, I don't know which." "Dat may be," replied Pompey; "But now you is only thirty years old; dat is what marser says you is to be." "I know I is more den dat," responded

the man. "I knows nothing about dat," said Pompey; "but when you get in de market, an anybody axe you how old you is, and you tell 'em forty-five, marser will tie you up an gib you de whip like smoke. But if you tell 'em dat you is only thirty, den he wont." "Well den, I guess I will only be thirty when dey axe me," replied the chattel.

"What your name?" inquired Pompey. "Geemee," answered the man. "Oh, Uncle Jim, is it?" "Yes." "Den you must have off dem dare whiskers of yours, an when you get to Orleans you must grease dat face an make it look shiney." This was all said by Pompey in a manner which clearly showed that he knew what he was about. "How old is you?" asked Pompey of a tall, strong-looking man. "I was twenty-nine last potato-digging time," said the man. "What's your name?" "My name is Tobias, but dey call me 'Toby'." "Well, Toby, or Mr. Tobias, if dat will suit you better, you is now twenty-three years old, an no more. Dus you hear dat?" "Yes," responded Toby. Pompey gave each to understand how old he was to be when asked by persons who wished to purchase, and then reported to his master that the "old boys" were all right.*[17]

Since there are three speakers of Black English in the passage, it is interesting to look separately at the dialect characteristics revealed in the speech of each of them. Pompey, the least sympathetic of the three, speaks the most in the passage, and the representation of his speech includes the greatest variety of Black English characteristics. His pronunciation of *th* is represented as *d* in *de, dat, dem dare*. There is one example of *v* represented as *b, gib* for *give*. And there are two examples of the recording of reduction

---

*POMPEY
Pronunciation Features
    1. Reduction of consonant clusters: *gentleman > gentman; and > an.*
    2. *th > d: the > de; that > dat; them there > dem dare.*
    3. *v > b: give > gib.*
    4. *asks > axe.*
Eye Dialect: *Does > Dus.*

Grammatical Features
Verbs
    1. Lack of subject-verb agreement; *I is, I knows, You is.*

GEEMEE
Pronunciation Features
    1. *the > d: than > den; that > dat; they > dey.*
    2. *ask > axe.*

Grammatical Features
Verbs
    1. Lack of subject-verb agreement: *I is.*

TOBY
Pronunciation Features
    1. *th > d: they > dey.*

Grammatical Features
    None.

of consonant clusters: *gentman* and *an*. In addition, Pompey uses *axe* for *ask*. In this passage Brown uses only one example of eye dialect—*dus* for *does*. The grammatical characteristics represented affect verbs only. Lack of subject-verb agreement can be seen in *I is, I knows,* and *You is.*

Geemee (whose very name is recorded in eye dialect) and Tobias, or Toby, the slaves for sale with whom the reader is to empathize, are capable, rather inconsistently and unrealistically, of speaking in both Standard English and in dialect. In fact, Geemee's most complex utterance appears in Standard English: " 'If I live to see next corn-planting time I will either be forty-five or fifty-five, I don't know which.' " And Toby reveals his real age in the following Standard English sentence: " 'I was twenty-nine last potato-digging time.' "

In their sentences in dialect, both of the slaves for sale are represented as using only one pronunciation feature of Black English: *th* is represented as *d*. Geemee is recorded as saying *den* for *than, dat* and *dey,* and Toby says *dey.* Brown has Geemee use one example of Black English verb formation—lack of subject-verb agreement in *I is,* while Toby, who admittedly has less to say, is not represented as using Black English verbs at all. Brown's purpose in using Black English dialect is very much like Stowe's—to create a vaguely realistic atmosphere in which the dark-skinned slaves, at least, do not speak Standard English. But "bad" blacks are shown to speak "blacker" English than good blacks. And, as was the case with Stowe, the light-skinned slaves, notably Currer and her daughters, "tragic mulattos" as they clearly are, speak flawless Standard English.

Significantly, anti-slavery polemicists like Brown and Stowe—whether black or white—attempted to reduce the extent of their representation of the characteristics of Black English speech when they sought to establish in the reader an empathy for black characters. They perceived—as Mark Twain's Jim would later put it in a discussion of Frenchmen—that if a character is to be recognized as human, he must "*talk* like a man,"[18] and not like something "special." They were also aware that manipulation and limitation of the use of Black English dialect help to determine the degree of empathy the reader will feel toward its various speakers.

After the Civil War, American fiction moved gradually toward a greater concern for the representation of things as they are, or were. Literary realism for American writers would not really manifest itself until the 1880s. Realism would then come to require the accurate representation of the speech as well as the lives of real people. But before modern realism established itself in the newly populous and industrialized American cities, a concern over the disappearance of the older ways of a rural and provincialized America, and a wish to preserve the realities and its regional speech, would come to be manifest in what is today called the "local color" movement. Since black people who spoke in dialect would in the years immediately following the war generally remain in the South, it would be southern writers (most of whom were white) who would be most interested and best qualified to represent Black English speech in literature in those years.

The local color literature of the decades after the war seemed to follow two different directions. One direction was toward realism. The "realistic" writers attempted to record accurately the pattern of life they observed. Often, as in the work of George Washington Cable, there was an attempt to analyze the relationships between the races. And Joel Chandler Harris's retelling of the folk tales of his region was—at least in part—an attempt to preserve actual stories that were rapidly becoming lost in a changing society.

The other strain in "local color" writing was a retrospective sentimentalism, a continuation of the Romantic strain that had been so evident in American writing earlier in the century. Novels and stories such as those by Thomas Nelson Page glorified life in the ante-bellum South. As with earlier novels in this sentimental tradition, man—including black rural man—was represented as basically good. Yet many of the writers of this tradition also regarded slavery as a benign institution, a social arrangement that brought out the best in both races.

Any literary celebration of a fading regionalism is by its nature conservative, for writers who write about a dying culture, if only to preserve its characteristics for literary appreciation, concern themselves with the values of the past rather than with those appropriate to the present and the future. "Local color" writing itself had a rather modest and somewhat temporary appeal. It takes an unusually skilled and much more cosmopolitan writer, a writer such as Mark Twain (or later, William Faulkner) to be able to grasp the essence of a particular locale fully, to record the various dialects associated with a specific region, and at the same time to transcend the limitations of localism by engaging significant and universal philosophical, psychological, and moral issues. And many of the local colorists of the 1880s and 1890s were themselves limited by the perspectives of their own regions.

The writers of the South who undertook to represent the "local color" of Black English speech produced widely varying results. The variety in their representations reflected the variousness of black speech in the different regions of the South. Black speech in Louisiana was represented as marked by French and-or creole influences. In the representations of Gullah (or Geechee) speakers from the Sea Islands of Georgia may be seen traces of African dialectal influence.

The Black English dialects represented in the passages to be examined here are all examples of provincial and rural Black English speech. These dialects are widely separated geographically. It is not until after the turn of the century, after large numbers of black people moved North and established themselves in an urban setting, that Black English as a unified dialect could be linguistically defined. Still, it is interesting to see how many features of what comes to be known as Black English in the twentieth century can be identified in the passages that follow. For the purpose of better examining the treatment of dialect within similar geographical areas, strict chronological order of the examples will be temporarily abandoned.

Because of the mixture of ethnic groups that could be found in Louisiana at the time of the Civil War—French, Spanish, Scots-Irish, and Anglo-Saxon Americans, as well as blacks—both the New Orleans area and the "Bayou," west of New Orleans, were places associated with the unusual and the picturesque, qualities valued by the regional writers of the latter half of the nineteenth century. George Washington Cable, born in New Orleans, but of New England stock, a southerner with a Puritan conscience, an "outsider" and yet an "insider" in New Orleans, a severe critic of slavery and an objective and knowledgeable observer of the relationships between the races, wrote of this region in what Louis D. Rubin has called the first "modern" southern novel, and described as "an uncompromising attempt to deal honestly with the complexity of Southern racial experience."[19] *The Grandissimes,* published in 1880, and set in 1803, is a novel about two men with the same father and the same name, Honoré Grandissime; one, however, is a quadroon and the other a white. The relationship between the two half brothers and their contrasting treatment by society offers Cable the opportunity of examining and ultimately of criticizing the social and racial problems of ante-bellum New Orleans. Although Cable's material is exotic in nature, his approach is decidedly realistic, and his analysis of New Orleans society under slavery is insightful. Realism is enhanced by his skill in distinguishing between the dialects of the characters. Cable was particularly proud of his representation of Creole dialect.[20] There are, of course, a number of black characters in Cable's novel. One of these is a beautiful quadroon, Palmyre Philosophe, who is respected for her knowledge of voodoo. In the passage that follows, Palmyre speaks her own version of French to the apothecary, Frowenfeld, an outsider to New Orleans society who replies in Standard English.

> *"Bon soi', Miché."* [Monsieur.] A rather hard, yet not repellent smile showed her faultless teeth.
> Frowenfeld bowed.
> *"Mo vien c'erc'er la bourse de Madame."*
> She spoke the best French at her command, but it was not understood.
> The apothecary could only shake his head.
> *"La bourse,"* she repeated, softly smiling, but with a scintillation of the eyes in resentment of his secrutiny.
> *"La bourse,"* she reiterated.
> "Purse?"
> *"Oui, Miché."*
> "You are sent for it?"
> *"Oui, Miché."*
> He drew it from his breast pocket and marked the sudden glisten of her eyes, reflecting the glisten of the gold in the silken mesh.

"*Oui, c'est ça,*" said she, putting her hand out eagerly.

"I am afraid to give you this to-night," said Joseph.

"*Oui,*" ventured she, dubiously, the lightning playing deep back in her eyes.

"You might be robbed," said Frowenfeld. "It is very dangerous for you to be out alone. It will not be long, now, until gun-fire." (Eight o'clock P.M.—the gun to warn slaves to be in-doors, under pain of arrest and imprisonment.)

The object of this solicitude shook her head with a smile at its gratuitousness. The smile showed determination also.

"*Mo pas compren',*" she said.

"Tell the lady to send for it to-morrow."

She smiled helplessly and somewhat vexedly, shrugged and again shook her head. As she did so she heard footsteps and voices in the door at her back.

"*C'est ça,*" she said again with a hurried attempt at extreme amiability; "Dat it; *oui;*" and lifting her hand with some rapidity made a sudden eager reach for the purse, but failed.[21]

In speaking French, Palmyre is shown as having a tendency to drop *r* (also a characteristic of Black English pronunciation), as in her individualized pronunciation of *Miché* for *Monsieur,* and to reduce consonant clusters as in *compren'* for *comprend* (or perhaps this is simply eye dialect for the Standard French). At the point in the exchange at which she is most frustrated and yet most determined, she is shown expressing herself in a typical Creole mixture of English and French: *Dat it, oui.* Palmyre's dialect reflects her position in society. As a quadroon, she attempts to speak French in formal situations with an outsider—but she has not mastered the language. She is more comfortable with Creole—the mixture of French and English—and she reverts to it on occasion.

Another "black" woman in the novel is an old *marchande des calas,* a cake seller, named Clemence, who had been separated from her mother in Virginia and had been sold "down river." In the passage that follows, she wins a verbal exchange with a local doctor and an unidentified white man.

Doctor Keene, in the old days of his health, used to enjoy an occasional skirmish with her. Once, in the course of chaffering over the price of *calas,* he enounced an old current conviction which is not without holders even to this day; for we may still hear it said by those who will not be decoyed down from the mountain fastnesses of the old Southern doctrines, that their slaves were "the happiest people under the sun." Clemence had made bold to deny this with argumentative indignation, and was courteously informed in retort that she had promulgated a falsehood of magnitude.

"W'y, Mawse Chawlie," she replied, "does you s'pose one po' nigga kin tell a big lie? No, sah! But w'en de whole people tell w'at ain' so—if dey know it, aw if dey don' know it—den dat *is* a big lie!" And she laughed to contortion.

"What is that you say?" he demanded, with mock ferocity. "You charge white people with lying?"

"Oh, sakes, Mawse Chawlie, no! De people don't mek up dat ah; de debble pass it on 'em. Don' you know de debble ah de grett cyount-'feiteh? Ev'y piece o' money he mek he tek an' put some debblemen' on de under side, an' one o' his pootiess lies on top: an' 'e gilt dat lie, and 'e rub dat lie on 'is elbow, an' 'e shine dat lie, an' 'e put 'is bess licks on dat lie; entel ev'ybody say: 'Oh, how pooty!' An' dey tek it fo' good money, yass—and pass it! Dey b'lieb it!"

"Oh," said some one at Doctor Keene's side, disposed to quiz, "you niggers don't know when you are happy."

"Dass so Mawse—*c'est vrai, oui!*" she answered quickly: "we donno no mo'n white folks!"

The laugh was against him.*[22]

Clemence's speech is represented as including many of the pronunciation and grammatical characteristics usually associated with modern Black English. Cable has her pronounce voiced *th* as *d*, as in *dey* and *de*, and *v* as *b*, as in *debble* and *b'lieb*. As her speech is represented, *r* is lost; *Master Charlie* is recorded as *Mawse Chawlie* and *sir* as *sah*. There are a number of examples of reduction of consonant clusters in the passage, as in *don'* for *don't* and *bess* for *best*, and an initial unstressed syllable is occasionally dropped, as in *s'pose* and *bout*. The primary grammatical feature is a regularization of the third person singular present tense, as in *he mek* and *he tek*, and there is one example of a double negative: *we donno no mo'n white folks*.

But the most distinctive feature in the above passage is Clemence's French expression, *c'est vrai, oui;* she utters it naturally, totally unaware that it is an expression from a different language from that which she was speaking earlier. It is the admixture of French and English in the speech of black people of New Orleans that identifies them with their specific locale. The examples of Palmyre's and Clemence's speech illustrate clearly that although French is considered more aristocratic than English, practically

Pronunciation Features

1. Reduction of consonant clusters: *Master > mawse; don't > don'; and > an; best > bess; ain't > ain'; more than > mo'n.*

2. *th > d: they > dey; the > de; then > den; that > dat.*

3. Loss of r: *Master Charlie > Mawse Chawlie; poor nigger > po' nigga; sir > sah; or > aw; pretty > pooty; every > ev'y; for > fo'.*

4. *v > b; devil > debble; believe > b'lieb.*

5. Loss of initial unstressed syllable: *suppose > s'pose; about > bout.*

6. Vowel fronting: *can > kin.*

Grammatical Features

Verbs

1. Regularization of third person singular present tense: *he mek; he tek; 'e gilt; 'e rub; 'e shine; 'e put; ev'y body say.*

2. Lack of subject-verb agreement: *does you s'pose.*

Negative

1. *ain'.*

2. Double negative: *we donno no mo'n white folks.*

speaking, the two languages are interfused to form a distinctive regional dialect.

Unlike George Washington Cable, who was born in New Orleans and represented that society in his literary work from the perspective of a qualified "insider," Kate Chopin, writing in the 1890s about the Bayou country west of New Orleans, was introduced to the area only after her marriage. Yet, despite the fact that she was born in St. Louis and actually did not write about Louisiana until she returned to St. Louis after her husband's early death, her two collections of short stories and her novel are admired for their sensitive presentation of the culture of the Acadians, or Cajuns, the French who came to Louisiana from Canada, in contrast to the more aristocratic Creole French who could trace their ancestry to the original French settlers.

Like Cable, Chopin uses dialect realistically, to indicate differences of social class among her characters. In one of her short stories, "At the 'Cadian Ball," taken from *Bayou Folk* (1894), Alcée Laballière, who is distraught because a cyclone has destroyed nine hundred acres of rice he had planted, sets out in the middle of the night for the Acadian Ball—without informing his mother's godchild, Clarisse, who loves him. In the passage that follows, Alcée's black servant, Bruce, recounts for Clarisse the conversation he had with his master before he rode away.

> He say, "I kin mak out to stan' up an' gi' an' take wid any man I knows, lessen hit's John L. Sulvun. But w'en God A'mighty an' a 'oman jines fo'ces agin me, dat's one too many fur me." I tell 'im, "Jis so," whils' I'se makin' out to bresh a spot off w'at ain' dah, on he coat colla. I tell 'im, "You wants li'le res', suh." He say, "No, I wants li'le fling; dat w'at I wants; an I gwine git it. Pitch me a fis'ful o' clo'es in dem 'ar saddlebags." Dat w'at he say. Don't you bodda, missy. He jis' gone a-caperin' yonda to de Cajun ball. Uh—uh—de skeeters is fair' a-swarmin' like bees roun' yo' foots!*[23]

Pronunciation Features
  1. Reduction of consonant clusters: *Sullivan > Sulvun; Almighty > A'mighty; little > li'le; rest > res'; fistful > fis'ful; clothes > clo'es; stand > stan'; round > roun'; just > jis'.*
  2. th > d: *that > dat; the > de; then > den; there > dah; with > wid; bother > bodda.*
  3. Loss of >r: *forces > fo'ces; bother > bodda; yonder > yonda; your > yo'; collar > colla; there > dah.*
  4. Nasalization: *going to > gwine; a-swarming > a-swarmin'; a-capering > a-caperin'; making > makin'.*
  5. Loss of initial unstressed syllable: *mosquitoes > skeeters.*
  6. Loss of glide: *joins > jines.*
  7. Vowel fronting: *can > kin; against > agin; get > git; just > jis'.*

Grammatical Features
Verbs
  1. Regularization of third person singular present tense: *he say.*
  2. Lack of subject-verb agreement: *de skeeters is; I knows; I wants; You wants.*
  3. Zero copula: *he jes' gone a-caperin'; dat wa't he say.*
Negative
  1. *ain'*
Nominative pronoun as possessive: *he coat colla.*
Hypercorrection: *your feet > yo' foots.*

The representation of Bruce's speech is filled with the pronunciation and grammatical features associated with Black English. His pronunciation of voiced *th* is recorded as *d,* as in *den, de, wid,* and *r* is omitted in *fo'ces, bodda, yonda, colla.* In Bruce's speech Chopin has recorded a number of examples of reduction of consonant clusters, as in *Sulvun, res',* and *stan'* and several examples of nasalization, as in *gwine* and *makin'.*

The grammatical characteristics Chopin records in Bruce's speech are more varied than those Cable represented in New Orleans Black English speech. Lack of subject-verb agreement is, as usual, the dominant feature, as in *I knows, I wants,* but there are also examples of zero copula, as in *he jis' gone a-caperin'.* As expected, Chopin's representation of Bruce's speech includes *ain'.* She also uses the nominative instead of the possessive pronoun form: *he coat colla.* And there is a single example of hypercorrection, in *yo' foots.*

Although there is no suggestion of French in Bruce's speech (as there often is with Chopin's white speakers, just as there is with Cable's Creoles), she does have a tendency to record the fronting of back vowels, as in *kin* instead of *can, bresh* instead of *brush, jis'* for *just, jines* for *joins.* These characteristics of a regional pronunciation are broadly associated with the nonstandard speech of the deep South.

Thus the speech representations of Chopin's characters seem to conform generally to that of Black English speakers today. Kate Chopin—who perhaps heard the blacks of St. Louis speak more frequently than those of Cajun Louisiana—gained the peculiarly regional flavor in her literary dialect by representing general characteristics of Black English for black speakers and setting that representation beside the dialect speech of the white Cajun speakers with whom they spoke.

If George Washington Cable and Kate Chopin helped to familiarize the American public with the variety of Louisiana dialects, Joel Chandler Harris became the most popular recorder of the black dialect of Middle Georgia. Harris's *Uncle Remus: His Songs and His Sayings,* first published in 1880, was a collection of black folk tales, analogues for which have been found in American Indian folklore and in the folklore of Europe, Asia, and Africa. These stories are told by a black slave narrator who lives a life of apparent racial harmony on a southern plantation.[24] But the "hero" of Uncle Remus's tales is usually Brer Rabbit, an "underdog" in the animal hierarchy who is able to survive because of his quickness of foot and wit. Thus on one level the reader is invited to read the stories as allegories that define the complex relationship between the races. Depending upon one's point of view, Harris may be perceived as supportive of the southern plantation system or as profoundly ironic in his treatment of it. And Uncle Remus can be seen as a satisfied slave, well cared for and happy with his white "master," or as an American Aesop, a subversive slave-fabulist teaching a white child the hidden realities of life and of black-white relations on the plantation. Perhaps like his hero, Brer Rabbit, Uncle Remus (or even Harris) could outwit a more powerful adversary; perhaps Uncle Remus is giving the child, and the reading public, an early lesson in post–Civil War race relations.

Harris prided himself on his accurate recording of dialect. In the introduction to his first book of Uncle Remus stories, *Uncle Remus: His Songs and His Sayings,* Harris states that his purpose is not only to record dialect realistically; he also intends to use dialect to convey what he considers to be innate character traits of blacks: their "poetic imagination," their "quaint and homely humor," and "a certain picturesque sensitiveness."

> The dialect, it will be observed, is wholly different from that of the Hon. Pompey Smash and his literary descendants, and different also from the intolerable misrepresentations of the minstrel stage, but it is at least phonetically genuine. Nevertheless, if the language of Uncle Remus fails to give vivid hints of the really poetic imagination of the Negro; if it fails to embody the quaint and homely humor which was his most prominent characteristic; if it does not suggest a certain picturesque sensitiveness—a curious exaltation of mind and temperament not to be defined by words—then I have reproduced the form of the dialect merely, and not the essence, and my attempt may be accounted a failure.[25]

Harris's representation of dialect is illustrated in the following excerpt from his well-known "The Wonderful Tar-Baby Story."

> "Didn't the fox *never* catch the rabbit, Uncle Remus?" asked the little boy the next evening.
> "He come mighty nigh it, honey, sho's you born—Brer Fox did. One day atter Brer Rabbit fool 'im wid dat calamus root, Brer Fox went ter wuk en got 'im some tar, en mix it wid some turkentime, en fix up a contrapshun wat he call a Tar-Baby, en he tuck dish yer Tar-Baby en he sot'er in de big road, en den he lay off in de bushes fer to see wat de news wuz gwineter be. En he didn't hatter wait long, nudder, kaze bimeby here come Brer Rabbit pacin' down de road—lippity-clippity, clippity-lippity—dez ez sassy ez a jay-bird. Brer Fox, he lay low. Brer Rabbit come prancin' 'long twel he spy de Tar-Baby, en den he fotch up on his behime legs like he wuz 'stonished. De Tar Baby, she sot dar, she did, en Brer Fox, he lay low.*[26]

*Pronunciation Features
   1. Reduction of consonant clusters: *after* > *atter; Brother* > *Brer; have to* > *hatter; just as* > *dez ez; and* > *en.*
   2. *th* > *d: neither* > *nudder; that* > *dat; the* > *de; then* > *den; there* > *dar; this* > *dish; with* > *wid.*
   3. Loss of *r: work* > *wuk; sure* > *sho'.*
   4. Nasalization: *by and by* > *bimeby; going to* > *gwineter; behind* > *behime; pacing* > *pacin'; prancing* > *prancin'.*
   5. Loss of initial unstressed syllable: *astonished* > *'stonished; until* > *twel.*
Eye Dialect: *as* > *ez; contraption* > *contrapshun; was* > *wuz.*

The excerpt above illustrates Harris's intention to convey both realism and humor. The dialect representation includes a number of pronunciation and grammatical features usually associated with Black English. Uncle Remus's pronunciation of voiced *th* is rendered as *d*, as in *nudder* for *neither* and *dish* for *this*. *R* is often lost, as in *wuk* for *work*, and consonant clusters are reduced, as in *atter* for *after* and *Brer* for *Brother*. Representation of nasalization is frequent, as in *bimeby, gwinter,* and *behime,* and there are two representations of the omission of an initial unstressed syllable, as in *'stonished* and *twel*. The occasional examples of eye dialect, as in *contrapshun, wuz,* and *ez,* are surprising in the work of one as knowledgeable about dialect as Harris.

The Black English grammatical features in the above excerpt all involve verbs. Regularization of the third person singular present tense form, as in *he come, here come Brer Rabbit* is represented, as is the omission of the final *-ed* suffix to indicate past tense—in *he fix,* instead of *he fixed,* and *he spy* instead of *he spied*. Finally, there is a single example of the representation of zero copula, *sho's you born*.

Yet it is in the figurative language and in the vocabulary and rhythmic patternings that Harris really conveys the sensitivity, humor, and poetic imagination of his black narrator. *Turkentime* for *turpentine* is probably an example of folk etymology; it sounds very much like *turkeytime*. *Lippity-clippity, clippity-lippity* is onomatopoetic, and the substitution of *wat* for *who* is an example of reduction, of depersonalization. It may also be a fusion of two relative pronouns, *that* and *who*. But here *wat* is a neologism; its use makes it unnecessary for a speaker to distinguish between traditionally distinctive pronouns. And the rhythms and repetition of *Brer Fox, he lay low,* establishes an almost metered refrain for the story.

The combination of the dialectal characteristics and folk features locate Uncle Remus's dialect, even to someone totally unfamiliar with Southern speech, in the plantation South. Although it might take a dialectologist to locate it specifically in Middle Georgia, the general reader can easily distinguish it from the speech of Louisiana discussed earlier.

If Uncle Remus's speech is to be associated with Middle Georgia, another character Harris created, an old African named Daddy Jack, speaks Gullah, the dialect of blacks from the Sea Islands of Georgia and the Carolinas. In *Nights with Uncle Remus* (1881), Daddy Jack often converses with Uncle Remus and the little boy and sometimes he tells a story himself. The following excerpt is from "Why the Alligator's Back is Rough."

Grammatical Features
Verbs
   1. Regularization of third person singular present tense: *he come; here come Brer Rabbit.*
   2. Loss of *-ed* suffix to indicate past tense: *[he] fix; he fotch; [he] mix; he spy; Brer Rabbit fool.*
   3. Zero copula: *sho's you born.*

"B'er Rabbit, 'e do blow un 'e do ketch um bre't'. 'E pit one year wey Dog is bin-a bark; 'e pit one eye 'pon B'er 'Gater. 'E lissen, 'e look; 'e look, 'e lissen. 'E no yeddy Dog, un 'e comforts come back. Bumbye B'er 'Gater, e' come drowsy; 'e do nod, nod, un 'e head sway down, tel ma'sh-grass tickle 'e nose, un 'e do cough sem lak 'e teer up da crik by da root. 'E no lak dis place fer sleep at, un 'e is crawl troo da ma'sh 'pon dry lan'; 'e is mek fer da broom-grass fiel'. 'E mek 'e bed wid 'e long tail, un 'e is 'tretch 'ese'f out at 'e lenk. 'E is shed 'e y-eye, un opun 'e mout', un tek 'e nap.[27]

Linguists today assert that Gullah (which Daddy Jack speaks) is, of all the varieties of Black English, the dialect most closely related to African languages, the least decreolized of the Black English dialects. Harris would have agreed; in his introduction to *Nights with Uncle Remus,* he explains some of the dialectal features to be found in the representations of Daddy Jack's speech in passages like the one above.

The dialect of Daddy Jack, which is that of the negroes on the Sea Islands and the rice plantations, though it may seem at first glance to be more difficult than that of Uncle Remus, is, in reality, simpler and more direct. It is the negro dialect in its most primitive state—the "Gullah" talk of some of the negroes on the Sea Islands, being merely a confused and untranslatable mixture of English and African words. . . . A key to the dialect may be given very briefly. The vocabulary is not an extensive one—more depending upon the manner, the form of expression, and the inflection, than upon the words employed. It is thus an admirable vehicle for story-telling. It recognizes no gender, and scorns the use of the plural number except accidentally. " 'E" stands for "he" "she" or "it," and "dem" may allude to one thing, or may include a thousand. The dialect is laconic and yet rambling, full of repetitions, and abounding in curious elisions, that give an unexpected quaintness to the simplest statements.[28]

In linguistic circles, Harris's name has become synonymous with accurate representation of the late nineteenth-century Georgia dialects. To the more literarily inclined, Harris has gained a lasting reputation as a local colorist who regarded the representation of dialect both as a means for conveying a sense of realism in his stories and as a medium for the communication of the peculiarly subtle, humorous, and poetic linguistic capability of Georgia blacks.

Just before the end of the century, in 1899, Charles W. Chesnutt, a black of North Carolina ancestry, published his first book, *The Conjure Woman,* a collection of tales told by a former slave, Uncle Julius McAdoo. Although modeled on Uncle Remus, Uncle Julius is a less stereotyped character, obviously shrewder, more apparently self-interested, and more overtly aware of the realities of slavery before the Civil War. His stories are not animal fables, but are "true" accounts of people and local events, events whose outcome is often determined by a "conjure." Although Uncle Julius claims that his stories are true, there is usually a motive in their telling. In "The Grey Wolf's Ha'nt," for instance, Uncle Julius hopes by telling the story to retain for himself the exclusive use of a particularly productive beehive. In the following selection from the story, Uncle Julius begins to relate the tale of Dan, one of "Mars Dugal' McAdoo's" slaves, who was turned into a gray wolf by a conjure man whose son Dan had killed.

> "Way back yander befo' de wah," began Julius, "ole Mars Dugal' McAdoo useter own a nigger name' Dan. Dan wuz big en strong en hearty en peaceable en good-nachu'd most er de time, but dange'ous ter aggervate. He alluz done his task, en nebber had no trouble wid de w'ite folks, but woe be unter de nigger w'at 'lowed he c'd fool wid Dan, fer he wuz mos' sho' ter git a good lammin'. Soon ez eve'ybody foun' Dan out, dey did n' many un 'em 'temp' ter 'sturb 'im. De one dat did would 'a' wush' he had n', ef he could 'a' libbed long ernuff ter do any wushing'."*[29]

Chesnutt's representation of Uncle Julius's dialect reveals many characteristics typical of modern Black English speech. His pronunciation of voiced *th* is recorded as *d* in *de* and *wid,* and his pronunciation of *v* as *b* in *libbed* for *live.* There are several examples of the recording of his tendency to drop *r*—as in *befo', wah,* and *sho',* and of his tendency to reduce consonant clusters in *ole, mars, foun', mos',* and *wush* rather than *wished.* He is generally represented as nasalizing words ending in *-ing,* as in *lammin'* and *wushin'* and he is represented as dropping his initial unstressed syllables in *'sturb, 'lowed,* and *temp'.* In addition to representing these "real pronunciation features," Chesnutt also relies heavily on eye dialect in the above passage to represent Uncle Julius's speech: *wuz, w'ite, w'at, c'd,* and *alluz* are all examples.

The verbs in this passage do not reveal the usual Black English charac-

Pronunciation Features

1. Reduction of consonant clusters: *old > ole; master > mars; found > foun'; most > mos'; wished > wush.*
2. *th > d: the > de; with > wid.*
3. Loss of *r: before > befo'; war > wah; dangerous > dange'ous; sure > sho'; everybody > eve'ybody; good-natured > good-nachu'd.*
4. *v > b: lived > libbed.*
5. Nasalization: *lamming > lammin'; wishing > wushin'.*
6. Loss of initial unstressed syllable: *disturb > 'sturb; allowed > 'lowed; attempted > temp'.*
Eye Dialect: *was > wuz; white > w'ite; what > w'at; could > c'd; always > alluz; as > ez; aggravate > aggervate.*

Grammatical Features
Verbs

1. Loss of *-ed* suffix to indicate past tense: *named > name'; attempted > temp'; used to > useter.*
2. Loss of *-ed* suffix to indicate past participle *would' 'a' wush'.*
3. Past participle instead of past tense: *He alluz done.*
Negative
1. Double negative: *he . . . never had no trouble.*

teristics of lack of subject-verb agreement and zero copula. However, Chesnutt does employ two other features affecting verbs. He indicates that Uncle
Julius does not pronounce final -*ed* in the past tense form, as in *name'* for
named or *temp'* for *attempted*. Furthermore, he represents Uncle Julius's
use of the past participal form in place of the expected past tense, as in *he
. . . done* rather than *he did*. There is one example of the double negative in
this passage: *he . . . never had no trouble*.

The last local colorist is the only example to be considered here of a
writer whose commitment is clearly to the tradition-oriented "romantic"
rather than the "realist" tradition. Thomas Nelson Page was born in
Hanover County, in eastern Virginia, and represented that area and its Black
English dialect in his stories of the Old South. Page sentimentalized the days
before the Civil War and depicted Virginia slavery as a benevolent feudalism. His stories, collected in *In Ole Virginia,* published in 1887, are filled
with nostalgia for a heroic past, a time when blacks accepted their "place" as
slaves and enjoyed making white people comfortable.

In Page's most famous story, "Marse Chan," which takes place after the
war, Sam, an old black man, pathetically bemoans the glorious past when he
served his master. Now that his master is dead, there is no life for Sam other
than to tend the graves of his master and his master's beloved, and to
continue to care for his master's old dog. Without recognizing the implications of his grief, Sam laments the passing of an idyllic life; his lament seems
to indicate his inability to adjust to his changed situation and to know how to
behave as a free man. In the following passage, Sam begins to tell the
traveler who has stopped him about his former master.

> "Well, when Marse Chan wuz born, dey wuz de grettes' doin's at
> home you ever did see. De folks all hed holiday, jes' like in de Chris-
> 'mas. Ole marster (we didn' call 'im *ole* marster tell arfter Marse Chan
> wuz born—befo' dat he wuz jes' de marster, so)—well, ole marster, his
> face fyar shine wid pleasure, an' all de folks wuz mighty glad, too,
> 'cause dey all loved ole marster, and aido' dey did step aroun' right
> peart when ole marster was lookin' at 'em, dyar warn' nyar han' on de
> place but what, ef he wanted anythin', would walk up to de back poach,
> an' say he warn' to see de marster. An' ev'ybody wuz talkin' 'bout de
> young marster, an' de maids an' de wimmens 'bout de kitchen wuz
> sayin' how 'twuz de purties' chile dey ever see; an' at dinner-time de
> mens (all on 'em hed holiday) come roun' de poach an' ax how de missis
> an' de young marster wuz, an' ole marster come out on de poach an'
> smile wus'n a 'possum, an' sez, 'Thankee! Bofe doin' fust rate, boys;'
> an' den he stepped back in de house, sort o' laughin' to hisse'f, an' in a
> minute he come out ag'in wid de baby in he arms, all wrapped up in
> flannens an' things, an' sez, 'Heah he is, boys.' "[*30]

*Pronunciation Features
   1. Reduction of consonant clusters: *old > ole; and > an'; child > chile; round > roun';
greatest > grettes'; just > jes'; Christmas > Chris'mas.*

As a "Note" to *In Ole Virginia,* Page inserted a brief description of the black dialect of Eastern Virginia that Sam speaks.

> The dialect of the negroes of Eastern Virginia differs totally from that of the Southern negroes, and in some material points from that of those located farther west.
>
> The elision is so constant that it is impossible to produce the exact sound, and in some cases it has been found necessary to subordinate the phonetic arrangement to intelligibility.
>
> The following rules may, however, aid the reader:
>
> The final consonant is rarely sounded. Adverbs, prepositions, and short words are frequently slighted, as is the possessive. The letter *r* is not usually rolled except when used as a substitute for *th,* but is pronounced *ah.*
>
> For instance, the following is a fair representation of the peculiarities cited:
>
> The sentence, "It was curious, he said, he wanted to go into the other army," would sound: " 'Twuz cu-yus, he say, he wan'(t) (to) go in(to) 'turr ah-my."[31]

The most distinctive feature in Page's list is probably the elision; the other features Page mentions correspond with a contemporary description of Black English. In the above excerpt, Page represents Sam's voiced *th* as *d,* in *day* for *they, aldo'* for *although, dyar* for *there,* and unvoiced *th* as *f,* in *bofe.* He frequently represents Sam's silent *r,* in *poach* for *porch* and *fust* for *first* and *heah* for *here.* There are several examples of reduction of consonant clusters, as in *chile* for *child, Chris'mas* for *Christmas,* and *ole* for *old,* and of nasalization, as in *flannens* for *flannels,* and *Chan* for *Channing.* Sam also is recorded as dropping an occasional initial unstressed syllable, as in *'cause* and *'bout. Ax* substitutes for *ask.* There are a number of examples of eye dialect: *sez* for *says, ag'in* for *again, wuz* for *was.*

The grammatical features in this representation of Sam's speech are

   2. Changes in *th:*
     a. *th* (voiced) > *d: they > dey; the > de; that > dat; although > aldo; there > dyar.*
     b. *th* (unvoiced) > *f: both > bofe.*
   3. Loss of *r: before > befo'; porch > poach; worse than > wus'n; first > fust; here >* *heah; everybody > ev'ybody; prettiest > purties'.*
   4. Nasalization: *flannels > flannens; Channing > Chan; doings > doin's; laughing >* *laughin'; looking > lookin'; talking > talkin'; saying > sayin'.*
   5. Loss of initial unstressed syllable: *because > 'cause; about > 'bout.*
   6. *ask > ax.*
   7. Diphthongization: *fair > fyar; there > dyar; nerrya > nyar.*
Eye Dialect: *was > wuz; had > hed; says > sez; again > ag'in.*

Grammatical Features
Verbs
   1. Present (regularized) instead of past tense: *he come.*
Negative
   1. Double negative: *dyar warn' nyar han'.*
Nominative pronoun as possessive: *in he arms.*
Hypercorrection: *wimmens; mens.*

varied. Page has Sam use present instead of past tense in *de mens . . . come,* instead of *came.* There is one example of a double negative: *dyar warn' nyar han'.* But Page does not limit the grammatical features in Sam's dialect to those involving verbs and negatives. There is an example of the use of the nominative instead, the possessive pronoun form, as in *in he arms,* and two examples of hypercorrect forms: *wimmens* and *mens.*

Page's representation of Eastern Virginia Black English dialect differs from that of the other black dialects from the other regions of the South discussed so far. In his representation of diphthongization, words such as *fyar* for *fair(ly), dyar* for *there, heah* for *here,* and *nyar* for *nerrya,* and the "drawl" effect obtained by the phrase *dyar warn' nyar han' on de place,* are quite different from the other representations of the other southern black dialects. Nor has this feature been identified in the historical black speech of Louisiana, Georgia, or North Carolina. Page's is a full representation; it is replete with pronunciation features and does not avoid syntactic idiosyncracies. It is similar to much nineteenth-century dialect writing in that it seems to be bent on representing black speech as "special" and on suggesting the "illiteracy" of the black speaker—on eliciting from the reader a patronizing attitude rather than one of empathy.

Although a number of writers would continue to work within the traditions of "local color"—and to represent Black English speech regionally until well into the twentieth century—the movement seemed to lose its momentum as the nineteenth century came to a close. Yet the movement gave impetus to one writer who transcended its limitations and—with a dialect-novel—took his place among the greatest in our literature. Mark Twain's *Huckleberry Finn* was rooted in a particular time and place, and in the dialects of that time and place. The novel is set in Hannibal, Missouri, where Samuel L. Clemens, its author, had spent his childhood, and on the lower Mississippi, where as a young man he had worked as a steamboat pilot.

While his literary predecessors and contemporaries had usually regarded the days before the war with a clear but certain point of view—either with nostalgia, as did Page, or with criticism, as did Stowe and Cable—Twain's perspective, as in most situations, was ambivalent. He repudiated the historical significance of the Civil War, in which he was only briefly involved, and the values of the Old South, which his parents had claimed as their place of origin; yet he also rejected the New America, with its tasteless rich and its grasping and greedy middle class. He resisted the American impulse toward simplification and saw instead the infinite complexities experience offered. These complexities are evident in *Adventures of Huckleberry Finn,* published in 1885. The novel is concerned with a number of provocative themes—the relationship between the individual and society, the contrast between life on the river and life on land, the relationship between father and son, and the distortion of societal values, especially of those regarding race. But the subject of most interest to this discussion is the characterization of the escaped slave, Jim, Huck's traveling companion on his trip down the river, and the representation of his speech.

Critics have reacted in conflicting ways to Jim. Some perceive him as a child. Others see him as Huck's surrogate father. Still others see him as Huck's teacher. Certainly Jim functions in the role of teacher, and one lesson Jim surely teaches and Huck less surely learns is that in order to be truly free and to understand fully the meaning of being human, one has to separate himself from society and its values. And society's racial values are very much at issue. Central to Huck's education is his learning to relate to Jim as a "man" instead of as a "nigger."[32]

One of the remarkable facts about *Adventures of Huckleberry Finn* is that, since it is entirely narrated by Huck, it is written entirely in dialect. Yet, since the novel contains direct speech, not one dialect, but several, are represented. In an explanatory note at the beginning of the novel, "The Author" sets forth his intentions and procedures as regards these dialects. He claims to have undertaken to distinguish between a number of different dialects in the novel, all of them associated with the Central Mississippi River Valley.

> In this book a number of dialects are used, to wit: the Missouri negro dialect; the extremest form of the back-woods South-Western dialect; the ordinary "Pike-County" dialect; and four modified varieties of this last. The shadings have not been done in a hap-hazard fashion, or by guess-work; but pains-takingly, and with the trustworthy guidance and support of personal familiarity with these several forms of speech.
>
> I make this explanation for the reason that without it many readers would suppose that all these characters were trying to talk alike and not succeeding.[33]

Although from his own statement—and indeed from the text—it is unclear how many dialects Twain has sought to distinguish, whether he claims a minimum of three or a maximum of seven, one critic, Curt M. Rulon, is of the opinion that there are basically only two, "a mixture of Caucasian (South) Midland and Southern speech on the one hand, and a mixture of Negro (South) Midland and Southern speech on the other hand."[34] So of Mark Twain's dialects here, certainly at least one of them is a localized Black English.

The passage that follows is taken from chapter 14, when Huck and Jim are relaxing on the island just after their escape. Huck has read to Jim about "kings and dukes and earls and such"[35] and then Jim tells Huck his interpretation of the story of King Solomon and of the two women who both claimed the same newborn child.

> "I doan k'yer what de widder say, he *warn't* no wise man, nuther. He had some er de dad-fetchedes' ways I ever see. Does you know 'bout dat chile dat he 'uz gwyne to chop in two?"
> "Yes, the widow told me all about it."

"*Well,* den! Warn' dat de beatenes' notion in de worl'? You jes' take en look at it a minute. Dah's de stump, dah—dat's one er de women; heah's you—dat's de yuther one; I's Sollermun; en dish-yer dollar bill's de chile. Bofe un you claims it. What does I do? Does I shin aroun' mongs' de neighbors en fine out which un you de bill *do* b'long to, en han' it over to de right one, all safe en soun', de way dat anybody dat had any gumption would? No—I take en whack de bill in *two,* en give half un it to you, en de yuther half to de yuther woman. Dat's de way Sollermun was gwyne to do wid de chile. Now I want to ast you: what's de use er dat half a bill?—can't buy noth'n wid it. En what use is a half a chile? I would'n give a dern for a million un um."*[36]

Jim's speech is carefully marked by Black English pronunciation and grammatical features. As expected, Mark Twain records voiced *th* as *d,* as in *dat, den,* and *dish-yer,* and unvoiced *th* as *f,* as in *bofe.* Jim's pronunciation deletes *r,* as in *heah* for *here* and *dah* for *there.* The pronunciation feature Mark Twain represents most frequently is reduction of consonant clusters, which usually involves dropping a final *d* or *t,* as in *chile* for *child,* *worl'* for *world,* or *doan* for *don't* and *mongs'* for *amongst.* Jim is also recorded as nasalizing, as in *gwyne* for *going to,* and with occasionally dropping an initial unstressed syllable, as in *bout* and *mongs'.* In the above passage, Mark Twain uses only one example of eye dialect, *'uz* for *was.*

The Black English grammatical features represented in the passage all involve verbs. Jim is represented as using the present tense instead of the past tense—*I ever see* instead of *saw.* Jim's speech is also represented as being marked by lack of subject-verb agreement as in *does you know* and *what does I do?* As Curt Rulon points out, the paletalized stop [ky] in *k'yer,* which is recorded in Huck's speech as well as Jim's, helps to identify the dialect as South-Western.[37]

Mark Twain's representation of Jim's dialect is certainly extremely well done. The curious spellings, the alterations in syntax, the strange figuration and vocabulary individuate Jim; if his speech were set beside Standard

Pronunciation Features
   1. Reduction of consonant clusters: *child* > *chile; world* > *worl'; don't* > *doan; just* > *jes'; amongst* > *mongs'; wouldn't* > *wouldn'; dad-fetchedest* > *dad-fetchedes'; beatenest* > *beatenes'; and* > *en; around* > *aroun'; find* > *fine; hand* > *han'; sound* > *soun'; ask* > *ast.*
   2. Changes in *th:*
      a. *th* (voiced) > *d: that* > *dat; the* > *de; then* > *den; there* > *dah; this-here* > *dish-yer.*
      b. *th* (unvoiced) > *f: both* > *bofe.*
   3. Loss of *r: here* > *heah; there* > *dah.*
   4. Nasalization: *going to* > *gwyne; don't* > *doan.*
   5. Loss of initial unstressed syllable: *about* > *bout; amongst* > *mongs'.*
Eye Dialect: *was* > *uz.*

Grammatical Features
Verbs
   1. Regularization of third person singular present tense: *de widder say.*
   2. Lack of subject-verb agreement: *does you know; I am* > *I's; what does I do?*
   3. Present instead of past tense: *I ever see.*

English, it might well have made him the object of ridicule. But, of course, it is not so juxtaposed. For the whole novel is in dialect, and Jim's speech, although highly individuated, cannot be judged against any standard. Huck's speech is similarly without a Standard English context. For both Huck and Jim speak dialects that are, while clearly nonstandard, also clearly and "specially" articulate. It is not necessary to reiterate what so many critics— Henry Nash Smith not the least of these—have said of Huck's and Jim's language. But it might well be wise here to recall Melville's Fleece for a moment. For the "specialness" of dialect in *Huckleberry Finn* also gives the reader a fresh perspective. The reader, deprived as he is of received linguistic standard, must—like Huck—perceive experience anew.

Although *Huckleberry Finn* can clearly be considered part of the "realistic" tradition as far as the treatment of natural speech is concerned, Twain has achieved a fusion of form and content in the novel that had not been so fully accomplished earlier in American literature. Such fusion of dialect speech and characterization, such organic and individuated dialect transmission, was hardly to become the practice of the novelists of the late nineteenth century who wrote after *Huckleberry Finn* was published. More usual was the development of a conventionalized, almost stylized method of dialect representation, drawn, often indiscriminately, from the "stock" of the recorded black dialect speech features of the local colorists or from the stage artificialities of the rather mannered "Negro" speech employed by the "locutors" of the minstrel shows, an indigenous form of comic entertainment then gaining widespread acceptance on American stages.

One late nineteenth century writer who was clearly not influenced by the possibilities for dialect explored in *Huckleberry Finn* is Stephen Crane. Crane is not usually remembered as a regionalist, nor as a comic writer, nor even as a dialect writer (although much of his finest work is shot through with dialect passages). Indeed, Stephen Crane almost certainly would have bridled at the suggestion that he be identified as a retrospective local colorist. Crane is more usually regarded as a precursor of twentieth-century realism, or as an impressionist whose awareness of the essentially subjective nature of reality pointed the way to the fiction of the 1920s. Sometimes he is seen as a literary naturalist whose darkened awareness committed him to examination of the unspeakable and the undisclosed in American life. He is known primarily for his "naturalistic" (and rather vigorously dialectal) war novel, *The Red Badge of Courage;* for his dialect novel of the Irish slums of New York, *Maggie: A Girl of the Streets;* or for a few distinguished short stories, most of which take place in the West or in an open boat at sea. In few of these works do black characters appear.

However, Crane did write at least one set of stories in which a number of black characters appear and speak in dialect and of which several are distinguished. These *Tales of Whilomville,* written in the late 1890s and set in "Whilomville," an upstate New York town closely modeled on Port Jervis, where Crane had spent some of his boyhood, are retrospective tales, realistic but centered on the experiences of boys and of blacks. One of the stories, "The Monster," is a radically expressionistic and strikingly modern story—certain to remain among Crane's finest works. But it is strange to see how this progressive, realistic, modernist writer, when undertaking to represent the dialect speech of black characters, reverts to stereotypical, almost "minstrel show" speech and language.

"The Knife," one of the *Tales of Whilomville,* is an example. The story is based on the tired joke about the black man who is irresistibly attracted to a ripe watermelon patch. As the story opens, Si Bryant, a white man, is cultivating his watermelons. A black man, Peter Washington, pauses to admire the ripe fruit.

> "Take your eye off them there melons, you rascal," said Si placidly.
> The negro's face widened in a grin of delight. "Well, Mist' Bryant, I raikon I ain't on'y make m'se'f covertous er-lookin' at dem yere mellums, sure 'nough. Dey suhtainly is grand."
> "That's all right," responded Si with affected bitterness of spirit. "That's all right. Just don't you admire 'm too much—that's all."
> Peter chuckled and chuckled. "Ma Lode, Mist' Bryant, y-y-you don' think I'm gwine come prowlin' in dish yer gawden?"
> "No, I know you hain't," said Si with solemnity. "B'cause if you did, I'd shoot you so full of holes you couldn't tell yourself from a sponge."
> "Um—no seh! No seh! I don' raikon you'll git chance at Pete, Mist' Bryant. No seh. I'll take an' run 'long an' rob er bank 'fore I'll come foolishin' 'roun' *your* gawden, Mist' Bryant."*[38]

Since the story is set in New York State, there is no clearly defined regional dialect to be associated with Peter Washington's speech—other than that Crane probably conceived of it as unspecifically southern. A few characteristics usually associated with Black English speech are apparent. As usual, Peter is represented as pronouncing voiced *th* as *d,* in *dem* for *them* and *dish* for *this.* But less usually, *there,* when it occurs as part of the

---

Pronunciation Features
1. Reduction of consonant clusters: *myself > m'se'f; don't > don'.*
2. *th > d: them > dem; this > dish.*
3. Loss of *r: Mister > Mist'; Lord > Lode; garden > gawden; sir > seh; certainly > suhtainly.*
4. Nasalization: *going to > gwine; prowling > prowlin'.*
5. Loss of initial unstressed syllable: *along > 'long; before > 'fore; around > 'round; enough > 'nough.*

Grammatical Features
Verbs
1. Present instead of past tense: *I ain't on'y make.*
Negative
1. *ain't.*

phrase *them there,* is recorded *yere,* as in *dem yere,* a feature not represented in any southern Black English dialect in this study. (Mark Twain uses *dish-yere* for *this here;* but he does not use *y* for voiced *th.*) Peter is recorded as dropping his *r* in *Mist'* for *Mister, Lode* for *Lord, gawden* for *garden,* and Crane here records two examples of reduction of consonant clusters: Peter's pronunciation of *myself* is represented as *m'se'f,* and *don't* as *don'.* Crane also represents nasalization in *gwine* and *prowlin',* and he omits several initial unstressed syllables, as in *'long, 'fore,* and *'round.*

The characteristics of Black English grammar in the above example of Peter's speech are minimal. Crane records one use of present tense instead of past tense, and in the same sentence, he represents *ain't; I ain't on'y make m'se'f covertous er-lookin' at dem yere mellums, sure 'nough.*

Crane also represents several dialectal indicators that have nothing to do with Black English, but whose presence reinforces the stereotype of the subservient black man. In the first place, Peter is made to stutter in the presence of Si Bryant: *y-y-you don' think I'm gwine come prowlin' in dish yer gawden?* When confronted with Bryant's threat that if he stole a watermelon, Bryant would shoot him "full of holes," Peter is made to repeat, in a frightened, humiliated way, *Um—no seh! No seh!* Furthermore, Peter is recorded as pronouncing *reckon* very strangely, as *raikon,* and finally, Crane has him use a totally improbable word, *foolishin'* which confirms his absurdity: *"I'll take an' run 'long an' rob er bank 'fore I'll come foolishin' round your gawden, Mist' Bryant."*

The fact that Crane wrote "The Knife" while living in England may account for its dialectal strangeness, but this fact can hardly excuse his undertaking such work. Yet, with no reality against which he could test his memory, Crane in "The Knife" also reverted to dialectal convention, to curious phonetic spelling, and to manipulation of verb forms. That there is nothing particularly realistic about Crane's dialect representation is beside the point; what is significant is the effect produced by such foolishness. Crane's dialect representation, in the context of a story narrated in Standard English, diminishes beyond human recognition the black characters who are made to speak it. Such caricatures are blackface absurdities; their utterers are only to be laughed at and can never be taken seriously by the reader.

Consideration of the representation of black dialectal speech in American fiction over the course of the nineteenth century is likely to present a rather disturbing picture. In the years before the Civil War few writers, white or black, seemed committed to the individuation of blacks as fictional characters, whether by representation of the idiosyncrasy of speech or otherwise. With Herman Melville the one distinguished and notable exception, the early nineteenth-century American novelists and short story writers considered here seemed content to isolate certain recurrent phonological features and an occasional syntactic characteristic, to manipulate orthography and to establish a conventionalized representation of black speech designed to show the speaker as comic, as somewhat less than hu-man. The polemic novelists of the abolitionist movement, in their quest for a responsive awareness of the black in servitude, only reduced the nonstan-dard characteristics of Black English speech in their representation. They did little else to individuate it.

After the war, the picture is not much improved. The "local colorists," intent on regional individuation and linguistic accuracy, were unable to make much creative headway in their use of the ante-bellum period, to which they were sometimes imaginatively committed. Only a few writers—George Washington Cable and Mark Twain are notable among them—were able to exploit the characteristics of Black English dialect speech to thematic purpose through their method of representation.

It is little wonder that as the twentieth century began and black writers of fiction appeared in print in increasing numbers, avoidance of the old ways of representing dialect and experimentation with a variety of other ap-proaches increasingly became the order of the day. It is also no wonder that in Harlem of the 1920s, after so many black Americans undertook the migra-tion from the provinces to the industrialized and standardized northern cities, and after a new dialect, a more regularized Black English, was coming to be shaped from the babel of the regional black dialects, a new and racially distinct and self-aware black literary movement finally was to come into being. Then the attitudes toward literary dialect and the representation of that dialect could begin to change.

NOTES

1. Joel Chandler Harris, *Uncle Remus: His Songs and His Sayings* (New York: Heritage Press, 1957), p. 78.
2. Zora Neale Hurston, *Their Eyes Were Watching God* (Urbana: University of Illinois Press, 1937; 1965), p. 158.
3. *Journal of Negro Education* 2 (January 1933): 180–201; reprinted in *Dark Symphony*, ed. James A. Emanuel and Theodore L. Gross (New York: The Free Press, 1968), p. 140.
4. Hugh Henry Brackenridge, *Modern Chivalry,* ed. Lewis Leary (New Haven, Conn.: College and University Press, 1965), pp. 130–31.
5. "Slavery in the United States," in *The Complete Works of Edgar Allan Poe,* ed James A. Harrison, (New York: Thomas Y. Crowell, 1902), 8: 271.
6. Edgar Allan Poe, "The Gold Bug," in *The Complete Poems and Stories of Edgar Allan Poe* (New York: Alfred A. Knopf, 1946), 1: 452–53.
7. See Eric Stockton and Killis Campbell, eds., *Poe's Short Stories* (New York: Harcourt, Brace, 1927), p. xx.
8. See the example of Daddy Jack's speech in the discussion of Joel Chandler Harris later in this chapter.
9. For a comprehensive discussion of Poe's use of dialect in "The Gold Bug," see Eric Stockton, "Poe's Use of Negro Dialect in 'The Gold Bug,'" in Juanita V. Williamson and Virginia M. Burke, *A Various Language* (New York: Holt, Rinehart, and Winston, 1971), pp. 193–214, esp. p. 214.

10. Ibid., p. 204.

11. Herman Melville, *Moby-Dick or The Whale,* ed. Charles Feidelson (New York: Bobbs-Merrill, 1964), p. 387.

12. Ibid., p. 391.

13. Harriet Beecher Stowe, *Uncle Tom's Cabin,* ed. Kenneth S. Lynn (Cambridge, Mass.: The Belknap Press of Harvard University Press, 1962), p. 101.

14. Ibid., p. 106.

15. Tremaine McDowell has pointed out Stowe's inability to record distinguishing linguistic features for her characters from different social or racial backgrounds. As he says, the speech of "Mrs. Stowe's slaves closely resembles that of her lower-class whites, particularly her Ohio River folk." Tremaine McDowell, "The Use of Negro Dialect by Harriet Beecher Stowe," *American Speech* 6 (1931): 322.

16. The first American edition was in 1867.

17. William Wells Brown, *Clotel, or, The President's Daughter* (New York: Arno Press and The New York Times, 1969), pp. 176–77.

18. Samuel Langhorne Clemens [Mark Twain], *Adventures of Huckleberry Finn,* 2d ed., ed. Sculley Bradley, Richmond Croom Beatty, E. Hudson Long, and Thomas Cooley (New York: W. W. Norton, 1977), p. 67.

19. Louis D. Rubin, *George W. Cable* (New York: Pegasus, 1969), p. 78.

20. When the Boston *Literary World* criticized the way Creoles talked in "Jean-ah Poquelin," Cable wrote to the editor of the *Literary World,* May 31, 1875, that he thought the accusation "does me real injustice. If I may do so I assure you that scarce a day has passed since the publication of 'Jean-ah-Poquelin' that I am not told by persons who have been accustomed to hear the 'dialect' from their earliest days, and many of whom speak it, that I have rendered it capitally. . . ." See Rubin, *George W. Cable,* p. 80.

21. George W. Cable, *The Grandissimes* (New York: Scribner's Sons, 1880), pp. 71–72.

22. Ibid., pp. 328–29.

23. Kate Chopin, "At the 'Cadian Ball," *Bayou Folk* (Boston: Houghton Mifflin, 1934), p. 268.

24. It should be remembered that at least two of Harris's other stories, "Free Joe and the Rest of the World" and "Where's Duncan?" depict a less-than-idyllic South.

25. Joel Chandler Harris, *Uncle Remus: His Songs and His Sayings,* p. xiii.

26. Ibid., p. 5.

27. Joel Chandler Harris, *Nights with Uncle Remus* (Boston: Houghton Mifflin, 1881), p. 146 .

28. Ibid., pp. xxviii–xxix. Harris also includes a glossary and additional explanation of sounds peculiar to Gullah.

B'er, brother

Beer, bear.

Bittle, victuals.

Bre't, breath.

Buckra, white man, overseer, boss.

Churrah, churray, spill, splash.

Da, the, that

Dey-dey, here, down there, right here.

Dey, there.

Enty, ain't he? an exclamation of astonishment or assent.

Gwan, going

Leaf, leave.

Lif, live.

Lil, lil-a, or *lilly,* little.

Lun, learn.

Mek, make.

Oona, you, all of you.

Neat', or *nead,* underneath, beneath.

Sem, same

Shum, see them, saw them.

Tam, time.

'Tan', stand.

Tankee, thanks, thank you.

Tark, or *tahlk,* talk

Tek, take.

Teer, tear.

T'ink, or *t'ought,* think, thought

Titty, or *titter,* sissy, sister.

T'row, throw.

Trute, truth.
Turrer, or *tarrah*, the other.
Tusty, thirsty.
Urrer, other.
Wey, where.

Wun, when.
Wut, what.
Y'et or *ut*, earth.
Yeddy, or *yerry*, heard, hear.
Yent, aint, isn't.

The trick of adding a vowel to sound words is not unpleasing to the ear. Thus: "I bin-a wait fer you; come-a ring-a dem bell. Wut mek-a (or mekky) you stay so?" "Yeddy," "yerry," and probably "churry" are the result of this—heard-a, yeard-a, yeddy; hear-a, year-a, yerry; chur-a churray. When "eye" is written "y-eye," it is to be pronounced "yi." In such words as "back," "ax," *a* has the sound of *ah*. They are written "bahk," "ahx" (pp. xxix–xxx).

29. Charles Waddell Chesnutt, *The Conjure Woman* (Ridgewood, N.J.: The Gregg Press, 1968), pp. 168–69.

30. Thomas Nelson Page, *In Ole Virginia* (Chapel Hill: University of North Carolina Press, 1969), pp. 4–5.

31. Ibid., facing p. 1.

32. See the Introduction to Samuel Clemens in Cleanth Brooks, R. W. B. Lewis, and Robert Penn Warren, *American Literature* (New York: St. Martin's Press, 1973), 2: 1281. The final section of this novel, as a number of critics have pointed out, does not easily contribute to a consistent interpretation of Huck's character, since his relationship to Jim changes when they settle down on land in the final chapters.

33. Clemens, *Huckleberry Finn*, p. 2. As has been frequently noted, the so-called Colonel Sherburn episode is the only moment in the novel in which narrative consistency seems to be violated; interestingly enough, it is only in this episode that Standard English is employed extensively.

34. Curt M. Rulon, "Geographical Delimitation of the Dialect Areas in *The Adventures of Huckleberry Finn*," in Williamson and Burke, *A Various Language*, p. 219.

35. Clemens, *Huckleberry Finn*, p. 64.

36. Ibid., pp. 65–66.

37. Rulon, "Geographical Delimitation," p. 219.

38. Stephen Crane, "The Knife," *Tales of Whilomville*, ed. Fredson Bowers (Charlottesville: The University Press of Virginia, 1969), p. 184.

4
Black English in Fiction, 1900–1945:
Dialect and Social Change

BETWEEN 1900 and 1940 the conditions of life for black people changed in many ways in America. The agrarian economy of the Old South was converted in part into the industrial economy of the New South. Instead of working in the cotton or rice fields, an increasing number of blacks were employed in a variety of industrial or government jobs. Thousands migrated North—to Detroit, Chicago, New York City, the East coast, to California and the plains states—in search of better pay. Even before the First World War a black bourgeoisie had developed in a number of urban areas, and Harlem was establishing itself as a center of black experience.

A significant result of the movement northward was the emergence of a new black image and self-image. No longer did blacks regard themselves simply as provincial agricultural workers or house servants. With the arrival of a new century came a racial rather than a regional, a proletarian rather than a peasant, an urban rather than a rural identity. Out of the mixture of regional accents in the cities a new urban Black English emerged—a dialect that became identified with race rather than with region.

Four basic directions were taken by writers wishing to represent black speech. Although occasional experimenters with the representation of post-migration Black English speech can be identified, the general literary trend gradually evolved out of nineteenth-century traditions. Throughout the first forty years of the century, one group of writers continued to portray the black stereotypes that had surfaced in nineteenth-century literature and developed them into caricature. Beginning before World War I and extending through the Harlem Renaissance of the 1920s, another group, in reaction to literary stereotyping of blacks, committed itself to the idea of moral, social, and economic "uplift" of black people and rejected all representation of black dialect in literature. Frustrated with and annoyed by the stringent requirements of the "uplift" movement, another group of writers advocated the exploration of "real" black life still to be found in rural black villages and settings yet untouched by "progress" and white industrialization. In such settings the preservation of Black English dialect was the key to authenticity. Finally, during the late 1920s and 1930s, interest in literary realism was extended to black urban life. The majority of writers in this group considered representation of the dialect of the black proletariat as central to the realities of black urban experience.

Of the literary trends that it is possible to identify, experimentation with dialect representation as a means of character definition is often seen in the work of Gertrude Stein. Stein was certainly one of the striking members of the literary avant-garde of the prewar years, years in which poetic and narrative experimentation set the stage for postwar literary flowering. Gertrude Stein experimented with new procedures in syntactic representation; particularly, she experimented with the relation between perception and its articulation, with impressionistic realism in fiction. One of the points of view with which she experimented most successfully was that of blacks.

Until 1909, when Gertrude Stein published "Melanctha," one of the portraits of women that make up *Three Lives,* the representation of black dialect in American literature, as indicated in the last chapter, had been characterized by elaborate phonological and grammatical features whose purpose was to identify a speaker by race, social class, and region. But Stein, tutored in the psychological theories of William James and intent on capturing the rhythms of casual speech in her writing, experimented with ways in which language could be used to reflect perception. "Melanctha" is the story of a young mulatto woman who tries repeatedly to understand and to establish a mutually satisfying relationship with Dr. Jefferson Campbell and with others of her acquaintance. Although several times the two come close to finding a balance between passion and wisdom, they repeatedly back away and Melanctha finally dies alone in a home for consumptives. Her failures, however, cannot be explained by her race, her social class, or her regional origins, but only by her limitations as a flawed but sympathetic human being struggling to understand and to be understood.

Much of the power in Melanctha's characterization lies not only in Stein's capacity to delineate a black character compassionately, as a human being who cannot find meaning in her life, but also in her representation of black speech. Without elaborately recording accepted or idiosyncratic pronunciation features as her literary predecessors had done, Stein records significant grammatical features of Black English, particularly the lack of subject-verb agreement *(you was)* and the double negative *(you ain't never ashamed).* Furthermore, she captures the essence of black dialectal speech by using a very simple vocabulary, a vocabulary uncluttered with readily recognizable dialectal words. She also repeats significant words that emphasize the psychological concerns of the speakers. In the passage that follows, for instance, Melanctha struggles to understand Jeff's definition of "good people," but she cannot. She says, " 'I certainly don't understand what you meant by what you was just saying,' " and later, " 'I certainly don't understand just what it is you mean by all that you was just saying to me.' " Then, " 'I can't say as I see just what you mean . . .,' " and finally, " 'I certainly don't just see what you mean by what you say.' " Although in this passage each statement is slightly different from the others, the similarities between them reflect Melanctha's struggling commitment to understand the man she is trying to love.

Finally, the last sentence in the passage that follows is a fused sentence that simulates the fluidity of informal speech and also, perhaps, suggests the overlapping relationship of a number of related ideas in Melanctha's mind. Although portraying the psychology of the character is all-important for Stein, as is illustrated in this passage, she is also able to convey with force and conviction the essential characteristics of black speech.

> "About what you was just saying Dr. Campbell about living regular and all that, I certainly don't understand what you meant by what you was just saying. You ain't a bit like good people Dr. Campbell, like the goodpeople you are always saying are just like you. I know good people Dr. Campbell, and you ain't a bit like men who are good and got religion. You are just as free and easy as any man can be Dr. Campbell, and you always like to be with Jane Harden, and she is a pretty bad one and you don't look down on her and you never tell her she is a bad one. I know you like her just like a friend Dr. Campbell, and so I certainly don't understand just what it is you mean by all that you was just saying to me. I know you mean honest Dr. Campbell, and I am always trying to believe you, but I can't say as I see just what you mean when you say you want to be good and real pious, because I am very certain Dr. Campbell that you ain't that kind of a man at all, and you ain't never ashamed to be with queer folks Dr. Campbell, and you seem to be thinking what you are doing is just like what you are always saying, and Dr. Campbell, I certainly don't just see what you mean by what you say."*[1]

The above passage clearly illustrates Stein's "experimental" style in the representation of dialect. She has ignored the phonological features of Black English dialect; she has also manipulated syntax and repeated significant phrases in order to emphasize the nature of the speaker's awareness. Most important, perhaps, she has shaped her representation of dialect to empha-

---

Pronunciation Features
None.

Grammatical Features
Verbs
    1. Lack of subject-verb agreement: *you was.*
Negative
    1. ain't.
    2. Double negative: *you ain't never ashamed.*
Adjectival form substituted for adverb: *regularly > regular.*

size, not the "specialness" of black speech, but the nature of awareness experienced by a character in a specific situation.

Despite the fact that Gertrude Stein's representation of dialect was innovative and undeniably powerful, she seemed to be too far ahead of her time to attract imitators. Even though "Melanctha" was a literary success, Stein never again returned to the subject of black people or the representation of black dialect. And none of her contemporaries followed her example of trying to convey dialect without recording phonological features. Perhaps they distrusted the technique of this strange expatriate, leader of the literary avant-garde in Paris who was geographically removed from the American scene and from a direct acquaintance with black folk and their speech. Years later, Richard Wright read "Melanctha" and recognized its truth and its force. Even so, he did not choose to imitate Stein's style in his own recording of dialect speech. Whatever the reason for Stein's inability to attract imitators in her own time, fifty-odd years passed after publication of "Melanctha" before American fiction writers of the 1960s and 1970s began similarly to experiment with simplified representations of black dialect. Other approaches would have to be tried and found wanting before American writers could break away from the conventional insistence on emphasizing pronunciation features in their representation of Black English speech.

The local color movement, in which black speakers were usually treated sympathetically, realistically, and, although Thomas Nelson Page is an exception, without condescension, was clearly finished by the close of the nineteenth century. Since in the new century experimentation with the representation of black characters and their speech, which so intrigued Gertrude Stein, did not catch fire in the literary world, another approach was needed. The one that attracted the most attention, and that can be seen as a degeneration of the local color movement, is the characterization of rural southern blacks as stereotypes of either the "bad Negro" or the "good Negro." White criteria would, of course, determine the categories. One of the earliest and most successful of such writers was Thomas Dixon, a Southerner, who was born ten years before Gertrude Stein (1864) and died in the same year that she did (1946). But Dixon had quite a different background and interests from Gertrude Stein. Whereas Stein, an experimenter by nature, did not write conventionally, and was, if anything, ahead of her contemporaries in imposing what she knew about human psychology on literary form, Dixon used a conventional novel form to make his peace with the past. His political and literary views were formed by his experience in the South during Reconstruction, and he devoted his life to interpreting "truthfully" a historical period that he considered the most tragic in American history.

Dixon's career was varied. He was a lawyer, a minister, a lecturer, a novelist, a playwright, and a motion picture producer. Although his experience seemed diverse, all of his careers were directed toward the polemic.

His interest in writing fiction had nothing to do with writing a novel of literary value. Instead, he saw the novel as a medium through which he could impose a "moral" interpretation on history, particularly on the Reconstruction period.

Dixon wrote in a highly romantic style. His novels are filled with sensationalism, sentimentality, and coincidence. His white characters are as stereotyped as his black ones; the acceptable men are staunch defenders of the Southern way of life, romantic knights of the Ku Klux Klan, and the acceptable women are pure, simple, naive, rigidly virginal, and without humor. Although Dixon was opposed to slavery, he believed in segregation; for Dixon the differences between the races made full equality impossible. In his opinion the black man had two choices—either to submit to the superiority of whites or to be completely separated from contact with whites.[2] No other alternatives existed. In his fiction he stereotypes blacks in two ways: either as "bad"—incorrigible, grasping, and beastly, or as "good"—fully mindful of their place and faithful to their former masters.

Dixon wrote three novels based on the Reconstruction period. The first two of his trilogy, *The Leopard's Spots* (1902) and *The Clansman* (1905), attained the greatest notoriety, and later became the basis for the plot of *The Birth of a Nation,* the still controversial film directed by D. W. Griffith in 1915. In *The Clansman* Dixon's message is clearly articulated: the death of Lincoln led to a betrayal of the South by the North, and resulted in the sudden rise to power of a group of uneducated, crude, grasping blacks. These blacks could not be content with the seizure of political power; because of their uncontrollable animal passion, recently freed blacks were a serious threat to the purity of white womanhood. Given the chaos of the situation, the only action possible for the white man of honor was to take the law temporarily into his own hands and, through the Klan, to put the blacks and the intruding northerners in their places, thereby restoring order to the community.[3]

The white characters follow the usual dominant stereotype—the men are valiant and noble and fight for their land and the honor of their women. The black characters conform to the conventional, but less attractive stereotypes for the dominated. The "bad Negro" seeks to usurp the political power of the white man and desires sexual union with a white woman; the "good Negro" is sexually quiescent, submissive to the white man, and demands no change within the social order.

In the passage that follows, two black men confront one another at the polls. The "bad Negro," Aleck, ambitious for political power, assumes the role of a judge who determines voting eligiblity. His behavior is intended to be pompous and vulgar. The other, Jake, who is ultimately denied voting rights, plays the role of the "good Negro." Jake has no ambition to be other than what the history of slavery and his experience have made him. Both men speak a very similar Black English dialect, which is not surprising since both come from the same geographical region in South Carolina. While Dixon has decorated their speech with a variety of phonological features, he has used only an occasional distinctive verb or negative form to suggest Black English grammatical features.

Although in the passage that follows, Aleck has the upper hand because of his social and newly acquired political position, Jake, the faithful servant, is given an opportunity, by manipulation of his pronunciation and of word meanings, to outwit his opponent. Aleck asks Jake to explain "'ter dis cote,'" by which he means "court." And Jake replies, with a deliberate pun, "'What cote? Dat ole army cote?'" Although Aleck has the authority to arrest Jake, he is temporarily humiliated before his peers. A full version of the passage follows.

> The troopers brought Jake before the judge.
> "Tryin' ter vote, is yer?"
> "'Lowed I would."
> "You hear 'bout de great sassieties de Gubment's fomentin' in dis country?"
> "Yas, I hear erbout 'em."
> "Is yer er member er de Union League?"
> "Na-sah. I'd rudder steal by myself. I doan' lak too many in de party!"
> "En yer ain't er No'f Ca'liny gemmen, is yer—yer ain't er member er de 'Red Strings'?"
> "Na-sah, I come when I'se called—dey doan' hatter put er string on me—ner er block, ner er collar, ner er chain, ner er muzzle—"
> "Will yer 'splain ter dis cote—" railed Aleck.
> "What cote? Dat ole army cote?" Jake laughed in loud peals that rang over the square.
> Aleck recovered his dignity and demanded angrily:
> "Does yer belong ter de Heroes ob Americky?"
> "Na-sah. I ain't burnt nobody's house ner barn yet, ner hamstrung no stock, ner waylaid nobody atter night—honey, I ain't fit ter jine. Heroes ob Americky! Is you er hero?"
> "Ef yer doan' b'long ter no s'iety," said Aleck with judicial deliberation, "what is you?"
> "Des er ole-fashun all-wool-en-er-yard-wide nigger dat stan's by his ole marster 'cause he's his bes' frien', stays at home, en tends ter his own business."*⁴

*ALECK
Pronunciation Features
   1. Reduction of consonant clusters: *gentleman > gemmen; society > s'iety.*
   2. Changes in *th:*
       a. *th* (voiced > *d: this > dis; the > de.*
       b. *th* (unvoiced) > *f: North > No'f.*
   3. *v > b: of > ob;* (and reduction of consonant clusters): *government > gubment.*
   4. *r:*
       a. Loss of *r: North Carolina > No'f Ca'liny; court > cote.*
       b. Addition of r: *to > ter; you > yer; a > er; of > er; Master > marster.*
   5. Nasalization: *trying > tryin'; fomenting > fomentin'.*
   6. Loss of initial unstressed syllable: *about > 'bout; explain > 'splain; because > 'cause.*

Analysis of the speech of both characters, as set forth below, confirms the widespread use of the phonological features traditionally associated with Black English. But beyond a recording of the actual features used, Dixon's inclusion of dialect in his novel is significant for dramatic purposes and for emphasis of his "moral" point. As with most dialect literature, the juxtaposition of the black dialect against the thoroughly standardized speech of whites suggests the "difference" of blacks from whites and thus serves to reinforce the point of view that former slaves are unprepared and unsuited to assume responsibility in a predominantly white society. And the contrast between the orthography used to represent the speech of the characters further suggests the "substandard" nature of black speech. Because Dixon's novels were more sensational and vicious than most, his rather obvious stereotyping of blacks through the representation of their speech was particularly offensive to black readers. It was this use of dialect to stereotype blacks that black writers and intellectuals would later take pains to counteract.

Not all of the literary stereotypes that appeared in the early part of the

Eye Dialect: *belong > b'long; don't > doan'.*

Grammatical Features
Verbs
    1. Lack of subject-verb agreement: *What is you?; is yer er member.*
    2. Zero copula in a question. *You hear (?).*
Negative
    1. *ain't.*

JAKE
Pronunciation Features
    1. Reduction of consonant clusters: *have to > hatter; old > ole; this here > des er; stands > stan's* (the apostrophe is exceedingly peculiar here); *best friend > bes' frien'; old fashioned > ole-fashun; and > en.*
    2. Changes in *th:*
        a. *th > d: the > de; they > dey; that > dat; this > des; rather > rudder.*
        b. Loss of *th: them > 'em.*
    3. *v > b: of > ob.*
    4. *r:*
        a. Loss of *r: no sir > na-sah.*
        b. Addition of *r: about > erbout; a > er; have to > hatter; at > atter.*
    5. Nasalization: *don't > doan'.*
    6. Loss of initial unstressed syllable: *allowed > 'lowed.*
    7. Loss of vowel glide: *yes > yas; join > jine; like > lak.*
Eye Dialect: *coat > cote; old fashioned > ole fashun.*

Grammatical Features
Verbs
    1. Lack of subject-verb agreement: *I am > I'se.*
Negative
    1. *ain't.*
    2. Double negative: *I ain't burn nobody's house ner barn yet, ner hamstrung no stock, ner waylaid nobody atter night. . . .*

twentieth century emphasized the "bad Negro." Frequently they focused on the comic, simple, happy, carefree black, who may have been first imaginatively represented in the early minstrel shows.[5] The minstrel show may have originated on the plantation, first as a means of entertainment by the slaves for themselves and later as a more stylized performance for their masters and their guests, or it may have grown out of nineteenth-century circus performances. Whatever its origin, it developed rapidly into a ritualized three-part form performed by white men in black face to burlesque the black. The image of the black man that grew out of the minstrel show, which became confused with reality in the minds of many Americans, was of a carefree entertainer who could sing about jumping Jim Crow and later moan "Mammy" with Al Jolson.

Nathan Irvin Huggins, in his book *Harlem Renaissance,* describes the minstrel show characters—particularly Jim Crow with his ragged costume and Jim Dandy, dressed in the height of fashion—as vulgar comic stereotypes that defined the Afro-American as white Americans chose to see him.[6] Huggins describes the "stage Negro" in some detail:

> The audience (one should say the popular culture) had ingrained in its imagination a view of the Negro that was comic and pathetic. The theatrical darky was childlike; he could be duped into the most idiotic and foolish schemes; but like a child, too, innocence would protect him and turn the tables on the schemers. His songs were vulgar and his stories the most gross and broad; his jokes were often on himself, his wife or woman. Lazy, he was slow of movement, or when he displayed a quickness of wit it was generally in flight from work or ghosts. Nevertheless, he was unrestrained in enthusiasm for music—for athletic and rhythmical dance. Likewise, he was insatiable in his bodily appetites; his songs and tales about food would make one think him all mouth, gullet, and stomach. Indeed, performers gave themselves grotesque lips, creating the illusion of cavernous mouths. The stage Negro went into ecstasy over succulent foods—pork, chicken, watermelon—"lip-smacking," "mouth-watering." Whether he played in the Jim Crow or the Jim Dandy tradition, he never left these bounds.[7]

The characterization of the "stage Negro" was not limited to the stage however; the popular mind had so completely accepted the stage image that it began to appear in literature. Octavus Roy Cohen was one writer who transferred that image to the printed page. For thirty-five years, between 1919 and 1955, Cohen burlesqued Birmingham, Alabama, blacks in his journalistic pieces, short stories, and novels. The plots of his stories are derived from jokes—jokes that rely for their effect on the comic caricature of the Negro. Cohen was not interested in psychological motivation or in the growth of a character as the result of his experiences. In his work black characters are presented as pretentious and impressed by bourgeois material values; their greatest pleasure in their pursuit of material riches is to outwit one another. Ultimately, the characters are rendered ridiculous by their names, their values, and their misuse of language. All of them come off badly.

In "Auto-Intoxication," the first story in Cohen's *Highly Colored* (1919), Mr. Anopheles Ricketts, recently married to Clarissy, enters a car race. His intention is to win the race so that he can buy his wife, who is occasionally impressed by the car of her former fiancé, Adam Shooks, a touring car of her own. Anopheles "borrows" Adam Shooks's car and wins the race, but he does so because his lack of experience as a racing car driver prevents him from being afraid of obvious dangers. As a result of his foolhardy determination, he beats four professional drivers who are too much aware of the danger Anopheles poses on the track to challenge him seriously. Before the race Anopheles's rival, Adam Shooks, who had tried to prevent Anopheles from using his car by taking both the car and Clarissy on a ride out of town, had also been outwitted by his friend. By coincidence Anopheles had found the car parked outside a restaurant and had borrowed it for the race. After their lunch, when Adam and Clarissy discovered that the car had disappeared, they had no choice but to walk eighteen miles back to Birmingham. Thus, at the end of the story, when Anopheles presents his wife with the second-hand roadster he has bought for her with his prize money, she is too tired to enjoy it. Indeed, now that the car is hers, she no longer wishes even to sit in a car. The humor of the plot, which is built largely on coincidence, is achieved—as in the minstrel show—through comic stereotypes. All three characters are represented as fools, and the author and his audience can have a good laugh at their expense.

Huggins considers the language of the minstrel show a "cloak of travesty for the stage Negro."

> The use, or misuse, of ponderous latinate words, the stiff, formal, pompous diction of the minstrels' interlocutor (that name itself, indeed) served the pretense and exposed it all at once. The audience was asked to look at blackfaced performers (Ethiopian Delineators as they sometimes called themselves) occasionally pretending to be civilized, and they laughed because the frequent malapropisms and misunderstandings made the pretense ludicrous. The language of the minstrel was, throughout, the language of social pretense.[8]

A similar treatment of language can be found in Cohen's short story. There are puns on both the title of the short story, "Auto-Intoxication," and on the title of the book, *Highly Colored*. The travestied names of the characters— Mr. Anopheles Ricketts, Mr. Adam Shooks, Mr. Florian Slappey—and the fact that they preserve a formal relationship with one another, addressing each other as "Mr." and "Missus," is evidence of their ridiculous pretension. In the speech of the characters, malapropisms abound. At one point in his negotiation with Adam Shooks, Anopheles says that he is willing " 'to take the matter under devisement.' "[9] He also gives "Brother Shooks" " 'pre-zac'ly ten minutes' "[10] to sign the contract to borrow Shooks's car for the race. And the car that Anopheles presents to Clarissy he describes as a " 'Rollins towerin' car.' "[11] Although much of the humor relies on mispronunciations, the manipulation of grammatical structure also contributes to the caricature. In the passage from "Auto-Intoxication" that follows, Mr. Anopheles Ricketts tells Clarissy, his car-struck wife, " 'automobiles is the on'y things you don't talk 'bout nothin' else but.' " The position of "but" at the end of the sentence is an awkward usage that emphasizes the nonstandard nature of Anopheles's speech, but it is not a significant characteristic of Black English. Also, the repetition of "got" in Clarissy's next speech exaggerates her excessive reliance on a single verb form: " 'We is got money enough to buy us a car, honey. Lots of folks which ain't got as much as what we got is got automobiles.' " Anopheles's reply, " 'You jes' quit talkin' with yo' mouth' " is a stylized redundancy. Here is the passage in full:

> "I 'clare to goodness gracious, Clarissy," he remarked irritably, "automobiles is the on'y things you don't talk 'bout nothin' else but."
> Clarissy pouted. "We is got money enough to buy us a car, honey. Lots of folks which ain't got as much as what we is got is got automobiles."
> "Yeh—reckon they is. An' lots of folks is got bills which ain't paid, but we ain't. You jes' quit talkin' with yo' mouth bouten automobiles. 'Tain't gwine git you nowheres, an'—"
> "I could of had a automobile," flared Clarissy suddenly. "I sho' could of had a ninety-hawss-power Conley-Detroit if'n I had of chose."*[12]

*Anopheles
Pronunciation Features
1. Reduction of consonant clusters: *just > jes'; and > an.*
2. Loss of *r: your > yo'.*
3. Nasalization: *nothing > nothin'; talking > talkin'; going to > gwine; only > on'y.*
4. Loss of initial unstressed syllable: *declare > 'clare; about > 'bout.*

Grammatical Features
Verbs
1. Lack of subject-verb agreement: *automobiles is; they is; folks is got.*
Negative
1. *ain't.*
2. Double negative: *'Tain't gwine get you nowheres; you don't talk 'bout nothin' else but.*

Clarissy
Pronunciation Features
1. Loss of *r: horse > hawss.*

Grammatical Features:
Verbs
1. Lack of subject-verb agreement: *we is got; lots of folks is got.*
2. *have > of: could have > could of.*
3. Past tense instead of past participle: *chosen > of chose.*
Negative
1. *ain't.*

Although Cohen understands the underlying pronunciation and grammatical structures of Black English, he cannot resist overdoing his representation of dialect in order to make the speakers objects of humor. Cohen's stereotyping of blacks may not be so malicious as Dixon's, but the end result, to make blacks appear ridiculous, is equally distorted and insulting.

Another portrayer of the comic black in fiction was Roark Bradford. Publishing in the years after the First World War, Bradford attempted to depict American blacks as he had remembered them from his childhood in Tennessee. Whereas Cohen depicted southern urban blacks in the minstrel mode of slapstick comedy, Bradford's representation was a throwback to the southern plantation tradition. His blacks were rural types who originated in the folk tradition rather than the minstrel show. In his popular collection of tales, *Ol' Man Adam an' His Chillun* (1928), the source for Marc Connelly's popular play *The Green Pastures* (1930), a black narrator adapts a number of Bible stories to what Bradford considers the real-life situation of blacks. The biblical characters, including "de Lawd," are black and speak in Black English.[13] Stereotypes abound—of pretentious characters who use language too elevated for the situation, of country-bumpkin types who are easily duped, of seductive women who win their men, of country black folk who love a fish fry. In one story, "The Adulteration of Old King David," Bathsheba, while still the wife of Uriah, tries to seduce King David by undressing and taking a bath in a tub on her front porch—in full view of King David, who sits in a rocking chair on his own front porch. Although King David at first accuses her of trying to "'adulterate My Majesty,'" by the middle of the story he has been distracted by her charms from writing another psalm.

The humor in the story arises partly from the fact that southern rural black people assume the roles of royal and-or heroic biblical characters in settings and situations familiar to the rural black narrator. King David sits on his front porch in his rocking chair and is later joined by "de Lawd"; Bathsheba goes about her routine of bathing on Saturday and washing clothes on Monday. Uriah is conveniently killed in an obscure and distant battle when he "got mixed up" with one of the enemies of "de Lawd." The actions and motivations of the characters are thus interpreted so as to be recognizable to the narrator, and the narrator seems simple and childlike to the reader. What most offended the black critic Sterling Brown about these characters was Bradford's burlesque of black religion. Specifically, there is nothing reverent about "de Lawd"; he is seen as naively as the others. As Brown says,

The difference between the personified God in the spirituals and God with a fedora upon his head and a ten-cent segar in his mouth should be apparent to anyone in the least familiar with Negro believers and their dread of sacrilege.[14]

The humor is also based on the characters' use of language. It is a combination of casual dialect speech—the women are frequently addressed as "gal"—and pretentious malapropisms, such as that used by King David when he threatens to put Bathsheba in jail for " 'tryin' to adulterate My Majesty.' " In the passage that follows, Bathsheba, King David, and the narrator all have the same range of dialect characteristics. There seems to be more variety in the Black English characteristics that Bathsheba uses, but the fact that in this passage she speaks more than the others may be significant.

> "Good mawnin', King David, Yo' Majesty," she say, sweetenin' up her voice.
> "Good mawnin', sister," say ole King David. "What can I do for you dis mawnin'?"
> "Well," say Miz Uriah, casual-like, "I comed over to ax you does you yar somethin' 'bout my husband. He ain't much husband, but he better'n no husband a-tall. I guess he's about all a ugly ole gal like me kin git, anyway. I wish I was a good-lookin' gal."
> "You don't look so bad, gal," say ole King David.
> "Aw, hysh up, Yo' Majesty," say Miz Uriah. "You know I ain't no good-lookin' gal. Jest look at 'at ole ugly laig. Look at 'at flat chest—" and she started twistin' herse'f round, showin' off.
> But David is a good man and he know what she's up to, so he say: "Git on back home, gal, befo' I puts you in jail for tryin' to adulterate My Majesty. Git home! You yar me?"*15

*KING DAVID
Pronunciation Features
    1. Loss of *r: morning > mawnin'; before > befo'*.
    2. Nasalization: *morning > mawnin'; trying > tryin'*.
    3. Vowel fronting: *get > git*.

Grammatical Features
Verbs
    1. Lack of subject-verb agreement: *I puts*.

BATHSHEBA
Pronunciation Features
    1. Reduction of consonant clusters: *at all > a-tall; old > ole; at that > at 'at; better than > better'n*.
    2. *th > d: this > dis*.
    3. Loss of *r: your > yo'; morning > mawnin'*.
    4. Nasalization: *morning > mawnin'; something > somethin'; good-looking > good-lookin'*.
    5. Loss of initial unstressed syllable: *about > 'bout*.
    6. Vowel fronting: *hush > hysh; get > git; can > kin; just > jest*.
    7. Diphthongization: *leg > laig*.
    8. *ask > ax*.

Grammatical Features
Verbs
    1. Lack of subject-verb agreement: *does you; I wish I was*.
    2. Zero copula: *he better'n*.
    3. Regularization of past tense of irregular verb: *I comed over*.

Although the black stereotypes Bradford uses are hardly outspokenly insulting, as they are in the work of Dixon or Cohen, a certain patronizing attitude is manifest through the representation of black speech. And this same attitude can be found as late as 1936, in Margaret Mitchell's historical romance, *Gone With the Wind,* one of the most successful bestsellers ever written. Mitchell drew her material from old newspaper accounts and pamphlets of the Civil War and postwar periods, but also from the conversations she remembered of her parents and their friends who had grown up during Reconstruction. The white society she portrays, in the only novel she ever wrote, assumes values not unlike those Dixon espoused when he published *The Clansman* in 1905. Mitchell's novel, the love story of Scarlett O'Hara and Rhett Butler and its eventual dissolution, is set against the background of the decay of the plantation South as a result of the Civil War. While white people are romanticized, although at times lightly satirized, blacks are generally stereotyped as either "good" or "bad"; "good Negroes" are those, like "Mammy," who remained faithful to their white families even after they were freed, and "bad Negroes" are those who lived as outlaws in shantytowns near Atlanta and were capable of displaying a streak of "meanness" toward whites and, in an extreme, of behaving violently.

It is extraordinary that seventy years after the end of the Civil War a book that so vividly portrayed the values of the Old South could have found such widespread popularity. For the reputation of black people, this popularity was threatening. As Sterling Brown said in 1937, the year in which *Gone With the Wind* was awarded the Pulitzer Prize and was selected by the American Booksellers Association as the most distinguished novel of 1936, novels like *Gone With the Wind* "encourage slavery in a world where slaves are still too numerous."[16]

For the book's admirers, however, the novel offered the comfort of escape and at the same time a sentimentalized portrayal of the collapse of a traditional culture in those late Depression years in which parallels could be drawn to the experiences of the readers themselves. To do this, to capture the imagination of the retrospectively oriented reader, Mitchell made use of traditional techniques of narration; in her representation of black dialect she was equally traditional.

In the passage that follows, the traditional southern attitudes toward

Negative
    1. *ain't.*

NARRATOR
Pronunciation Features
    1. Reduction of consonant clusters: *herself* > *herse'f* (and loss of *l*); *missus* > *miz.*
    2. Nasalization: *sweetening* > *sweetenin'; twisting* > *twistin'; showing* > *showin'.*

Grammatical Features
Verbs
    1. Regularization of third person singular present tense: *she say; say ole King David; say Miz Uriah; he know; he say.*

blacks are verbalized and accepted by Sam, a former slave at Tara, Scarlett's family plantation. Sam served a Yankee Colonel in the Civil War; although he was taken North by the Colonel, he did not like Yankee ways and found his way back to Atlanta. Sam, whose "big black face" is described as "stupid and as easily read as a child's"[17] has other characteristics that caricature him as a big dog rather than a human being.

> Sam galloped over to the buggy, his eyes rolling with joy and his white teeth flashing, and clutched her outstretched hand with two black hands as big as hams. His watermelon-pink tongue lapped out, his whole body wiggled and his joyful contortions were as ludicrous as the gambolings of a mastiff.[18]

Sam takes Scarlett O'Hara by surprise one day as she is driving near shantytown, and tells her of his wish to return to Tara. The implication, of course, is that he was happy as a slave and prefers dependency to autonomy. He is convinced that the Yankees never could understand his loyalty to his former southern masters.

> "W'en Ah tell dem dat an' tell dem how good Miss Ellen ter de niggers, an' how she set up a whole week wid me w'en Ah had de pneumony, dey doan b'lieve me. An', Miss Scarlett, Ah got ter honin' fer Miss Ellen an' Tara, tell it look lak Ah kain stan' it no longer, an' one night Ah lit out fer home, an' Ah rid de freight cahs all de way down ter 'Lanta. Ef you buy me a ticket ter Tara, Ah sho be glad ter git home. Ah sho be glad ter see Miss Ellen and Mist' Gerald agin. Ah done had nuff freedom. Ah wants somebody ter feed me good vittles reg'lar, and tell me whut ter do an' whut not ter do, an' look affer me w'en Ah gits sick. S'pose Ah gits de pneumony agin? Is dat Yankee lady gwine tek keer of me? No, Ma'm! She gwine call me 'Mist' O'Hara' but she ain' gwine nuss me. But Miss Ellen, she gwine nuss me, do Ah git sick an'—"*[19]

Pronunciation Features
    1. Reduction of consonant clusters: *when > w'en; after > affer; and > an'; stand > stan'*.
    2. *th > d: them > dem; that > dat; the > de; with > wid*.
    3. *r:*
        a. Loss of *r: cars > cahs; sure > sho; Mister > Mist'; nurse > nuss*.
        b. Addition of *r: to > ter*.
    4. Nasalization: *don't > doan; going > gwine; ain't > ain'*.
    5. Loss of initial unstressed syllable: *Atlanta > 'Lanta; enough > nuff; believe > b'lieve; suppose > s'pose*.
    6. Vowel fronting: *for > fer; like > lak; get > git*.
    7. Diphthongization: *can't > kain*.

Grammatical Features
Verbs
    1. Lack of subject-verb agreement: *Ah wants; Ah gits*.
    2. Zero copula: *Miss Ellen ter de niggers; Ah sho be glad; Ah done had; She gwine call; she gwine nuss*.
    3. Regularization of past tense of irregular verb: *Ah rid*.
Negative
    1. *ain't > ain'*.
    2. Double negative: *Ah kain stan' it no longer*.

Mitchell relies on both phonological and grammatical features in her rendering of Sam's Black English dialect. There are, however, a few peculiarities in her recording of the phonological features. She has Sam pronounce *and,* for instance, both as *an'* and as *and.* And a strange word like *pneumonia,* whose pronunciation has little to do with its spelling, is recorded in Sam's "illiterate" speech as *pneumony.* Since the rest of his pronunciation is carefully phoneticized, one may well wonder how he pronounced the Greek root, *pneu.*

At the beg- of the 20th century)

The tendency to stereotype blacks by description, behavior, and language, as it existed in the fiction of Dixon, Cohen, Bradford, and Mitchell, was threatening to the reputation of black people. And it would be black writers who would have to object to such stereotyping and to offer an alternative. The first alternative presented itself toward the beginning of the twentieth century by a man who was to assume an important role in the leadership of American blacks, W. E. B. DuBois.

Born in 1868, a man whose life spanned almost a century, W. E. B. DuBois had a number of careers: he was a professor, lecturer, founder of the Niagara Movement and of the N.A.A.C.P., journal editor, essayist, book reviewer, and novelist. In all his roles he regarded himself as a spokesman for his race, and dedicated himself to fighting prejudice and to asserting the dignity and right to equality of the American black man. His most influential years were between 1910 and 1934, when he served as editor of *The Crisis,* the journal of the N.A.A.C.P. Editor for a quarter of a century, DuBois was responsible for bringing critical and often controversial issues before his reading public, of introducing the work of young black writers to a receptive black audience, and of helping form the political and literary views of educated black people.

DuBois recognized the power of the word and took seriously his mission of defining and then criticizing the work of black writers. Stereotypes of the Negro in fiction written by whites offended him deeply. But, ironically, the use of polemic so pervasive in Dixon's work also pervades DuBois's writing. Both men, although their attitudes toward the racial situation were diametrically opposed, recognized the propagandistic potential of literature. Dixon, of course, wrote to establish the superiority of the white man; DuBois, to insist upon the humanity of the black.

Writing in the October 1926 issue of *The Crisis,* DuBois said,

all art is propaganda and ever must be, despite the wailing of the purists. I stand in utter shamelessness and say that whatever art I have for writing has been used always for propaganda for gaining the right of black folk to love and enjoy. I do not care a damn for any art that is not used for propaganda. But I do care when propaganda is confined to one side while the other is stripped and silent.[20]

His purpose, as he saw it, was to encourage black writers to speak out and to write about themselves in a way that would convince both white and black readers of the humanity and seriousness of the black man. DuBois wished these writers to contest the unfavorable stereotypes of black people that had been established in the work of white authors.

> the white public today demands from its artist, literary and pictorial, racial pre-judgment which deliberately distorts truth and justice, as far as colored races are concerned, and it will pay for no other.[21]

DuBois's own first novel, *The Quest of the Silver Fleece* (1911), although published fifteen years before the "art is propaganda" statement in *The Crisis,* is a clear illustration of his propagandistic intentions. The plot of the novel is strongly influenced by Frank Norris's books, *The Octopus* (1901) and *The Pit* (1903), two novels of a trilogy about the effects of the economics of wheat production on individuals associated with it. In DuBois's novel, cotton replaces wheat as the determinant in a decaying economy, but in both novels the "little" man's life is controlled by decisions made by the interests of large conglomerates. In order to survive, DuBois's black hero and heroine must demonstrate strength, pride, and intelligence. DuBois's populist and socialistic sympathies are evident here, for within the context of the novel, the way to survive is for the working classes—rural and urban, black and white—to join forces against the impersonal business interests. The novel can also be read as an answer to Dixon's *The Clansman* and its treatment of race relations, as a satire of the southern white aristocracy, and as an assertion of the noble qualities of a black hero and heroine.

Set against the background of the cotton economy of Toomsville, Alabama, the main plot depicts the love story of Bles Alwyn and Zora Cresswell. Bles is a black boy, educated in the South, who rises to a point of being considered as the first black Secretary of the Treasury, but refuses to compromise himself in order to find political favor; he returns to Alabama and dedicates his life to educating his people. Although Bles has the broader experience, Zora is the stronger, more interesting character. At the beginning of the novel Zora is a child of nature, an "exotic primitive" type who, while very young, was forced to sleep with her employer's son. In Bles's view, she is tainted. But Zora does not allow an early sexual indiscretion to affect her ethical view; she sees right and wrong in terms of her responsibilities toward others. She is convinced that "Right" for her is to dedicate her life to the betterment of her people—to their education and to their economic self-sufficiency. She also possesses the business sense to bring her dreams to fruition. As a leader of her people, Zora seems to have almost superhuman powers. In the melodramatic conclusion, Bles finally recog-

nizes that he loves "the best woman in all the world,"²² Zora, but it is she, the
natural leader, in forgiving him for his former intolerance of her, who proposes marriage.

If the novel is conceptually derivative, it is also flawed in its literary
execution. The black characters are noble, but they are stereotypes—
simplistically conceived, predictable, and somewhat wooden in their behavior and speech. DuBois's treatment of dialect is intricately related to his
depiction of character. Throughout the novel Bles speaks no dialect. He is
already a schoolboy when the novel begins and his standard speech is intended to suggest his potential for leadership. Zora speaks in dialect in her
early scenes, but DuBois's representation of her dialect is far from convincing. In almost haphazard fashion DuBois includes random characteristics of
southern black dialect in her speech. But within the symbolic framework of
the novel, Zora's early use of dialect suggests her primitive, almost savage
quality—she lives in a shack in the woods with a mother who is regarded as a
witch. The use of dialect also implies for DuBois that the speaker—in this
case Zora—has not yet freed herself from her past, from mental as well as
physical slavery.²³ In DuBois's view, this freedom can be found through
education—not through the limiting vocational education advocated by
Booker T. Washington, but by what has come to be known as a humanistic
or "liberal" education.

In the passage that follows, in which Zora, the child, speaks intimately
to Bles, only two pronunciation features appear—the loss of *th* in *them* and
the omission of the unaccented first syllable in *because*. Both features,
although sometimes associated with Black English, are not distinctive characteristics. The only grammatical feature included is occasional lack of subject-verb agreement. But even that feature is not used consistently. Within a
single sentence Zora says *a devil come,* in which the subject and verb do not
agree, while in the more complex structure of a relative clause, the subject
and verb do agree: *a big red flower that grows.*

> "Yes, they is devils down yonder behind the swamp," she would
> whisper, warningly, when, after the first meeting, he had crept back
> again and again, half fascinated, half amused to greet her; "I'se seen
> 'em, I'se heard 'em, 'cause my mammy is a witch.". . . .
> "One night a devil come to me on blue fire out of a big red flower
> that grows in the south swamp; he was tall and big and strong as any-
> thing, and when he spoke the trees shook and the stars fell. Even
> mammy was afeared; and it takes a lot to make mammy afeared, 'cause
> she's a witch and can conjure. He said, 'I'll come when you die—I'll
> come when you die, and take the conjure off you,' and then he went
> away on a big fire."*²⁴

*Pronunciation Features
  1. Loss of *th: them* > *'em.*
  2. Loss of initial unaccented syllable: *because* > *'cause.*

As soon as Zora enters school, her dialect miraculously disappears and her speech becomes as stilted as that of the other characters. Suddenly, her language is abstract and somewhat obscure. She speaks of "Truth" and "Beauty" and of the necessity of finding "The Way," her idealized vision of moral life. She becomes, in fact, a spokesman for DuBois himself.

> "I do not belong in this world where Right and Wrong get so mixed. With us yonder there is wrong, but we call it wrong—mostly. Oh, I don't know; even there things are mixed."[25]

DuBois's treatment of dialect in this early novel is a prefiguration of his disapproval of the use of dialect in literature, a disapproval that he reiterated throughout his career. He associated the assignment of dialect speech with the degradation of black characters; such literary representation, DuBois firmly believed, would do nothing to help improve conditions for "the race." Thus the novel illustrates DuBois's belief that fiction was an effective medium for propaganda. The message of the novel is that happiness for Bles and Zora will be derived from the recognition that the greatest good will arise from a life of service, from their joint commitment to improving the lives of black people. First they would enlighten the people by educating them. Then, by arranging for black farmers to unite with poor whites against the capitalistic cotton producers, the economic situation of the historically downtrodden could be improved. Thus the novel illustrates DuBois's conviction that through education and political activism the lives of the formerly enslaved could be morally "uplifted." For DuBois "moral uplift" meant liberating black minds from a demeaning self-image and avoiding, as a medium for expression, dialectal speech, the speech of their shameful past.

DuBois's moral stance determined every position he articulated. Implicit in his work is an admiration for the respectable black and contempt for the black masses. DuBois took advantage of his position as editor of *The Crisis* to review favorably those books that advocated his "aesthetic" position. He praised those which presented middle-class professional blacks in a favorable light and criticized severely those books that presented uneducated "low life" characters in an exotic, colorful, or even underworld setting. The novels he tended to review favorably during his *Crisis* days generally did not use dialect speech at all—books such as Nella Larsen's novels of middle-class mulatto women, *Quicksand* (1928) and *Passing* (1929), and Jessie Fauset's novels of black bourgeois life, *There is Confusion* (1924) and *Plum Bun* (1929). These novels did not consider the problems of the black lower classes; the "talented tenth" characters interacted either

Grammatical Features
Verbs
    1. Regularization of third person singular present tense: *devil come.*
    2. Lack of subject-verb agreement: *they is; I'se seen.*

with others of the same background as themselves or with whites. In DuBois's view such novels presented "truth" and "beauty" about black life. DuBois called *Quicksand*

> the best piece of fiction that Negro America has produced since the heyday of Chesnutt, and stands easily with Jessie Fauset's *There is Confusion,* in its subtle comprehension of the curious cross currents that swirl about the black American.[26]

In his review of *Plum Bun,* he stated,

> It will not attract those looking simply for the filth in Negro life, but it will attract and hold those looking for the truth.[27]

Although DuBois favorably reviewed the society fiction written by young black women, he was extremely critical of any work that mentioned the "filth," as he called it, associated with lower-class life. In his review of Claude McKay's *Home to Harlem,* his objection is strongly stated:

> Claude McKay's *Home to Harlem* . . . for the most part, nauseates me, and after the dirtier parts of its filth I feel distinctly like taking a bath.[28]

And later,

> He has used every art and emphasis to paint drunkenness, fighting, lascivious sexual promiscuity and utter absence of restraint in as bold and as bright colors as he can.[29]

DuBois criticized Arna Bontemps's *God Sends Sunday* for similar reasons:

> Arna Bontemps' first venture in fiction is to me a profound disappointment. It is of the school of *Nigger Heaven* and *Home to Harlem.* There is a certain pathetic touch to the painting of his poor little jockey hero, but nearly all else is sordid crime, drinking, gambling, whoremongering, and murder. There is not a decent intelligent woman; not a single man with the slightest ambition or real education, scarcely more than one human child in the whole book. Even the horses are drab. In the "Blues" alone Bontemps sees beauty. But in brown skins, frizzled hair and full contoured faces, there are to him nothing but ugly, tawdry, hateful things, which he describes with evident caricature.[30]

DuBois even rejected Langston Hughes's novel of rural lower-class black life, *Not Without Laughter,* for he disapproved of Hughes's choice of subject: "It touches dirt, but it is not dirty and it ends with the upward note."[31]

DuBois, the leader of the black literati and a determiner of black taste, held a limited view of the purpose of black literature. Fiction that failed to endorse his political views he criticized harshly. For him the purpose of black literature was to portray the Negro as a respectable citizen, to establish a positive model for blacks. And in rejecting literature that concerned itself with the lower classes, DuBois was in fact rejecting the use of Black English dialect.

DuBois edited *The Crisis* in the years that have come to be known popularly as the Harlem Renaissance—the period that, depending on whose authority one follows, spans the 1920s, and perhaps the 1930s, a time in which a growing group of black writers saw black life as a legitimate subject for their own work. One of the men behind the Harlem Renaissance, the sociologist Charles S. Johnson, editor of *Opportunity,* the house organ of the Urban League during the Renaissance years, was probably more responsible than others of the period for directing the attention of talented black writers and artists to opportunities in the arts. For Johnson, according to David Levering Lewis, only in the arts was creative expression still relatively untrammelled by the conventions of American racism.

> No exclusionary rules had been laid down regarding a place in the arts. Here was a small crack in the wall of racism, a fissure that was worth trying to widen. Not only was this a tactic admirably suited to the ability and temperament of educated Afro-Americans, it seemed to be the sole battle plan affording both high visibility and low vulnerability.[32]

Through honest literary and artistic representations of black life, Johnson believed, racial stereotyping could be confronted head-on, and a reconsideration of the rôle of the black in American life would be possible.

Actually, the Harlem Renaissance can be viewed as one of the happier consequences of the migration by blacks from the rural South to the northern cities between 1890 and 1920. Gunnar Myrdal has estimated that during this period more than two million blacks "left the farm for the factory."[33] The emigration North introduced them to the problems of urban poverty—crowded and unsanitary housing, economic uncertainty—without alleviating the troubles they had seen—discrimination, exploitation, violence. Adjustment to the new life was demanding and difficult. To complicate matters, The United States entered the First World War in 1918, and blacks, many of whom saw the war with a foreign enemy as an opportunity (as DuBois put it) to "close ranks"[34] with white Americans and fight together for their country, were disillusioned with the treatment they received. Regiments were segregated, and although provisions were made to train black officers, once trained they were allowed only to lead black troops. Although the soldiers found that they were warmly received by the French during the war, when they returned home they were subjected to the same indignities they had grown to expect before they left. Jim Crow, they discovered, still ruled their lives, and they seemed powerless to do anything about it.

The political reaction to this frustration was generally twofold. On the one hand, a political response was developed that shaped the formation and activities of the N.A.A.C.P. and gave birth to the Urban League and to

Opportunity, its journal. Generally, the direction was leftist and as-similationist. On the other hand, there were the separatists, those around Marcus Garvey, who sought to lead an exodus back to Africa.

But there was another reaction—not directly political, rather, instead, literary. The political, social, and economic conditions in contemporary black life proved a vital source of literary material. The black intelligentsia, many of whom had settled in Harlem, were eager to write of their experiences and to publish what they wrote. These writers believed that artistic representation of the lives of black people would help to humanize them in the minds of the white public. And so black writers began to write about black experience; and in part because white readers were curious about black life in the "exotic" Harlem at their doorstep, their books were published by white publishers. What is called the Harlem Renaissance, or the Negro Renaissance, or the vogue of "the New Negro" was on its way. Although it has been traditional to regard the stock market crash of 1929 as the end of the Harlem Renaissance, many of the young black writers who had begun to publish their work in the 1920s actually were to do their best work in the 1930s. But whatever dating one follows, and whatever terminology one uses, the period after the First World War saw an awakening of a black literature that is today considered to be the foundation of a more recent black literary expression.

While DuBois judged literature by its potential as propaganda, Alain Locke, a professor at Howard University and the editor of a representative collection of fiction, essays, and poetry by black writers entitled *The New Negro* (1925), became the spokesman for a different aesthetic. Locke was an academic and a literary man, not a political thinker, and that background and bias are evident in his writing. It was Locke who located the "Renaissance" in Harlem, which he saw as a "race capital," a center for the literary expression and cultural self-definition of black people in America.

> In Harlem, Negro life is seizing upon its first chances for group expression and self-determination. It is—or promises at least to be—a race capital. That is why our comparison is taken with those nascent centers of folk-expression and self-determination which are playing a creative part in the world to-day. Without pretense to their political significance, Harlem has the same rôle to play for the New Negro as Dublin has had for the New Ireland or Prague for the New Czechoslovakia.[35]

Locke believed that the black writers of the 1920s were quite different from earlier black writers. In his mind, the work of the new writers reflected the "new mentality for the American Negro":

> In this new group psychology we note the lapse of sentimental appeal, then the development of a more positive self-respect and self-reliance; the repudiation of social dependence, and then the gradual recovery from hyper-sensitiveness and "touchy" nerves, the repudiation of the

double standard of judgment with its special philanthropic allowances and then the sturdier desire for objective and scientific appraisal; and finally the rise from social disillusionment to race pride, from the sense of social debt to the responsibilities of social contribution, and offsetting the necessary working and commonsense acceptance of restricted conditions, the belief in ultimate esteem and recognition. Therefore the Negro to-day wishes to be known for what he is, even in his faults and shortcomings, and scorns a craven and precarious survival at the price of seeming to be what he is not.[36]

Black art for Locke would follow standards quite different from those set by DuBois. Although black literature could be concerned with racial issues, Locke, whom David Levering Lewis calls "the Proust of Lenox Avenue,"[37] believed it was more important that it concern itself with artistic expression first.

The newer motive, then, in being racial is to be so purely for the sake of art. Nowhere is this more apparent, or more justified than in the increasing tendency to evolve from the racial substance something technically distinctive, something that as an idiom of style may become a contribution to the general resources of art. In flavor of language, flow of phrase, accent of rhythm in prose, verse and music, color and tone of imagery, idiom and timbre of emotion and symbolism, it is the ambition and promise of Negro artists to make a distinctive contribution.[38]

Despite the fact that in *The New Negro* Locke included examples of dialect writing by black writers, he was aware of its dangers; in his introductory material, he, as had DuBois, stated a preference for nondialect literature. Both men firmly believed that dialect writing did not promote the most admirable image of the race. In describing the "New Negro" writers, Locke said,

They have shaken themselves free from the minstrel tradition and the fowling-nets of dialect, and through acquiring ease and simplicity in serious expression, have carried the folk-gift to the altitudes of art.[39]

Yet Locke had special praise for James Weldon Johnson's poem *Creation: A Negro Sermon,* because in it Johnson was able "to transpose the dialect motive and carry it through in the idioms of imagery rather than the broken phonetics of speech. . . ."[40] Johnson succeeded in preserving the "folk spirit" without distorting language, and that is an achievement Locke considered admirable.

Even though DuBois and Locke agreed in their disapproval of dialect writing, their views otherwise represented two contrasting directions available to black writers of the 1920s and 1930s; DuBois, the political philosopher, endorsed literature with a propagandistic purpose, while Locke, the aesthete, preferred literature with unquestioned artistic value. Although each had his enthusiastic supporters, many of the Harlem Renaissance writers chose to listen to no arbiter of taste and went their own separate ways. Despite the fact that the "leaders" made an effort to control the type of literature black writers were producing and to discourage dialect literature in order to advance the political and literary and cultural recognition of black people, many of the best black writers of the period ignored an externally imposed aesthetic and for one reason or another continued to write in dialect.

Generally, the dialect writers of the 1920s and 1930s were involved in one way or another with literary realism; they used dialect to suggest an atmosphere of actuality. The work of these dialect writers can be divided into two groups: one was concerned with rural southern settings and "local" dialects; the other focused on an urban setting—usually Harlem—and consequently upon a standardized urban speech.

Rural dialect writing of the 1920s and 1930s was quite different from the "local color" writing of the late nineteenth century. Although some of the writers attempted a kind of scientific precision in their representation of dialect, the dialect speaker was no longer the "plantation Negro" or the obedient servant left over from a pre–Civil War society; rather, his dialect speech identified him as a primitive or as an exotic, observed from a highly educated point of view. Often he was a character whom time had passed by, a character who was out of place in a post-World War I world and yet who had no other world to relate to.

A forerunner of the black dialect school who recognized the exotic potential of the literary use of folk or of primitive dialect (although he rarely used dialect in his own prose) was James Weldon Johnson. In 1912, while he was United States Consul in Nicaragua, Johnson published, under an assumed name, a remarkable novel, *The Autobiography of an Ex-Coloured Man*. The novel is the fictional account of a man whose light skin and European features make it possible for him to "pass" as a white man. By hiding his origins, he gains social and financial success, although he ultimately and ironically realizes he may have "sold [his] birthright for a mess of pottage."[41]

Since the narrator's intention is to "pass," his speech is not represented in dialect. The dialect occasionally included in the book, that of black people overheard by the narrator, adds a sense of authenticity to the situations described. The passage that follows indicates the narrator's admiration for the vitality of dialect speech and also records some examples of the speech of blacks in Atlanta, which in 1912 would still have been considered as a provincial city of the rural South:

> I had read some Negro dialect and had heard snatches of it on my journey down from Washington; but here I heard it in all of its fullness

and freedom. I was particularly struck by the way in which it was punctuated by such exclamatory phrases as "Lawd a mussy!" "G'wan, man!" "Bless ma soul!" "Look heah, chile!" These people talked and laughed without restraint. In fact, they talked straight from their lungs and laughed from the pits of their stomachs. And this hearty laughter was often justified by the droll humour of some remark. I paused long enough to hear one man say to another: "W'at's de mattah wid you an' yo' fr'en' Sam?" and the other came back like a flash: "Ma fr'en'? He ma fr'en'? Man! I'd go to his funeral jes' de same as I'd go to a minstrel show."*[42]

Although the examples recorded here are brief, it is interesting that Johnson has relied for dialectal effect almost entirely on pronunciation features; only one grammatical feature, zero copula, appears in the passage.

Thirteen years after Johnson's novel was published, in 1923, one of the earliest writers associated with the Harlem Renaissance, Jean Toomer, published his only novel, *Cane*. During the early twenties Toomer frequented Harlem with the black writers. Langston Hughes, in his autobiography, mentions Wallace Thurman, Dorothy Peterson, Aaron Douglas, and Nella Larsen[43] in connection with Toomer. But Toomer was also associated with the white writers of Greenwich Village, particularly Hart Crane, Waldo Frank, Gorham Munson, and Kenneth Burke. Later, as his interest in literature faded, Toomer turned to a study of the Russian mystic Gurdjieff; inspired by him, Toomer attempted to transcend the limitation of racial identity and to merge himself in a world consciousness. His association with Gurdjieff, and his turning away from interest in race as an issue, may help to account for the fact that in the later years of his life Toomer came to deny his blackness absolutely.

Cane, a collection of stories and poems, is reminiscent of Sherwood Anderson's *Winesburg, Ohio* (1919) in its examination of individual characters formed and deformed by their locale. In its use of black people to convey symbolic meaning, *Cane* also recalls W. E. B. DuBois's *The Souls of Black Folk*. Most frequently, *Cane* has been admired for its poetic and symbolic power. The style is experimental—the stories are interspersed with short poems; sentences are short and often convey a character's consciousness. The language is full of color and symbol; ideas are rarely directly stated; atmosphere and implication merge and move apart. Waldo Frank, in his foreword to the first edition of *Cane*, was the first to admire the poetic quality of Toomer's writing:

Pronunciation Features
1. Reduction of consonant clusters: *child > chile; just > jes'; friend > fr'en'*.
2. *th > d: with > wid; the > de*.
3. Loss of *r: Lord > Lawd; mercy > mussy; here > heah; your > yo'*.
4. Nasalization: *Go on > G'wan*.

Grammatical Features
Verbs
1. Zero copula: *He ma fr'en'?*

A poet has risen in that land who writes, not as a Southerner, not as a rebel against Southerners, not as a Negro, not as apologist or priest or critic: who writes as a *poet*. . . . He has made songs and lovely stories of his land . . . not of its yesterday, but of its immediate life. And that has been enough.[44]

"Esther," one of the short stories in *Cane,* relates the life of a girl between the ages of nine and twenty-seven, and her continuing fascination with a hauntingly large and very black man, Barlo. Barlo's African features and his ability to preach while he is in a religious trance intrigue the light-skinned, nine-year-old girl. His image is impressed on her young imagination. When she is sixteen she dreams that she bears Barlo's baby—ugly, but a symbol to her of his possessed self. As the years pass, Esther's fantasy of Barlo continues; it is an escape from the dull routine of her life as a clerk in her father's store. She loves both his good and his bad qualities; as they are described, both are distinctly masculine.

Best cotton picker in the county, in the state, in the whole world for that matter. Best man with his fists, best man with dice, with a razor. Promoter of church benefits. Of colored fairs. Vagrant preacher. Lover of all women for miles and miles around.[45]

Finally, when Esther is twenty-seven, Barlo returns to the town. Esther, convinced that if she wants him she must assert herself to gain him, seeks him out one midnight and finds him in the arms of a black woman. She is received with curiosity and surprise by the couple who, unlike Esther, speak in dialect.

"Well, I'm sholy damned—skuse me, but what, what brought you here, lil milk-white gal?"
"You." Her voice sounds like a frightened child's that calls homeward from some point miles away.
"Me?"
"Yes, you Barlo."
"This aint th place fer y. This aint th place fer y."
"I know. I know. But I've come for you."
"For me for what?"
She manages to look deep and straight into his eyes. He is slow at understanding. Guffaws and giggles break out from all around the room. A coarse woman's voice remarks, "So thats how th dictie niggers does it." Laughs. "Mus give em credit fo their gall."[*46]

*BARLO
Pronunciation Features
1. Reduction of consonant clusters: *little* > *lil.*
2. Loss of initial unstressed syllable: *excuse* > *skuse.*
3. Vowel fronting: *for* > *fer.*
Eye Dialect: *the* > *th; you* > *y.*

Grammatical Features
Verbs
None.

Shock, disbelief, and disillusionment overcome Esther; humiliated, she stumbles out of the room and into the street. Like the other women in *Cane,* there will be no pleasure and fulfillment in her life; now she will never find a place for herself. Her rebuff by blackness has overwhelmed her. Cursed by being neither black nor white in a society that insists upon this distinction, Esther, like her ancestor Cain, is destined to wander the earth.

The dialect used in this passage is used realistically, but it carries symbolic meaning as well. Barlo's dialect speech emphasizes his vitality, his "otherness," his exotic primitiveness for Esther, as does the blackness of his skin, which Esther finds so irresistible. Perhaps this primitiveness also implies a capacity for cruelty and insensitivity, which Barlo and his woman demonstrate in their final treatment of Esther. The contrast between the types is further emphasized by the fact that Barlo speaks in dialect and the light-skinned, educated Esther does not. The lack of communication that inevitably results seems a significant and tragic failure for Esther.

Although the style of *Cane* is experimental and highly symbolic, the representation of dialect in the story is entirely conventional. There is none of the conscious emphasis on grammatical features and reduction of phonological features that there was in Stein's "Melanctha." The dialectal features in "Esther" are minimal—enough pronunciation and grammatical features appear in Barlo's and the "other woman's" speech to make their conflict with Esther believable. But the strangeness of the speech is emphasized in ways that suggest meanings beyond simple realistic representation; omission of apostrophes throughout the dialect passage, for example, gives a visual strangeness to the passage but signals nothing significant in pronunciation.

Toomer, then, uses dialect for realistic effect, as did Johnson, but at the same time its symbolic significance cannot be ignored. Toomer's purpose in using dialect cannot be separated from his symbolic intentions for his characters. His selective use of dialect also tends to reinforce his representation of the sense of disillusionment and alienation that pervades the lives of the descendants of Cain in this rural Georgian "cane country."

At the center of the Harlem Renaissance were two writers, Langston Hughes and Zora Neale Hurston, who, during their youth, strongly dis-

Negative
1. *aint.*

WOMAN
Pronunciation Features
1. Reduction of consonant clusters: *must > mus.*
2. Loss of *th: them > em.*
3. Loss of *r: for > fo* (note Barlo says *fer*).

Grammatical Features
Verbs
1. Lack of subject-verb agreement: *niggers does.*

agreed with the propagandistic purpose for literature advocated by DuBois[47] and with the bourgeois aestheticism of Alain Locke. Instead of concerning themselves with the problems of the "talented tenth," the morality of "social uplift," and with the representation of the Standard English speech of economically and socially arrived black people, these writers turned their attention to what they considered the "realities" of black life—the life of poor blacks, and, of course, their speech.

In the summer of 1926 Hughes and Hurston, along with Wallace Thurman, Aaron Douglas, Bruce Nugent, Gwendolyn Bennett, and John P. Davis, came together to produce a journal that would express their aesthetic position as a response to DuBois and Locke. The product, *Fire!!*, a remarkable collection of poems, stories, drawings, and a play by Hurston, was intended to shock the black literary establishment and to attract interest in an alternative to the control over young black artists exerted by DuBois and Locke. For the most part, the journal was ignored. Hughes accused DuBois of "roasting" it,[48] but in fact DuBois never commented upon *Fire!!* in print. Most of the copies, ironically and unfortunately, were burned in a fire shortly after publication.

Fire!! did, however, contain a good bit of dialect writing, something that both Hughes and Hurston considered essential in the authentic portrayal of the lower classes and something they rightly assumed would alienate the black establishment. Although *Fire!!* did not have the impact they had hoped, it set forth the point of view of a new generation of black writers who saw the value of representing poor blacks and their speech in their writing.

As he describes the first twenty-eight years of his life in his autobiography, *The Big Sea* (1940), Langston Hughes emphasizes his dislike of the bourgeoisie and the establishment—whether in Mexico, where he visited his father, at Columbia University, or in Washington, D.C. He preferred his associations with the common people—musicians and restaurant help in Paris, black street people in Harlem, or sailors he met on freighters during his trips around the world. This love of ordinary people is evident in his poetry and his prose; it became the identifying characteristic of his literary work. Langston Hughes was the first black American to make his living by writing, and his writing is innovative because he tried to use the rhythms and sounds of ordinary black speech as part of the realistic representation of his characters. In Hughes's work the folk tradition—closely identified with dialect speech—again comes alive in modern settings.

Hughes's *Not Without Laugher* (1930), a novel with which Hughes himself was not entirely happy, and which has received considerable criticism for its simple plot and stereotyped characters, celebrates the capacity for joy and laughter of black people. Hughes purposely set his novel in Kansas; thus he avoided the stereotypes of rural Southern blacks. But despite the rather original setting for a black novel, the stereotypes remain. There is Hager, the old Christian washerwoman who has known slavery but believes in education as the catalyst for change for her children and her race. She has three daughters—Tempy, the eldest, who has social pretensions, lives in town and tries to imitate white folks, even if she cannot associate socially with them. Tempy considers dialect déclassé, and objects to her nephew, Sandy, speaking it. Interestingly enough, "the Negro" is represented on her bookshelf by "Chestnut's [sic] *House Behind the Cedars,* and the *Complete Poems* of Paul Lawrence [sic] Dunbar, whom Tempy tolerated on account of his fame, but condemned because he had written so much in dialect and so often of the lower classes of colored people."[49] The second daughter, Annjee, marries for love; her husband is a good-natured, musical loafer, Jimboy, who has trouble keeping a job, but who is able to laugh and enjoy life to its fullest. Their child, Sandy, spends his early years with his grandmother in Kansas because his parents cannot support him in Chicago. Hager's third daughter, Harriet, is very much like Jimboy; she sings and dances and enjoys life. Although Harriet began her career as a prostitute, her later success as a singer will make it possible for Sandy to attend college and thereby to fulfill Hager's dream. DuBois's "uplift" is clearly a motivating force for the older characters in the novel; nevertheless, Sandy, through his observation of the members of his family, remains committed to the values of music and laughter and warmth and love instilled in him by his father. Possibly his compromise is one that Hughes sees as necessary for his race; Sandy stays in touch with his own nature and with his origins, although through education he will transcend the humble living conditions associated with his family's past.

In the novel Hager, Annjee, Harriet, and Jimboy always speak in dialect. Sandy observes more than he speaks, but when he does speak his language reflects his schooling; he uses Standard English. When he slips at his Aunt Tempy's and says "ain't," Tempy quickly corrects him. But it is Hager who speaks dialect most frequently. In the following passage, she speaks of her past and her dreams of the future for Sandy.

> "Fo' nigh on forty years, even sence Cudge an' me come here from Montgomery. An' I been washin' fo' white folks ever' week de Lawd sent sence I been here, too. Bought this house washin', and made as many payments myself as Cudge come near; an' raised ma chillens washin'; an' when Cudge taken sick an' laid on his back for mo'n a year, I taken care o' him washin'; an' when he died, paid de funeral bill washin', cause he ain't belonged to no lodge. Sent Tempy through de high school and edicated Annjee till she marry that onery pup of a Jimboy an' Harriett till she left home. Yes, sir. Washin', an' here I is with me arms still in de tub! . . . But they's one mo' got to go through school yet, an' that's ma little Sandy. If de Lawd lets me live, I's gwine make a edicated man out o' him. He's gwine be another Booker T. Washington."*[50]

Pronunciation Features
  1. Reduction of consonant clusters: *and* > *an'; children* > *chillens; more than* > *mo'n; educated* > *edicated.*

Hughes clearly uses dialect selectively, for realistic purposes, but his attitude toward dialect differs dramatically from that of many other twentieth-century writers. In the first place, he does not use dialect purely to punctuate a passage, to keep the reader aware by occasional use of dialect that the characters are black and believable, as did Dixon and Margaret Mitchell. Nor is his purpose symbolic and suggestive, as is the case with Jean Toomer. For Hughes dialect speech is really part of the factual fabric of which the novel is woven; the characters are fully defined to a large extent because of their use or avoidance of dialect and they are aware of it as a defining characteristic of their race. The characters who use dialect in Hughes's novel speak frequently and in rather lengthy passages.

Furthermore, whereas earlier twentieth-century dialect writers had relied heavily on pronunciation features to indicate dialectal speech and included only an occasional grammatical feature—a double negative or an example of a lack of subject-verb agreement—Hughes has increased the number and range of grammatical features he records. He particularly concentrates on verb forms. In the above passage Hager frequently confuses tenses. She substitutes the past participle form for the past tense: *come* instead of *came* and *I taken care* in place of *I took care.* She also uses the present tense, *she marry* (note regularization of the third person singular present tense), instead of the past tense, *she married.* There are several examples of zero copula: *I been, when Cudge taken,* as well as the usual lack of subject-verb agreement: *I is.* The double negative is represented in Hager's speech: *he ain't belonged to no lodge,* as is the use of the objective pronoun *me,* both as a subject and as a possessive form: *me arms.*

Emphasis on the grammatical features marks a new phase in the representation of black dialect speech. In part, emphasis on the grammatical features reduces the difficulty of reading. Also, writers such as Langston Hughes, who was a close observer and participant in the type of life he wrote

2. *th > d: the > de.*
3. Loss of *r: for > fo'; near > nigh; Lord > Lawd; more > mo'; there's > they's.*
4. Loss of *v: of > o'.*
5. Nasalization: *going to > gwine; ordinary > ornery; washing > washin'.*
6. Loss of initial unstressed syllable: *because > cause.*
7. Loss of vowel glide: *my > ma.*

Grammatical Features
Verbs
1. Lack of subject-verb agreement: *here I is.*
2. Present instead of past tense: *till she married > till she marry;* (in present tense also note regularization of the third person singular present tense).
3. Past participle instead of past tense: *I taken care.*
4. Zero copula: *I been; when Cudge taken.*
Negative
1. *ain't.*
2. Double negative: *he ain't belonged to no lodge.*
Pronouns
1. Objective pronoun as subject: *me.*
2. Objective pronoun as possessive: *me arms.*

about, were becoming aware that grammatical features were at least as important as pronunciation features in the representation of dialect speech. But perhaps more important, as Hughes was undoubtedly aware, orthographical representation of pronunciation features had negative connotations. Through misuse at the hands of writers like Thomas Dixon, such representation had come to be associated with the anti-realistic black stereotype in American fiction. Also, orthographical peculiarity perhaps implied—or suggested—an ignorance on the part of the speaker associated with illiteracy. But Langston Hughes, committed as he was to the simple realistic value of dialect writing, found a way to put all those connotations behind him. With his emphasis on syntactic characteristics he began a new trend for others to follow.

Zora Neale Hurston maintained her friendship with Langston Hughes until the end of the 1920s, when they disagreed as joint authors of a play, *Mule Bone*.[51] Born in an all-black town, Eatonville, Florida, Hurston went North for high school and college; in 1928 she graduated from Barnard, where she studied anthropology with Franz Boas. As a graduate student, still under Boas's tutelage, she returned to the South to collect folklore materials, which she was to publish first in collections of folklore and then to transform in later years into fiction. She was known as a lively eccentric and storyteller among those whom she called the Harlem "niggerati."

Zora Neale Hurston was at her best when she shaped her folkloristic materials into fiction. The characters that result are convincing and realistic—and far removed from stereotype. She herself describes her choice of subject and style:

> I saw that what was being written by Negro authors was all on the same theme—the race problem, and saturated with our sorrows. By the time I graduated from college, I had sensed the falsity of the picture, because I did not find that sorrow. We talk about the race problem a great deal, but go on living and laughing and striving like everybody else. So I saw that what was being written and declaimed was a pose.[52]

Hurston, like Hughes, resisted the inhibiting restrictions on black writing imposed by DuBois and Locke. Instead, she turned to a region she knew well, Florida, and wrote of black people in a town whose center was the porch of the only store. There, in their own striking dialect, the men would recount tales and stories and exchange their views on local daily events. Hurston's childhood experiences in Florida, along with her formal training in anthropology and folklore under Boas, formed an unusual combination that made it possible for her to portray in fiction the liveliness of modern black rural culture. Her second and best novel, *Their Eyes Were Watching God* (1937), represents a coherent integration of folklore and fiction; at the same time, she makes a contemporary statement about the attainment of feminine autonomy and individuality.

Janie Crawford, the illegitimate heroine of the novel, is raised by her grandmother in a town in West Florida. An ex-slave and impressed by the values of education and respectability, the grandmother marries Janie off, before she can "get into trouble," to a much older man with sixty acres. He regards Janie as an extension of his property and works her unmercifully. Once Janie realizes the extent to which she is being used, she runs off with an assertive, ambitious outsider, Joe Starks, who takes her to an all-black Florida town. Joe quickly sets up a store and soon is elected mayor. He fully expects Janie, as "Mrs. Mayor," to act in a dignified manner, not to partici-pate in the storytelling that the men enjoy on the front porch of the store, and not to socialize with the townswomen. Cut off by her position from the community and alienated by the coldness of her husband, Janie is isolated and unhappy. When her husband dies after twenty years of marriage, she is still not fully mature as a woman.

After Joe Stark's death, Janie is courted by and marries a man much younger than she—a "Jimboy" character named Tea Cake, who is easygo-ing, who sings and laughs and enjoys life fully. With Tea Cake, Janie dis-covers a love of sharing, and as the two pick beans side by side "down on the muck" in the Everglades, their love grows deep and strong and transcends any human relationship that Janie had thought possible. In the climactic scene of the novel, during a hurricane, Tea Cake is bitten by a rabid dog and becomes crazed and violent, and it becomes necessary for Janie to kill her beloved husband in self-defense. She does so without regret and with the recognition that, despite the ending, no one could alter the perfection of her relationship with her third husband.

Within the novel all of the black characters speak in dialect. Hurston's ear for word usage as well as for pronunciation is evident in the delightful metaphoric language her characters speak. In the following passage Tea Cake is courting the recently widowed Janie, but because he is so much younger than she is, Janie is slow to comprehend the serious intention of his visit.

"See dat? You'se got de world in uh jug and make out you don't know it. But Ah'm glad tuh be de one tuh tell yuh."

"Ah guess you done told plenty women all about it."

"Ah'm de Apostle Paul tuh de Gentiles. Ah tells 'em and then agin Ah shows 'em."

"Ah thought so." She yawned and made to get up from the sofa. "You done got me so sleepy wid yo' head-scratchin' Ah kin hardly make it tuh de bed." She stood up at once, collecting her hair. He sat still.

"Naw, you ain't sleepy, Mis' Janie. You jus' want me tuh go. You figger Ah'm uh rounder and uh pimp and you done wasted too much time talkin' wid me."

"Why, Tea Cake! Whut ever put dat notion in yo' head?"

"De way you looked at me when Ah said whut Ah did. Yo' face skeered me so bad till mah whiskers drawed up."

"Ah ain't got no business bein' mad at nothin' you do and say. You got it all wrong. Ah ain't mad atall."

"Ah know it and dat's what puts de shamery on me. You'se jus' disgusted wid me. Yo' face jus' left here and went off somewhere else. Naw, you ain't mad wid me. Ah be glad if you was, 'cause then Ah might do somethin' tuh please yuh. But lak it is—"

"Mah likes and dislikes ought not tuh make no difference wid you, Tea Cake. Dats fuh yo' lady friend. Ah'm jus' uh sometime friend uh yourn."*53

Although Janie is the former mayor's wife and Tea Cake is a drifter, both clearly speak the same dialect. Pronunciation and grammatical features are quite evenly divided, with slightly more variety in both categories in Tea Cake's speech. Whereas there is only one example of verb variation in Janie's speech, the use of a past participle as a helping verb, as in *You done told* and *You done got*, in Tea Cake's speech four examples of verb variation are evident. He uses lack of subject-verb agreement in *You'se* (which could

*JANIE
Pronunciation Features
   1. Reduction of consonant clusters: *just > jus'*.
   2. *th > d: with > wid; that > dat, dats*.
   3. Loss of *r: your > yo'; for > fuh*.
   4. Nasalization: *scratching > scratchin'; being > bein'; nothing > nothin'; yours > yourn*.
   5. Loss of vowel glide: *I > Ah; my > mah*.
   6. Vowel fronting: *can > kin*.
Eye Dialect: *what > whut*.

Grammatical Features
Verbs
   1. Past participle used as helping verb: *You done told; you done got*.
Negative
   1. *ain't*.
   2. Double negative: *Ah ain't got no business; Mah likes and dislikes ought not tuh make no difference wid you*.

TEA CAKE
Pronunciation Features
   1. Reduction of consonant clusters: *just > jus'; figure > figger*.
   2. Changes in *th:*
      a. *th > d: that > dat, dats; the > de; with > wid*.
      b. Loss of *th: them > 'em*.
   3. Loss of *r: your > yo'*.
   4. Nasalization: *talking > talkin'; something > somethin'*.
   5. Loss of initial unstressed syllable: *because > 'cause*.
   6. Loss of vowel glide: *I > Ah; my > mah; like > lak*.
   7. Vowel fronting: *again > agin*.

Grammatical Features
Verbs
   1. Lack of subject-verb agreement: *You have > you'se; Ah tells; Ah shows; You was*.
   2. Past participle used as helping verb: *You done wasted*.
   3. Regularization of past tense of irregular verb: *drew > drawed*.
   4. *Be: Ah be glad*.
Negative
   1. *ain't*.

be either *You has* or *You is*), *Ah tells, Ah shows,* and *You was.* Like Janie, he uses the double past participle in *You done wasted.* He also forms the past tense *drawed* according to the regular rather than the irregular model, and uses *be* as a substitute for *am* in *Ah be glad.* It is Janie, however, who uses the double negative in this passage: *Ah ain't got no business* and *Mah likes and dislikes ought not tuh make no difference wid you,* whereas Tea Cake relies only on *ain't* for negative expression.

The balance between pronunciation and grammatical features in the novel follows the same pattern as in Langston Hughes's *Not Without Laughter.* But Hurston approached the problem from a different perspective than Hughes did. In the first place, she considered herself a professional collector of folk materials. And for her the language in which stories were transmitted was as important as the content of the stories and tales. Pronunciation and grammatical and lexical features indicated for her authenticity in the realistic portrayal of character and situation. Furthermore, Hurston, by nature a rebel and an individualist, could well have insisted on using literary dialect in simple defiance of the "Negro leaders" who cringed at the sight of dialect in literature.

Whatever her reason, the dialectal speech is perfectly integrated into the novel; here there is no separation between form and content. Here dialect does not stereotype its speakers. In fact, Hurston is so accomplished in her representation of character through speech that her people assert their individuality because of, never in spite of, their speech. *Their Eyes Were Watching God* is an example of dialect writing at its best; it is certainly one of the most successful novels that use dialect to have come out of the Harlem Renaissance.

Langston Hughes and Zora Neale Hurston did not confront racial issues head-on in their fiction; they did not use their art as propaganda. Instead, they used the modern rural setting as a backdrop for "real" black characters who lived in a black world and were concerned with defining the values and using the speech patterns that existed within that world. For their variety of literary realism they—particularly Hurston—were criticized by the "race leaders." Such lack of agreement about writing was typical of the Harlem Renaissance period. Far from being a unified literary movement, a "school," with the pupils educated according to an agreed-upon aesthetic, it was rather a period in which black writers with a variety of literary approaches and talents began to write and receive public recognition. As a group they agreed on very little—from the purpose of literature to the choice of setting, the use of dialect, or methods of characterization.

The critic Blyden Jackson has called the black novel a city novel;[54] indeed, many black writers in their eagerness to eradicate completely the "plantation Negro" image, chose to write of urban rather than of rural life.

For the black man of the 1920s, the city symbolized both escape from the oppressions of rural southern racism and a way out of an inhibiting and stereotyped self-image. The city seemed a Paradise in which a black Adam could be proud and could prosper. During the 1920s, when they accepted a qualified version of an American Dream, blacks did not anticipate the inevitable fall of this newly arrived black Adam. For them the city symbolized opportunity. In the city black people sought to shape for themselves a new identity and a new way of life. The "New Negro," as he would appear in fiction, was usually male, urban, verbally adroit, flamboyant in his dress and, more often than not, with shadowy underworld connections—in short, a black Gatsby. This romantic and picaresque hero often fascinated white readers by daring to overturn the dominant middle-class values. But all too frequently he distressed blacks who considered a positive and responsible literary racial image crucially important. For the Harlem Renaissance writers of the urban novel—Carl Van Vechten, Claude McKay, and Countee Cullen will be considered here—the "real" black urban character could be found in Harlem, for Harlem was the center of the modern black world in America's literary capital, New York.

One of the most influential—and controversial—writers associated with the Harlem Renaissance was Carl Van Vechten, a white midwesterner who had been fascinated by black culture since his childhood. As as adult in New York, he was known in literary and artistic circles; he collected paintings, wrote novels and essays, took photographs, and made a point of knowing anyone of importance in the arts. Always a figure of fashion, Van Vechten was famous for his parties, at which he brought together a wide variety of writers and artists, both black and white. Described somewhat ambiguously by Nathan Irvin Huggins as a "midwife" to the Harlem Renaissance,[55] he was also a generous man of some affluence, who did his best to help black writers—Langston Hughes, Walter White, Claude McKay, and Rudolph Fisher, among them—find publishers interested in their work. Van Vechten's interest in black life—and it was black city life with which he was acquainted—culminated in the writing of his fifth novel, *Nigger Heaven* (1926). Although Van Vechten intended for the novel to present a broad spectrum of black city life, one that would portray a diverse and realistic picture of Harlem, the title and prologue to the novel deeply offended a number of black critics, DuBois and Locke among them.

The offense in part seemed to be the result of a literal response to the title; Van Vechten believed his critics had missed the irony and the theatrical connotation that he had intended. He allowed his hero, Byron Kasson, to articulate that intent when he returned to Harlem after a walk through fashionable Manhattan:

> Nigger Heaven! Byron moaned. Nigger Heaven! That's what Harlem is. We sit in our places in the gallery of this New York theatre and watch the white world sitting down below in the good seats in the

orchestra. Occasionally they turn their faces up towards us, their hard, cruel faces, to laugh or sneer, but they never beckon. It never seems to occur to them that Nigger Heaven is crowded, that there isn't another seat, that something has to be done. It doesn't seem to occur to them either, he went on fiercely, that we sit above them, that we can drop things down on them and crush them, that we can swoop down from this Nigger Heaven and take their seats. No, they have no fear of that! Harlem! The Mecca of the New Negro! My God![56]

The main plot of *Nigger Heaven* turns around two highly intelligent, educated, young black people, Mary Love, a librarian, and Byron Kasson, a struggling writer. Their tragedy, as seen through Van Vechten's eyes, is that their education has interfered with their ability to be themselves, to act naturally, and to love one another; to put the problem succinctly, they are overcivilized. Instead of enjoying the freedom offered them by the city, they have repressed their emotional spontaneity. Clearly, their backgrounds inhibit them from speaking in dialect. Their speech is stilted, formal, and decidedly artificial. The more colorful and interesting characters are less respectable by middle-class standards. Lasca Sartoris, a *femme fatale* who moves in fashionable Harlem circles and therefore speaks no dialect, is a typical Van Vechten woman whose sexual attractiveness and love of self-indulgence nearly destroy Byron. Anatole Longfellow, or the Scarlet Creeper, nattily dressed in plaid suit, tan shoes, straw hat, and diamond tie pin, strolls through Harlem at the beginning of the novel. His flamboyant style attracts women; one "golden-brown" beauty is willing to pay him for his company.

> Everybody knows who you is, Mr. 'Toly, *everybody!* Her voice implored his attention.
> The Creeper continued to clap.
> Ah been jes' nacherly crazy to meet you.
> The Creeper was stern. What fo'? he shot out.
> You knows, Mr. 'Toly. I guess you knows.
> He drew her a little apart from the ring.
> How much you got?
> Oh, Ah been full o' prosperity dis evenin'. Ah met an ofay wanted to change his luck. He gimme a tenner.
> The Creeper appeared to be taking the matter under consideration. Ah met a gal las' night dat offer me fifteen, he countered. Nevertheless, it could be seen that he was weakening.
> Ah got annuder five in mah lef' stockin', an' Ah'll show you lovin' such as you never seen.
> The Creeper became more affable. Ah do seem to remember yo' face, Miss Silver, he averred. Will you do me duh favour to cling to mah arm.*[57]

*Miss Silver
Pronunciation Features
  1. Reduction of consonant clusters: *just* > *jes'*; *left* > *lef; naturally* > *nacherly; and* > *an'*.
  2. *th* > *d: this* > *dis; another* > *annuder*.

The Creeper and Miss Silver participate in the exciting cabaret life that so fascinated Van Vechten about Harlem. As one would expect from their style and their social class, they speak in dialect. Van Vechten's use of dialect is thoroughly conventional. As with earlier writers, he balances pronunciation and grammatical features in his representation of his characters' speech. The usual pronunciation features, voiced *th* pronounced as *d*, reduction of consonant clusters, and nasalization, are discernible, as are typical Black English grammatical features—lack of subject-verb agreement and zero copula. One feature that seems particularly out of place in Miss Silver's speech and that cannot be explained as hypercorrection is the insertion of *an* before a word beginning with a vowel: *an ofay*. The absurd combination of the slang (Pig Latin) word *ofay*, preceded by the proper Standard English article, *an*, seriously disturbs the realistic effect of the verbal interchange.

Throughout the prologue to the novel, usually in the narrated sections, Van Vechten cannot resist showing off his knowledge of Harlem slang: *monk* for *monkey-chaser* (a black from the British West Indies), *jig-chaser* (a white person who seeks the company of blacks), or its opposite, *pink-chaser* (a black who seeks the company of whites). All of these examples are explained in a glossary at the end of the novel. But the need for explanation emphasizes the fact that the book was written for a white audience and that Van Vechten was going out of his way to render his characters as exotics.[58]

The other dialect speaker in the novel is the Creeper's rival and enemy, a *nouveau riche* man with social pretensions. Randolph Pettijohn, the "Bolito King," a black Horatio Alger, began selling hot dogs in Harlem and then, making money at everything he touched, moved to real estate and

3. Loss of *v: of > o'*.
4. Nasalization: *evening > evenin'; stocking > stockin'; loving > lovin'; give me > gimme*.
5. Loss of vowel glide: *I > Ah; my > mah*.

Grammatical Features
Verbs
    1. Lack of subject-verb agreement; *who you is; You knows*.
    2. Zero copula: *You never seen; Ah been*.

Pronouns
    1. Omission of relative pronoun: *I met an ofay wanted to change his luck*.

ANATOLE (The Scarlet Creeper)
Pronunciation Features
    1. Reduction of consonant clusters: *last > las'*.
    2. *th > d: that > dat; the > duh*.
    3. Loss of *r: for > fo'; your > yo'*.
    4. Loss of vowel glide: *I > Ah; my > mah*.

Grammatical Features
Verbs
    1. Loss of *-ed* suffix indicate past tense: *offered > offer*.
    2. Zero copula: *How much you got*.

became the proprietor of one of Harlem's fashionable cabarets, the Winter Palace.

At a party at the beginning of the novel, immediately after Mary first meets Byron, Pettijohn corners Mary and proposes marriage to her. The impossibility of their union is accentuated by the contrast in their speech. Pettijohn's use of dialect repels the middle-class Mary.

> An' Ah got somethin' to say, an' dere ain' much time lef' to say et in, the King continued. Ah knows Ah ain' yo' kin', but you's mine. Ah wants a nice, 'spectable 'ooman for a wife . . . Mary opened her mouth to speak . . . Wait a minute. Ah ain't elegant. Ah ain' got no eddication lak you, but Ah got money, plenty of et, an' Ah got love. Ah'd mek you happy an' you'd give me what Ah wants, a 'spectable 'ooman. Ef you want to, we'd live on Strivers' Row . . .
>
> At last Mary succeeded in stopping him. I'm sorry, Mr. Pettijohn, she said, but it's no use. You see, I don't love you.
>
> Dat doan mek no difference, he whispered softly. Lemme mek you.
>
> I'm afraid it's impossible, Mary asserted more firmly.
>
> The Bolito King regarded her fixedly and with some wonder. You cain' mean no, he said. Ah's willin' to wait, an' to wait some time, but Ah gotta git you. You jes' what Ah desires.
>
> It's impossible, Mary repeated sternly, as she turned away.*[59]

As with the earlier conversation between the Creeper and his girl, Van Vechten's use of dialect is intended to create a realistic effect. A similar conventional balance of pronunciation and grammatical features can be seen in Pettijohn's dialect. Although the presentation of dialect is similar to that in the earlier example, the implications of Pettijohn's speech within the context of the plot are quite different. By proposing to Mary, Pettijohn is trying to transcend his origins; he sees marriage to a librarian as one more step up the ladder of success. His is a less spontaneous dialect speech than the Creeper's. He does not use the slang that the Creeper does and his speech is more

Pronunciation Features
1. Reduction of consonant clusters: *left > lef; education > eddication; just > jes'; and > an'; kind > kin'.*
2. *th > d: there > dere; that > dat.*
3. Loss of *r: your > yo'.*
4. Nasalization: *something > somethin'; let me > lemme; willing > willin'; don't > doan.*
5. Loss of initial unstressed syllable: *respectable > 'spectable.*
6. Loss of vowel glide: *I > Ah; like > lak.*
7. Vowel fronting: *make > mek; get > git.*
8. Diphthongization: *can't > cain'.*

Grammatical Features
Verbs
1. Lack of subject-verb agreement: *you are > you's; Ah wants; Ah desires; Ah's.*
2. Zero copula: *Ah got; You jes' what Ah desires.*
Negative
1. *ain'.*
2. Double negative: *dat doan mek no difference.*

self-conscious and stilted. He represents a transitional figure—one who, despite his social pretensions, has not been able to rid himself of the most obvious characteristic of class, his dialect speech. In a sense, bcause of that speech, he is a misfit—rejected both by the Harlem street world and by the educated middle class. Both contribute to his death at the end of the novel; the Creeper, his business rival, actually murders him, and Byron, his rival in love, first with Mary and then with Lasca Sartoris, stabs the dead body and, as could perhaps have been predicted, is immediately apprehended by the arm of the white man's law.

Although Van Vechten uses dialect conventionally in *Nigger Heaven,* he uses it for realistic effect. Still, the contribution that the book makes to the Harlem Renaissance is not in its use of dialect, but in the establishment of a new black stereotype. The Scarlet Creeper was destined to haunt the city streets of later black fiction.

Another writer of the Harlem Renaissance who was intrigued with the possibilities lower-class Harlem life offered the novelist was a Jamaican, Claude McKay, who had first gained American recognition for his poetry, much of it in dialect. In the late 1920s, McKay turned from poetry to fiction; between 1928 and 1933 he wrote three novels: *Home to Harlem, Banjo,* and *Banana Bottom.* Although McKay is considered in any serious discussion of the Harlem Renaissance, he was not a part of the Harlem literary establishment; his radical political and literary ideas were often at odds with those of DuBois and Locke. As his novels illustrate, he believed that the black lower classes were more in touch with their racial identity than the educated and pretentious middle classes. For McKay, blackness was a quality to be proud of, and the people of the street were the ones who expressed it with vigor and directness.

McKay chose Harlem as the setting and lower-class blacks as the characters of his first novel, *Home to Harlem* (1928). His Harlem, with its cabarets and its free-spirited, pleasure-seeking men and women, is reminiscent of Van Vechten's romanticized representation of city life. A female character in McKay's novel describes Harlem as a sexual Paradise:

> "What makes you niggers love Harlem so much? Because it's a bloody ungodly place where niggers nevah go to bed. All night running around speakeasies and cabarets, where bad, hell-bent nigger womens am giving up themselves to open sin."[60]

But James R. Giles rightly notes the positive quality of McKay's Harlem:

> Harlem is an oasis of pleasure and sensuousness for Jake; it is the one place in the world in which he can be free and comfortable. Europe was war and racism; white America is cold materialism, oppression of the black man, and a kind of spiritual sterility. But on Jake's return, and for most of the novel, Harlem is a haven that is almost "pure" because it is

comparatively uncontaminated by guilt, lust for power, or by materialism.[61]

The novel concerns the picaresque escapades of Jake, a World War I military deserter, recently returned to Harlem. On his first night home he meets a "little brown girl," appropriately named Felice, who charges him ten dollars for her sexual services. The next day, while strolling through Harlem, he discovers that she has returned his money. But by then he cannot remember her address. The remainder of the novel is directed to his sporadic and ultimately successful search for her.

The world McKay depicts is a male world, reminiscent of Hemingway's, although McKay denied any direct influence. Jake is a good-natured hedonist who uses women easily. Although he admits a commitment to Felice, he feels no need to resist other women—or she other men—until they find one another at the end of the novel.

In the final chapter, in retaliation for Jake's taking Felice, Zeddy, one of Jake's friends and Felice's last man, openly reveals that Jake is a deserter. Jake and Felice decide that they must leave Harlem to prevent Jake from being caught. Black resentment at being drawn into a white man's war is evident in both of their speeches.

> "He done lied about that, though," Jake said, angrily. "I didn't run away because I was scared a them Germans. But I beat it away from Brest because they wouldn't give us a chance at them, but kept us in that rainy, sloppy, Gawd-forsaken burg working like wops. They didn't seem to want us niggers foh no soldiers. We was jest a bunch a despised hod-carriers, and Zeddy know that."
> Now it was Felice's turn. "You ain't telling me a thing, daddy. I'll be slack with you and desert with you. What right have niggers got to shoot down a whole lot a Germans for? Is they worse than any other nation a white people? . . . You done do the right thing, honey, and Ise with you and I love you the more for that. . . . But all the same, we can't stay in Harlem no longer, for the bulls will sure get you."*[62]

*JAKE
Pronunciation Features
    1. Loss of *v: of > a.*
    2. Loss of *r: for > foh.*
    3. Diphthongization: *God > Gawd.*
    4. Vowel fronting: *just > jest.*

Grammatical Features
Verbs
    1. Regularization of third person singular present tense: *Zeddy know.*
    2. Lack of subject-verb agreement: *We was.*
    3. Past participle used as helping verb: *He done lied.*
Negative
    1. Double negative: *They didn't seem to want us niggers foh no soldiers.*
Pronouns
    1. Objective instead of demonstrative pronoun: *those > them Germans.*

McKay's representation of Black English dialect is quite different from Van Vechten's and actually more like Langston Hughes's. For instead of balancing pronunciation and grammatical features as Van Vechten and most of the dialect writers before him had done, McKay's written dialect, as had Hughes's, clearly emphasized grammatical over pronunciation features. A few pronunciation features are included in Jake's speech here—one example each of the loss of *v*, loss or *r*, diphthongization and fronting of the vowel, and, in Felice's speech a single example of loss of *v*. All of the other dialectal features are grammatical. They include examples of three key Black English grammatical features: lack of subject-verb agreement, use of the past participle as a helping verb, and the double negative.

Clearly, the trend toward simplification of written dialect that was evident in Langston Hughes's novel *Not Without Laughter* is continued in *Home to Harlem*. But whatever dialectal characteristics are recorded in writing, the intention of Van Vechten and McKay, as well as of Hughes and Hurston, was to reproduce the actuality of black speech.

Like Claude McKay, Countee Cullen was one of the foremost poets of the Harlem Renaissance. But unlike McKay he was a native New Yorker, the son of a minister, a Phi Beta Kappa graduate of New York University. He was also a master of poetic forms and a sometimes Keatsian, sometimes Tennysonian, spirit. He attempted only one novel, *One Way to Heaven* (1932), a rather awkward combination of the Van Vechten-McKay representation of Harlem street life on the one hand and the Wallace Thurman satire of the Harlem literati on the other.

The plot of Cullen's novel concerns a charming, one-armed con-man and gambler, Sam Lucas. As the novel opens, Sam finds himself broke and friendless on a cold winter night in Harlem. Opportunity strikes, however, when he discovers an evangelical church service in progress. A professional at dramatic conversions, Lucas waits for the proper moment, then strides up to the altar and discards his pistol and deck of cards. The congregation is jubilant, and one young woman, Mattie Johnson, who had been reluctant to be reborn, is so overwhelmed by his example that she converts also. Sam eventually marries Mattie; however, being a "travelin' man," he cannot stay long. He goes off with another woman, but returns to Mattie with a case of terminal pneumonia. Still the charmer, Sam arranges another conversion on

FELICE
Pronunciation Features
    1. Loss of *v: of* > *a*.

Grammatical Features
    1. Lack of subject-verb agreement: *Is they; Ise*.
    2. Past participle used as helping verb: *You done do*.
Negative
    1. *ain't*.
    2. Double negative: *We can't stay in Harlem no longer*.

his deathbed to please Mattie, but this time, ironically, the conversion "takes." Crudely woven into the main plot through Mattie, who is employed as a maid for Constancia Brandon of Harlem high society, is the subplot, a satire of middle-class Harlem life. For long periods Cullen deserts Sam and Mattie in order to represent the literary and artistic society of Constancia's salon. A lack of integration between the two plots flaws the novel seriously. And neither plot is substantial enough to stand on its own.

Another weakness in the novel is a lack of dialogue. There is clearly an overbalance of narration. The actions of the characters are described and then interpreted; only rarely do the characters speak. Since dialect is not appropriate at Constancia's gatherings, it can be found only in the Sam-Mattie plot, and for low-life characters they seem to speak very little. In the following passage, Sam selectively tells Mattie about his past.

> "I was born in Texas in a little town so small I don't need to tell its name, 'cause nobody would know it. 'Tain't on the map. Ma had a child every year, and paw was crazy tryin' to get enough to feed them, but they kept on comin'. I didn't have no schoolin'. I can read my name if it's writ big enough, but if you writ it small I wouldn't know it. There was ten of us when I left home over ten years ago, when I was eighteen. God knows how many there is now. Since then I've seen a heap of towns and places. I always liked travelin'. I'm what they call a travelin' man. I had my arm cut off by a train when I was stealin' a ride. Now I'm here in New York and I think it's so fine, and I think you're so nice, I wish my travelin' days was over. That's all about me."*[63]

Perhaps because of his middle-class background, perhaps because he wished to avoid conflict with DuBois and Locke, Cullen has radically simplified the dialectal features in his novel. He relies almost entirely on the dropping of the final *g* on present participles to suggest Black English pronunciation. The main grammatical feature he utilizes is lack of subject-verb agreement, although there are two examples of *writ*, one as past tense and one as past participle, and one example of the negative *'Tain't.* Even though the grammatical features outnumber the pronunciation features, as they did in the prose of Langston Hughes and of Claude McKay, there is evidence

Pronunciation Features
    1. Nasalization: *trying* > *tryin'; coming* > *comin'; schooling* > *schoolin'; traveling* > *travelin'; stealing* > *stealin'*.
    2. Loss of initial unstressed syllable. *because* > *'cause.*

Grammatical Features
Verbs
    1. Lack of subject-verb agreement: *There was ten of us; how many there is; I wish my travelin' days was over.*
    2. Regularization of past tense: *wrote* > *writ.*
    3. Regularization of past participle: *it's written* > *it's writ.*
Negative
    1. *'Tain't.*

that in trying to write in dialect Cullen was out of his element. It is hardly believable that a man of Sam's character would say, "'I think it's so fine, and I think you're so nice,'" for instance. Whereas Hughes and McKay rely heavily on dialectal speech to make their black characters convincing, Cullen avoids dialect whenever he can, and escapes for as long as possible into Constancia's comfortable parlor. The result is a novel that is less than satisfactory.

At the end of the Depression of the 1930s, on the eve of World War II, the urban ghetto was no longer seen as a place of escape for blacks. No longer was it a setting of carefree escapades for fictional or real Jakes and Sams. The war, widespread unemployment, crowded urban living conditions, racial prejudice, and the indifference of government agencies had turned this black Paradise into a teeming black Hell. And, in Harlem and other urban ghettos like it, hell produced monsters, distorted human beings, like Bigger Thomas, the protagonist of Richard Wright's major novel of 1940, *Native Son.*

Clearly, the most outstanding Afro-American writer of the Depression era was Richard Wright, a product of the poverty-stricken southern background he attributes to many of his black characters. He was born in 1908 on a plantation near Natchez, Mississippi. Because his father deserted the family and his mother was sickly, he lived as a child with one relative after another, learning well what it meant to be hungry and homeless. Although his formal schooling lasted only through the ninth grade, Wright became a voracious reader and recognized while he was still young that writing was a possible way out of a life of poverty. In 1927, when he found himself in Chicago, he quickly associated himself with the literary figures at the John Reed Club and was introduced there to the ideas of Marxism, which were later to influence his fiction. In 1938, he published a collection of short stories entitled *Uncle Tom's Children,* which centered on the violent relationship between blacks and whites in the rural South. The stories dramatize the growing resistance by blacks to white oppression. And everywhere there is blood and lynching and death.

Wright uses a great deal of dialect in these stories—a dialect that relies heavily on the most superficial of pronunciation features—dropping the last letter of a word for example, or excessive eye dialect—to suggest Black English speech. Grammatical features, however, are sparse. The following passage, an internal monologue, is taken from the first story of the collection, "Big Boy Leaves Home." In it Wright records Big Boy's thoughts, rather than his speech, in dialect, but he does not include a single example of a Black English verb form. Only two examples of the negative are evident: *ain* for *ain't* and the double negative: *ain no use.*

> He shifted, trying to get a crick out of his legs. Shucks, he wuz gettin tireda this. N it wuz almos dark now. Yeah, there wuz a little bittie star way over yonder in the eas. Mabbe tha white man waznt

dead? Mabbe they wuznt even lookin fer im? Mabbe he could go back home now? Naw, better wait erwhile. Thad be bes. But, Lawd, ef he only had some water! He could hardly swallow, his throat was so dry. Gawddam them white folks! Thas all they wuz good fer, t run a nigger down lika rabbit! Yeah, they git yuh in a corner n then they let yuh have it. A thousan of em! He shivered, for the cold of the clay was chilling his bones. Lawd, spose they found im here in this hole? N wid nobody t help im? . . . but ain no use in thinkin erbout tha; wait till trouble come fo yuh start fightin it. But if tha mob came one by one hed wipe em all out. Clean up the whole bunch. He caught one by the neck and choked him long and hard, choked him till his tongue and eyes popped out. Then he jumped upon his chest and stomped him like he had stomped that snake. When he had finished with one, another came.[64]

In a 1938 review of *Uncle Tom's Children,* Zora Neale Hurston, who was revolted by the excessive violence in the stories, criticized Wright for his representation of dialect:

Since the author himself is a Negro, his dialect is a puzzling thing. One wonders how he arrived at it. Certainly he does not write by ear unless he is tone-deaf.[65]

Two years later, in 1940, when Wright published *Native Son,* his locale as well as his treatment of dialect had changed radically. *Native Son* is the story of a poor black boy, Bigger Thomas, who, like his creator, had come to Chicago from the deep South. Indeed, Bigger is what Wright might have become without his own way of sublimating his feelings of violence, through writing.

The apparent "realism"—or even "naturalism"—in the novel's orientation and in Wright's method has been attributed to the influence of Dreiser's work, particularly his *An American Tragedy*[66] and its rather self-conscious symbolism, as well as to Wright's reading of Hawthorne and Poe.[67] Yet, given Wright's membership in the Communist Party during the 1930s, *Native Son* was also taken up by the Marxist press and praised as a "Marxist" novel.[68] Although there is perhaps more evidence for such a reading in the final section than in the earlier sections, such a label was never entirely a satisfactory one for *Native Son.* Wright himself was not comfortable with Communist Party doctrine, and his final break from the Party, which came in 1944, was preceded by several years of increasing disenchantment.[69] So, in 1947, when Wright, newly expatriated to Paris, was warmly received as an "existentialist" colleague by Jean-Paul Sartre and Simone de Beauvoir, *Native Son* gained a new label. Wright would remain a Parisian literary figure until his death in 1960, and *Native Son,* which had begun as a Chicago novel about a black American, gained an international reputation as an important "existentialist novel."

Although the experience of Bigger Thomas is clearly that of a black American, the literary treatment of his experience was not. As Wright himself acknowledged in "How 'Bigger' Was Born," an essay written after the novel was published, but usually printed as an introduction to the novel,

> This association with white writers was the life preserver of my hope to depict Negro life in fiction, for my race possessed no fictional works dealing with such problems, had no background in such sharp and critical testing of experience, no novels that went with a deep and fearless will down to the dark roots of life.[70]

The character of Bigger Thomas was a new and influential contribution to black American fiction, as was the compelling description of the city that formed him. After a rather Sandburgian adjectival sequence, Wright describes Chicago in vivid terms:

> huge, roaring, dirty, noisy, raw, stark, brutal; a city of extremes: torrid summers and sub-zero winters, white people and black people, the English language and strange tongues, foreign born and native born, scabby poverty and gaudy luxury, high idealism and hard cynicism! A city so young that, in thinking of its short history, one's mind, as it travels backward in time, is stopped abruptly by the barren stretches of wind-swept prairie! But a city old enough to have caught within the homes of its long, straight streets the symbols and images of man's age-old destiny, of truths as old as the mountains and seas, of dramas as abiding as the soul of man itself! A city which has become the pivot of the Eastern, Western, Northern, and Southern poles of the nation. But a city whose black smoke clouds shut out the sunshine for seven months of the year; a city in which, on a fine balmy May morning, one can sniff the stench of the stockyards; a city where people have grown so used to gangs and murders and graft that they have honestly forgotten that government can have a pretense of decency![71]

Bigger is a product of this city, and his life is entirely determined by it. His race and social class determine where he lives, whether he works, who his friends are, and even how he speaks. In his own mind and in that of society, he has no autonomous existence. Only after he has killed two women, one white and one black, and is the object of a city-wide search, does he begin to think of himself as an individual and begin to gain an identity. In the distorted world in which he lives, it is only through violence and destruction that he can understand what he is and who he is.

Like Richard Wright, his creator, Bigger ultimately does not find the teachings of Marxism satisfactory for interpreting his experience. Despite the persuasive arguments of Max, Bigger's Communist lawyer, that Bigger's behavior was determined by his class identity, Bigger, with his own death imminent, interprets his experience in an individualistic, even existential, way. " 'But what I killed for, I am,' "[72] asserts Bigger. By resting his identity on the murders he has committed, Bigger willingly isolates himself from the society that created him but will not claim him. As Robert Bone has pointed out, his tragedy lies in his need to isolate himself totally from the human condition in order to know himself.[73]

One of Bigger Thomas's characteristics is his inability to speak articulately. He actually speaks very little in the novel, and when he does speak he uses monosyllables and short sentences. In order to trace the development of Bigger's state of mind, Wright frequently has Bigger think in dialect, as Big Boy had done. Bigger's fear of not being able to express himself verbally contributes to his frustration and his resulting outbursts of violence. Not until the end of the novel, after Max, his lawyer, brings him the news that he is to die in the electric chair, does Bigger begin to speak fluently, to express what he has learned from his experience.

> "Well, it's sort of funny, Mr. Max. I ain't trying to dodge what's coming to me." Bigger was growing hysterical. "I know I'm going to get it. I'm going to die. Well, that's all right now. But really I never wanted to hurt nobody. That's the truth, Mr. Max. I hurt folks 'cause I felt I had to; that's all. They was crowding me too close; they wouldn't give me no room. Lots of times I tried to forget 'em, but I couldn't. They wouldn't let me. . . ." Bigger's eyes were wide and unseeing; his voice rushed on: "Mr. Max, I didn't mean to do what I did. I was trying to do something else. But it seems like I never could. I was always wanting something and I was feeling that nobody would let me have it. So I fought 'em. I thought they was hard and I acted hard." He paused, then whimpered in confession, "But I ain't hard, Mr. Max. I ain't hard even a little bit. . . ." He rose to his feet. "But . . . I—I won't be crying none when they take me to that chair. But I'll b-b-be feeling inside of me like I was crying. . . . I'll be feeling and thinking that they didn't see me and I didn't see them. . . ."*[74]

Clearly, the above passage is free of the decorative dialectal features of the earlier passage from *Uncle Tom's Children*. Here Wright has greatly simplified the pronunciation features and concentrated instead, as his friend Langston Hughes had done, on recording grammatical features. Only two pronunciation features appear in the passage: loss of *th* in *'em* for *them* and loss of the initial unstressed syllable in *'cause* for *because*. The grammatical features, although more in number than the pronunciation features, are clearly selective. There is a single example of lack of subject-verb agreement: *They was,* and one example of an adjective used instead of an adverb: *they was crowding in too close.* Although *ain't* is used as a negative—notice that Wright has restored the final *t* since *Uncle Tom's Children*—the most

*Pronunciation Features
1. Loss of *th: them* > *'em*.
2. Loss of initial unstressed syllable: *because* > *'cause*.

Grammatical Features
Verbs
1. Lack of subject-verb agreement: *They was.*
2. Adjective used instead of adverb: *closely* > *close*.
Negative
1. *ain't*.
2. Double negative: *I never wanted to hurt nobody; they wouldn't give me no room; I won't be crying none*.

significant feature in the passage is three examples of the double negative: *I never wanted to hurt nobody; they wouldn't give me no room;* and *I won't be crying none.*

Although *Native Son* marks a change in the representation of black character as well as in the possibilities for the black novel in the area of dialect, it illustrates the gradual tendency introduced by Gertrude Stein in 1909 with "Melanctha," a story that Wright much admired, to simplify the representation of black dialect in literature. With the birth of Bigger Thomas, the "plantation Negro" was definitely dead. And his dialect, which from the beginning had been heavily phonological, died with him.

Despite attacks on it by the "race leaders" of the Harlem Renaissance, the use of dialect in fiction had survived, but its representation and its connotations had changed. Hereafter dialect would be indicated in writing more by grammatical than by phonological features. It would represent the language of black folk, the poor, whether country or city people, and in the years after World War II would remain viable, later to become identified with literary assertions of black pride. Although the orthographical representation of phonological characteristics of black speech would come to be employed only for comic or satiric purpose, the Black English dialect, syntactically represented, was to become an identifying racial characteristic that later black writers would display with pride.

NOTES

1. Gertrude Stein, "Melanctha," in *Three Lives* (Norfolk, Conn.: New Directions, 1909, 1933), p. 120.

2. Raymond A. Cook, *Thomas Dixon* (New York: Twayne, 1974), p. 61.

3. Although Dixon supported the deeds of the Ku Klux Klan during Reconstruction, he strongly opposed using the Klan to justify irresponsible and malicious violence for its own sake. Therefore he refused to be associated with the activities of the Klan during the 1920s. For him the Klan was an organization of historical importance during Reconstruction; but after Reconstruction, it no longer had a justifiable purpose. See Cook, *Thomas Dixon,* p. 64.

4. Thomas Dixon, *The Clansman* (New York: A. Wessels, 1907), p. 250.

5. For a discussion of the development of the minstrel Negro from comic to racial stereotype, see Blyden Jackson, "The Minstrel Mode," in *The Waiting Years* (Baton Rouge: Louisiana State University Press, 1976), pp. 155–64.

6. Nathan Irvin Huggins, *Harlem Renaissance* (New York: Oxford University Press, 1971), p. 261. Walter M. Brasch, in *Black English and the Mass Media* (Amherst: University of Massachusetts Press, 1981), includes a brief discussion of the origins of the minstrel show (pp. 47–50) and its descendant, the *Amos 'n' Andy* radio show (pp. 221–25).

7. Ibid., p. 251.

8. Ibid., p. 265.

9. Octavus Roy Cohen, *Highly Colored* (New York: Dodd, Mead, 1921), p. 16.

10. Ibid., p. 20.

11. Ibid., p. 58.

12. Ibid., p. 1.

13. It is both confusing and peculiar that the illustrations to the first edition by A. B. Walker are clearly of white characters.

14. Sterling Brown, *The Negro in American Fiction* and *Negro Poetry and Drama* (New York: Arno Press, 1969), p. 126.

15. Roark Bradford, "The Adulteration of Old King David," in *Ol' Man Adam an' His Chillun* (New York: Harper and Brothers, 1928), pp. 230–31.

16. Brown, *The Negro in American Fiction,* p. 196.

17. Margaret Mitchell, *Gone With the Wind* (New York: Macmillan, 1936), p. 782.

18. Ibid., p. 779.

19. Ibid., p. 781.

20. W. E. B. DuBois, "Criteria of Negro Art," *The Crisis* 32 (October 1926): 290, 292, 294, 296–97 (repr. in Daniel Walden, *W. E. B. DuBois: The Crisis Writings* [Greenwich, Conn.: Fawcett, 1972], p. 288).

21. Ibid., p. 289.

22. W. E. B. DuBois, *The Quest of the Silver Fleece* (College Park, Md.: McGrath, 1969), p. 433.

23. Of course, the crudity of the dialect representation strongly suggests that it was written by a Northern author unfamiliar with Southern dialects and unskilled in their written representation.

24. DuBois, *Quest,* pp. 44–45.

25. Ibid., p. 328.

26. *The Crisis* 35 (June 1928): 202, 211 (repr. in Herbert Aptheker, ed., *Book Reviews by W. E. B. DuBois* [Millwood, N.Y.: KTO Press, 1977], p. 113).

27. *The Crisis* 36 (April 1929): 125, 138 (repr. in Aptheker, p. 129).

28. *The Crisis* 35 (June 1928): 202, 211 (repr. in Aptheker, p. 113).

29. Ibid. (repr. in Aptheker, p. 114).

30. *The Crisis* 38 (September 1931): 304 (repr. in Aptheker, p. 157).

31. *The Crisis* 37 (September 1930): 313, 321 (repr. in Aptheker, p. 150).

32. David Levering Lewis, *When Harlem was in Vogue* (New York: Alfred A. Knopf, 1981), p. 48.

33. Gunnar Myrdal, *An American Dilemma,* pp. 191–96; quoted in Robert Bone, *The Negro Novel in America* (New Haven, Conn.: Yale University Press, 1958), pp. 53–54.

34. See "Close Ranks," *The Crisis* 16 (July 1918): 111 (repr. in Walden, *W. E. B. DuBois: The Crisis Writings,* pp. 257–58).

35. Alain Locke, *The New Negro* (New York: Arno Press, 1968), p. 7.

36. Ibid., pp. 10–11.

37. Lewis, *When Harlem Was in Vogue,* p. 149.

38. Ibid., p. 51.

39. Ibid., p. 48.

40. Ibid., p. 51.

41. James Weldon Johnson, *The Autobiography of an Ex-Coloured Man* (New York: Knopf, 1927), p. 211.

42. Ibid., p. 56.

43. Langston Hughes, *The Big Sea* (New York: Hill and Wang, 1940), p. 241.

44. Waldo Frank, Introduction, Jean Toomer, *Cane* (New York: Boni and Liveright, 1923).

45. Ibid., p. 23.

46. Ibid., pp. 24–25.

47. Although Hurston throughout her life remained alienated from DuBois's belief that literature could be used most effectively as a tool for propaganda, Hughes, in his writings of the 1930s, actually moved closer to positions earlier advocated by DuBois. In a speech he made at the First American Writers' Congress in 1935, Hughes advocated that the work of black writers should be essentially propagandistic. See "To Negro Writers," *Good Morning Revolution,* ed. Faith Berry (New York: Lawrence Hill, 1973), pp. 125–26.

48. Hughes, *The Big Sea,* p. 237.

49. Langston Hughes, *Not Without Laughter* (New York: Knopf, 1930), p. 259.

50. Ibid., p. 145.

51. For an objective account, see Robert E. Hemenway, *Zora Neale Hurston* (Urbana: University of Illinois Press, 1977), pp. 136–57.

52. Stanley J. Kunitz and Howard Haycraft, *Twentieth-Century Authors* (New York: The H. W. Wilson Co., 1942), p. 695.

53. Zora Neale Hurston, *Their Eyes Were Watching God* (Urbana: University of Illinois Press, 1937, 1965), pp. 157–59.

54. Blyden Jackson, "The Ghetto of the Negro Novel: A Theme with Variations," in *The Waiting Years*, p. 180.

55. Nathan Irvin Huggins, *Harlem Renaissance* (London: Oxford University Press, 1971), p. 93. In an article "Carl Van Vechten Presents the New Negro," *Studies in the Literary Imagination* 7 (Fall 1974): 85–104, Leon Coleman systematically itemizes all that Van Vechten did to encourage the New Negro in an artistic atmosphere and to present his work to interested publishers and to an interested public.

56. Carl Van Vechten, *Nigger Heaven* (New York: Octagon Books, 1973), p. 149.

57. Ibid., p. 11.

58. This self-conscious use of Harlem slang was to some readers more offensive than the title. Zora Neale Hurston does something similar in a short story she wrote much later, in 1942, but she succeeds where Van Vechten fails in making the slang she uses sound natural. See "Story in Harlem Slang," *American Mercury* 55 (July 1942): 84–96.

59. Van Vechten, *Nigger Heaven*, p. 38.

60. Claude McKay, *Home to Harlem* (Chatham, N.J.: The Chatham Bookseller, 1928), p. 79.

61. James R. Giles, *Claude McKay* (Boston: Twayne Publisher, 1976), p. 73.

62. McKay, *Home to Harlem*, pp. 331–32.

63. Countee Cullen, *One Way to Heaven* (New York: Harper and Brothers, 1932), pp. 64–65.

64. Richard Wright, "Big Boy Leaves Home," in *Uncle Tom's Children* (New York: Harper and Row, 1936), p. 44.

65. *The Saturday Review*, April 2, 1938, p. 44.

66. Robert Bone, *The Negro Novel in America* (New Haven, Conn.: Yale University Press, 1958), pp. 142–43.

67. Dan McCall, *The Example of Richard Wright* (New York: Harcourt, Brace, and World, 1969), pp. 70–71.

68. Keneth Kinnamon, *The Emergence of Richard Wright* (Urbana: University of Illinois Press, 1972), pp. 148–51.

69. Ibid., pp. 153–57.

70. Richard Wright, "How 'Bigger' Was Born," in *Native Son* (New York: Harper and Row, 1940), p. xvi.

71. Ibid., p. xxvi.

72. Richard Wright, *Native Son*, pp. 391–92.

73. Robert Bone, *Richard Wright* (Minneapolis: University of Minnesota Press, 1969), p. 22.

74. Wright, *Native Son*, p. 388.

5
Black English in Fiction, 1945–Present:
Black Speech and Black Consciousness

IN contrast to the first forty years of the twentieth century, during which black people were increasingly segregated in northern urban ghettos and ignored as much as possible by the rest of the population, the period since 1940, although often turbulent, has brought black people more into the mainstream of American life. Once the courts upheld the guarantee of equal rights for all people, as stipulated in the Constitution, blacks began to assert themselves culturally and politically. Their attraction, first towards assimilation and then toward nationalism, is most dramatically illustrated in the literature of the last forty years.

The first decade of the period was dominated by World War II. Although at the beginning of the war the armed services still maintained segregated companies, blacks were widely recruited in the Navy, Air Force, Marines, WACs, and WAVEs, as well as in the Army. Black civilians, however, at least at the beginning of the war, found employment more difficult. Then, in response to A. Philip Randolph's planned March on Washington in 1941, President Roosevelt decreed that blacks be hired at defense plants under government contracts. The decision was significant in providing employment for the thousands of blacks who had left the South for northern cities with great expectations of finding meaningful jobs. As Richard Kluger has noted, "By 1940, one out of every four American blacks was living in the North or West."[1] C. Vann Woodward uses specific figures: "In the decade of the 'forties alone the number of Negroes living outside the South jumped from 2,360,000 to 4,600,000, an increase of nearly 100 percent."[2]

Life in the cities was crowded and harsh. Dreams of finding Eden, which had fired the imaginations of blacks coming North in the 1920s, were nonexistent now. Richard Wright's representation of city life for Bigger Thomas and his family and friends was a reality for too many people. The tense situation erupted during the Detroit riots of 1943, which pitted blacks against whites in undisguised racial conflict. Richard Kluger recites the results:

> It went on for two days as thirty-four were killed, twenty-five of them Negroes—and seventeen of them by policemen; three-quarters of the 600 injured were colored, as were 85 percent of the more than 1,800 arrested.[3]

The North as well as the South had shown itself to be racially volatile. In fact, violence seemed to be everywhere during the forties, both at home and abroad. And before the country had had time to recover from a second massive World War, it found itself, by 1950, embroiled in another foreign conflict, this time in Korea.

In race relations, the fifties were distinguished by a landmark decision by the Supreme Court. In 1954 *Brown* v. *Board of Education,* which provided for fully integrated education in all public schools, overturned the decision which, in 1897, had sanctioned segregated schooling, *Plessy* v. *Ferguson. Brown* v. *Board of Education* inaugurated the Civil Rights Movement in the country and introduced a decade of adjustment, particularly by the South, to the reality of integrated schools and, later, of integrated public facilities and restaurants.

The sixties were filled with more legislation and more violence, again both at home and abroad. Significant civil rights legislation, to which President Kennedy had committed his administration before he was assassinated, but which did not become law until President Johnson assumed office, included the Civil Rights Act of 1964, which was "aimed at racial discrimination in public accommodations, public schools, housing, labor unions, employment, and economic opportunity,"[4] and the Voting Rights Bill of 1965. C. Vann Woodward saw 1965 as a significant year:

> It did not mark the solution of a problem, but it did mark the end of a period—the period of legally sanctioned segregation of races.[5]

Unfortunately, only five days after the Voting Rights Act was passed, violence broke out in Watts, the black section of Los Angeles. Major cities—Detroit, New York, Chicago, Newark, Washington, D.C., among others—were to experience similar violence before the sixties had ended.

White resistance to Civil Rights legislation, the loss of a number of important leaders—Adam Clayton Powell, Malcolm X, Martin Luther King, as well as President John F. Kennedy and Attorney General Robert F. Kennedy, and American involvement in yet another unwanted, undeclared war—a war that blacks considered racist in origin—this time in Vietnam, gave black people sound reasons for their increasing alienation from a country in which they had always been regarded as outsiders.

Home-grown black alienation, perhaps combined with some of the more positive ideas regarding blackness that grew out of the Negritude Movement led by Leopold Senghor during the 1950s in Europe, was soon converted by a new generation of leaders—Stokely Carmichael, Eldridge Cleaver, Amiri Baraka among them—into a positive association of Black Power and Black Pride. Black nationalism, which had been used by Marcus Garvey in the 1920s as an alternative when hopes for assimilation were frustrated, had resurfaced. Not sure they wanted to be integrated into a society as degenerate and as corrupt as the one they saw before them, this new generation of blacks did not look to Africa as a place to resettle. Their intention was to seek a cultural identity for black people that would regard blackness as a positive quality, one by which they could overcome their years of oppression by the dominant culture. Instead of having their rights and privileges determined for them, they would determine what they wanted and how they were to get it themselves. Ironically, then, as opportunities were becoming increasingly available for blacks within the work force and within the society, black nationalist groups were insisting on asserting their separate cultural identity.

Although the black nationalist groups of the 1960s and early 1970s were numerous and fragmented,[6] the movement, particularly the more positive aspect of Black Pride, can be regarded as at least partially responsible for significant evidence of maturity in the fiction of recent black writers. The use of dialect, which was quickly reaching a dead end within the context of realism, became infused with new meaning and offered new possibilities for expression in black fiction.

This chapter will examine how Black English dialect has been handled by three groups of writers publishing after 1940. The first section will focus on white writers, the second on black writers who published before the Civil Rights Movement, and the third on writers of the 1960s and 1970s.

Three white writers of the past forty years, Eudora Welty, William Faulkner, and William Styron make up the first group. All are Southerners; all have chosen southern settings for the work of fiction under discussion; all use Black English dialect to represent the speech of rural black characters. Although all three writers can be identified as regional writers, carry-overs, perhaps, of the nineteenth-century local color tradition, all use techniques in the representation of black speech that are quite different from those of their nineteenth-century predecessors.

Eudora Welty considers "regional," in describing a writer, to be "a careless term, as well as a condescending one, because what it does is fail to differentiate between the localized raw material of life and its outcome as art."[7] Nevertheless, Welty is a writer, albeit an artful one, whose subject is life in her home state of Mississippi, a region she knows well. For Welty, a clearly defined place is central to successful fiction:

> The truth is, fiction depends for its life on place. Location is the cross-roads of circumstance, the proving ground of 'What happened? Who's here? Who's coming?'—and that is the heart's field.[8]

Furthermore, she believes, a clear sense of place is necessary for successful delineation of character.

> Besides furnishing a plausible abode for the novel's world of feeling, place has a good deal to do with making the characters real, that is, themselves, and keeping them so.[9]

Because of her concern with a specific, clearly defined locale, Welty, despite her objection to a concern with her regionalism, can be regarded as a contemporary local colorist. Her first book of short stories, *A Curtain of Green* (1941), illustrates her mastery of her locale and characters who are representative of all social classes—from the decaying planter class to poor, uneducated blacks.

However, although there is a "real" quality to her characters and their place, Welty cannot be regarded as a realistic writer. Her work is allusive and symbolic as well. Katherine Anne Porter has sensed this unique fusion in Welty's work, particularly in stories like "A Worn Path," one of the more famous of the stories collected in *A Curtain of Green*.

> Let me admit a deeply personal preference for this particular kind of story, where external act and the internal voiceless life of the human imagination almost meet and mingle on the mysterious threshold between dream and waking, one reality refusing to admit or confirm the existence of the other, yet both conspiring toward the same end.[10]

The story concerns the difficult cross-country journey at Christmas-time of an old black woman, Phoenix Jackson, from her home in the woods off the Natchez Trace to town to get medicine for her sickly grandson. Symbolism fills the story, from the name of the main character, Phoenix, to the meaning of her December journey, to the contrast between her encounter with the hunter who has killed a bird, who destroys life for his own entertainment, and her own mission of love, her hunt for medicine to save her grandson, whom she compares to a bird. But it is the use of dialect in the story that is of interest in this discussion. Welty uses dialect to convey the "real" quality of the situation and to make Phoenix Jackson a believable and sympathetic character. Toward the end of the story, having arrived at the clinic in the town, Phoenix speaks to a nurse about her grandson:

> Phoenix spoke unasked now, "No, missy, he not dead, he just the same. Every little while his throat begin to close up again, and he not able to swallow. He not get his breath. He not able to help himself. So the time come around, and I go on another trip for the soothing medicine."

"All right. The doctor said as long as you came to get it, you could have it," said the nurse. "But it's an obstinate case."

"My little grandson, he sit up there in the house all wrapped up, waiting by himself," Phoenix went on. "We is the only two left in the world. He suffer and it don't seem to put him back at all. He got a sweet look. He going to last. He wear a little patch quilt and peep out holding his mouth open like a little bird. I remembers so plain now. I not going to forget him again, no, the whole enduring time. I could tell him from all the others in creation."*[11]

Perhaps the most striking characteristic of Welty's use of dialect in the above passage is the absence of pronunciation features. Phoenix's dialect speech is conveyed entirely by grammatical features, particularly her use of verbs. Several examples of regularization of the third person singular present tense, lack of subject-verb agreement, and zero copula are evident. But Welty also uses stylistic features to add authenticity to Phoenix Jackson's speech. Phoenix's sentences, for instance, are short; furthermore, the repetition of sentence patterns creates a rhythmical effect frequently associated with Black English speech: *he not get his breath. He not able to help himself.* And later, *He got a sweet look. He going to last.*

As the above example illustrates, Eudora Welty uses dialect, as did the nineteenth-century local colorists, to enhance the "realness" of her main character, Phoenix Jackson. But what distinguishes her from the nineteenth-century local color tradition and clearly places her in the mid-twentieth century is her representation of dialect—her elimination of pronunciation features and her total reliance on grammatical and stylistic features in the depiction of Phoenix Jackson's speech.

Although other southern writers—Katherine Anne Porter and Carson McCullers among them—were contemporaries of Eudora Welty and also wrote about various aspects of southern life, it is William Faulkner whose fiction has received the highest praise. Cleanth Brooks, R. W. B. Lewis, and Robert Penn Warren describe Faulkner's work as the "culmination of the development of twentieth-century southern fiction."[12] The work they describe is largely in the form of stories, stories that, taken together, combine to make up novels. These novels, if they are taken together, can be seen as forming a great megafiction, a moral history of Faulkner's South.

*Pronounciation Features
   None.

Grammatical Features
Verbs
   1. Regularization of third person singular present tense: *throat begin; the time come; he sit; he suffer; he wear;* [he] *peep; it don't.*
   2. Lack of subject-verb agreement: *we is; I remembers.*
   3. Zero copula: *he not dead; he just the same; he not able; he not get; he going; I not going.*
   4. *got* substitutes for *has: he got.*
Double subject: *my little grandson, he.*

Of the many characters who play parts in this megafiction, not an inconsiderable number are black, and of course their speech is variously represented. But of all of his books, *Go Down, Moses,* Faulkner's last tragedy of Yoknapatawpha County, perhaps best illustrates his method in representing black speech. And *Go Down, Moses* is—not coincidentally—also the single work of Faulkner that most directly engages the history of black-white relationships over more than a hundred years of southern history.

Go Down, Moses is a collection of seven stories that many critics—Edmond Volpe is one—see as "cemented together by theme into a remarkably unified novel."[13] The book, a history of black-white relationships in the South among the descendents of Carothers McCaslin from the days of slavery to the present of 1942, can be read as turning around a single theme—the possession, both of the wilderness and of the blacks—by the white man. Yet there is another theme, inextricably linked with the first, for *Go Down, Moses* is also a representation of the increasing difficulty of communication between blacks and whites. This theme is manifest in Faulkner's recording of the speech of the novel's black characters.

Although there are occasional backward glances, as in part 4 of "The Bear," the stories are for the most part chronologically arranged. The first story, "Was," takes place before the Civil War; it is a comic account narrated from childhood memory by Ike McCaslin's guardian-cousin, McCaslin Edmonds, of the recovery of a runaway slave named Tomey's Turl, and the loss of Uncle's Buck's bachelorhood in one of the great poker hands in American literature. Turl is the only significant[14] black character that speaks in the story, and he speaks very little.[15] When he does speak (he speaks to McCaslin Edmonds), he uses Black English dialect:

> "Hah," Tomey's Turl said. "And nem you mind that neither. I got protection now. All I needs to do is to keep Old Buck from ketching me unto I gets the word."
> "What word?" he said. "Word from who? Is Mr Hubert going to buy you from Uncle Buck?"
> "Huh," Tomey's Turl said again. "I got more protection than whut Mr Hubert got even." He rose to his feet. "I gonter tell you something to remember: anytime you wants to git something done, from hoeing out a crop to getting married, just get the womenfolks to working at it. Then all you needs to do is set down and wait. You member that."*[16]

Pronunciation Features
    1. Loss of initial unstressed syllable: *remember > member.*
    2. Vowel fronting: *get > git.*
Eye Dialect: *what > whut.*

Grammatical Features
Verbs
    1. Lack of subject-verb agreement: *I needs; I gets; you wants; you needs.*
    2. *get, got* substitute for *have: I gets; I got.*
Negative
    1. Double negative: *And nem you mind that neither.*

Although the key dialectal features in the passage are grammatical—lack of subject-verb agreement in *I needs, I gets,* and a single example of the double negative: *nem you mind that neither,* there is one dialectal feature that particularly distinguishes Turl's speech, but that probably cannot be identified precisely with Black English; he uses three forms of a single verb, *got, get,* and *git.* The frequent repetition of these forms is used by Faulkner as a comic but ominous device that helps establish the central concern of "getting" and owning, not only for "Was," but for the remaining stories of *Go Down, Moses.*

Despite the fact that he is a half-brother to Uncle Buck and Uncle Buddy, Turl, because he is black, is perceived by his brothers less as a relative than as a piece of property. In this recognition lies the real tragedy of *Go Down, Moses.* But in "Was," the result is comedy, so it is not surprising that Turl, the "owned" black brother, would be made to speak in a rather exaggerated dialect by the tradition-oriented narrator of the story, McCaslin Edmonds.

Also, significantly, except for Turl's brief interchange with McCaslin, the blacks and whites within the story do not speak to one another. Turl and Uncle Buck have developed a ritual hunting pattern whenever Turl runs away; each is aware of the movements of the other, but the two rarely talk together, rarely communicate verbally. Each simply, and more or less mutely, acts out his part in a ritual hunt. The ritual does not provide for verbal communication between the hunter and the hunted. Introduced in the first story, this fact of noncommunication between blacks and whites will be developed in the stories to come.

In the second story, "The Fire and the Hearth," a black character, Lucas Beauchamp, a son of Tomey's Turl and Tennie Beauchamp, is the protagonist. Unlike Turl, Lucas can in no way be regarded as a stock black comic character. In fact, he is more realistically, fully, and sympathetically represented than any character in the earlier story. Lucas is a man who is aware and proud of his connection through the male line to old Carothers McCaslin; he is highly intelligent and capable of using his intelligence to manipulate others—both white and black—to do his bidding.

By way of dignifying Lucas, in emphasizing his intelligence, Faulkner has him speak a modified Black English—just enough to distinguish his speech from that of the whites. In the following quotation he is telling his white relative and landlord, Roth Edmonds, of having tricked the salesman of a machine supposed to locate buried gold into renting the machine from him.

"For twenty-five dollars a night," Lucas said. "That's what he charged me to use it one night. So I reckon that's the regular rent on them. He sells them; he ought to know. Leastways, that's what I charges."[17]

The only written indication that Lucas is speaking Black English is the lack of subject-verb agreement in *I charges*. The absence of excessive dialectal features in his speech clearly indicates that Faulkner has identified him as a character to be taken seriously.

The speech of George Wilkins, a black man who later marries Lucas's daughter, Nat, is represented quite differently in the story. George is a "low character," a comic figure, not so intelligent as Lucas and clearly dominated by Lucas. His speech, in contrast to Lucas's, is filled with dialectal features, including a number of mispronunciations. In the passage that follows, George apologizes to Lucas for getting him in trouble because Lucas has made illegal moonshine.

> "I dont rightly know, sir," George said. "It uz mostly Nat's. We never aimed to get you into no trouble. She say maybe ifn we took and fotch that kettle from whar you and Mister Roth told them shurfs it was and you would find it settin on yo back porch, maybe when we offered to help you git shet of it fo they got here, yo mind might change about loandin us the money to—I mean to leffen us get married."*[18]

Two pronunciation features commonly associated with Black English appear in George Wilkins's speech—loss of *r* and nasalization. But there are others that can probably be identified as local black pronunciation—*fotch, whar, uz, shurfs,* and the phrase *git shet*. Grammatical features in George's speech are relatively sparse. There is only one example of regularization of third person singular present tense and one example of a curiously ambiguous double negative.[19] With the speech of George and Lucas, Faulkner seems to be following the traditional approach to the representation of dialect—phonological features punctuate the dialect speech of low, comic characters, and their absence indicates a character's greater intelligence, social status, and dignity.

Two other characters in "The Fire and the Hearth" speak Black English—Molly, Lucas's wife, and their son, Henry. Molly's speech is more like Lucas's than George's, in that the distinguishing features of her dialect are grammatical rather than pronunciation features—regularization of the third person singular present tense and double negative, specifically. In the following passage, Molly complains of Lucas's behavior to Roth Edmonds and asks for a divorce from Lucas. Lucas, she says,

> "stays out all night with it, hunting that buried money. He dont even

*Pronounciation Features
    1. Loss of *r: your > yo, you; before > fo.*
    2. Nasalization: *if > ifn; setting > settin; loaning > loandin; letting > leffen.*

Grammatical Features
Verbs
    1. Regularization of third person singular present tense: *she say.*
Negative
    1. Double negative: *We never aimed to get you into no trouble.*

take care of his own stock right no more. I feeds the mare and the hogs and milks, tries to. but that's all right. I can do that. I'm glad to do that when he is sick in the body. But he's sick in the mind now. Bad sick. He dont even get up to go to church on Sunday no more. He'd bad sick, marster. He's doing a thing the Lord aint meant for folks to do. And I'm afraid."[20]

Henry, who is the same age as Roth Edmonds, and is inseparable from him until the boys are seven years old, also speaks in Black English; except for one pronunciation feature, an example of reduction of consonant cluster in *Les* for *Let's,* his speech is distinguished by grammatical features—here the lack of subject-verb agreement in *we was:*

"Les stay here," Henry said. "I thought we was going to get up when pappy did and go hunting."[21]

The fact that his speech differs from that of his white companion emphasizes the racial and resulting social distinctions between the two, which the seven-year-old Roth senses. He lives to regret the inevitable separation that he at seven insisted upon, but he makes no effort to correct the injustice when he has the opportunity in the final story of the novel, "Go Down, Moses."

Of all the black characters in "The Fire and the Hearth," it is Lucas who uses his verbal skills most successfully to get his way. He is able to outwit Zack Edmonds and the salesman from Memphis and to assert his will to Roth Edmonds in his decision to give up the divining machine and reclaim his wife. Lucas, in fact, seems to have a greater understanding of how white people behave and think, and thus how he can manipulate them, than the whites are capable of in regard to blacks. For the most part, however, each group remains isolated from the other.

The next story, "Pantaloon in Black," concerns a black tenant of the McCaslins, but does not involve any McCaslin directly. The plot is, however, tightly interwoven with the theme of communication. For Rider, the main character, speech is not a meaningful medium of expression. Rider is a black mill-hand and devoted husband, who is unable to deal with his grief over the death of his young wife, Mannie. Rider is not a verbally articulate man, and is thus unable to talk freely about his grief. When he speaks, he speaks Black English in very short sentences, and he uses language only to assert the simplest of facts and feelings. After the funeral, for instance, all he says is: " 'Ah'm goan home.' "[22] And to his dog,

"Us bofe needs to eat," he said, moving on though the dog did not follow until he turned and cursed it. "Come on hyar!" he said. "Whut you skeered of? She lacked you too, same as me."*[23]

*Pronunciation Features
1. *th* > *f: both* > *bofe.*
2. Nasalization: *going* > *goan.*
3. Loss of glide: *liked* > *lacked; I'm* > *Ah'm.*

Pronunciation features outnumber grammatical features in Rider's speech—traditionally an indication of the speech of comic characters. Rider, however, is an exception; he is an example of a "low" character whose speech is phonologically represented, but who is nevertheless tragic. With Rider it is clear that Faulkner is not stereotyping.

But the dominant characteristic of Rider's speech is that there is so little of it. Instead of speaking, Rider tries to deal with his grief and his frustration through physical violence; he frantically shovels dirt on Mannie's grave at the funeral; he appears at the sawmill before dawn the next day and tests his strength by singlehandedly lifting a log in a feat of superhuman strength; and, finally, after getting himself drunk, he slashes the throat of a white man named Birdsong, who cheated him in a crap game. Rider's only release after his frenzy of physicality and violence, is death; as expected, he is lynched by Birdsong's kinfolk. Rider's failure of articulation is thus the ultimate cause of his death; it is his tragedy. With bitter irony, Faulkner concludes the story by having a white sheriff, whose job is to police the actions of others, relate Rider's story to his indifferent wife. But the sheriff's insensitivity, his inability to understand Rider as a fellow kinsman and thus to empathize with the depth of Rider's love for his wife and the extent of Rider's grief, turns his description of the events into a gruesome parody. Once again words fail to serve the human need for articulate recognition of man for man.

The closest communication between blacks and whites in the novel can be discerned in the next two stories, "The Old People" and "The Bear," hunting stories that concern the initiation of the boy, Ike McCaslin, the son of Uncle Buck's old age, into the ways of the wilderness. Sam Fathers, a man of mixed Indian, black, and white blood, is Ike's teacher, Although Sam prefers to claim his descent from a Chickasaw Indian Chief, within the community his black blood determines his "place"; for seventy years "*he had had to be a negro.*"[24] His black blood also influences his speech, which, when he talks with his closest friend, Jobaker, a full-blooded Chickasaw, is described as "a mixture of negroid English and flat hill dialect."[25] To young Ike McCaslin, Sam describes the characteristics of old Ben, the bear himself, the object of the hunt:

> "He dont care no more for bears than he does for dogs or men neither. He come to see who's here, who's new in camp this year, whether he can shoot or not, can stay or not. Whether we got the dog yet that can

4. Diphthongization: *here > hyar.*
Eye Dialect: *what > whut.*

Grammatical Features
Verbs
    1. Lack of subject-verb agreement: *Us bofe needs.*
Pronouns
    1. Objective pronoun as subject: *us bofe.*

bay and hold him until a man gets there with a gun. Because he's the head bear. He's the man."*[26]

Significantly enough, because Sam Fathers, like Lucas Beauchamp, is regarded with respect and not with humor by the community, his speech is not represented phonologically. Two typical Black English features are evident, however—regularization of the third person singular present tense and the triple negative.

Uncle Ash, the cook on the hunting trip, also speaks a Black English in which are emphasized features similar to those in Sam Fathers's speech.

> "Cep Lion," Ash said. "Lion dont need no nose. All he need is a bear."
> . . . "He run a bear through a thousand-acre ice-house. Catch him too. Them other dogs dont matter because they aint going to keep up with Lion nohow, long as he got a bear in front of him."**[27]

As in Sam Fathers's speech, the dominant dialectal features are grammatical, and the selection of grammatical features—regularization of third person singular present tense and the double negative—are the same.

Two other black characters appear in "The Bear" and as usual their speech, or the lack of it, is significant. One of them, a rather shadowy figure who later runs away from the area and is never traced, is Tennie's Jim, Lucas Beauchamp's brother. Jim speaks only two words—a characteristically black utterance, "Yes, sir"—in the story. But the remaining black is much more important.

This last black is unnamed, and he appears in the story when, in part 4, he offers himself to Ike as a suitor to Fonsiba,[28] another black relative of the McCaslins, who is the sister of Lucas and Tennie's Jim. In so presenting

---

*Pronunciation Features
    None.

Grammatical Features
Verbs
    1. Regularization of third person singular present tense: *he dont; he come.*
Negative
    1. Triple negative: *He dont care no more for bears than he does for dogs or men neither.*

Page 271
**Pronunciation Features
    1. Loss of initial unstressed syllable: *except > cep.*

Grammatical Features
Verbs
    1. Regularization of third person singular present tense: *Lion dont; he need; He run.*
Negative
    1. *aint.*
    2. Double negative: *Lion dont need no nose; they aint going to keep up with Lion nohow.*
Objective instead of demonstrative pronoun: *Them other dogs.*

himself, he flies in the face of the McCaslin proprietary presumptions concerning their black relatives. And his anomalous behavior is established by the fact that his speech, far from being in Black English, is pretentiously standard. Ike's response to him is tragically characteristic; he refuses to deliver the inheritance to Fonsiba directly, but uses an indirect means of delivery, a trust, to satisfy his responsibility. The full implications of Ike's response to this anomalous figure, whose dialectal insistence upon recognition as a fellow human, which provokes only evasion on Ike's part, will not be fully seen until "Delta Autumn."

"Delta Autumn" is set in 1942, when Ike McCaslin is an old man. It concerns his trip to the retreating and now possessed wilderness when he is nearly eighty and no longer able to participate in the actual hunt. Left alone in the tent while the younger men hunt, Uncle Ike is visited by a young woman (who, like Fonsiba's husband, remains unnamed). The woman is carrying a baby, and she is looking for Roth Edmonds. The young woman is black, although not obviously so; she identifies herself as the granddaughter of Tennie's Jim. Yet she does not speak Black English; rather, her speech is recorded in Standard English, without a trace of dialect. Ike calls attention to this fact when he says,

> "You sound like you have been to college even. You sound almost like a Northerner even, not like the draggle-tailed women of these Delta peckerwoods."[29]

Her male child (who has been fathered by Roth Edmonds) is thus another miscegenetic McCaslin offspring; he will prove to be the youngest and last McCaslin in *Go Down, Moses*. Yet to Ike the union that produced the child represents a horrible repetition of the past, when Carothers McCaslin sired an illegitimate line through his union with his slave mistress. Disturbed, Ike thinks to himself:

> *Maybe in a thousand or two thousand years in America. . . . But not now! Not now!*[30]

Ike, who until this point in the novel has been perceived as something of a saint who has eschewed possessions and isolated himself from his community to avoid perpetuating the sins of his forefathers, almost hysterically advises the woman to leave, to go North, and to marry " 'a man in your own race. . . . Marry a black man.' "[31] As the nameless young woman and her unnamed baby, whose face is never revealed, leave, the young woman comments that Ike is incapable of love. Clearly, Ike has paid a price for his saintly isolation.

Faulkner's imaginative use of dialect to emphasize his themes is even more dramatically illustrated in the final and title story of the novel. "Go Down, Moses" concerns the grief of Mollie Worsham Beauchamp,[32] the wife of Lucas Beauchamp, at the time of the execution of her grandson, Samuel Worsham Beauchamp ("Butch"), for having killed a white policeman in Chicago.[33] Mollie is obsessed with the idea of bringing her grandson's body back to Mississippi for a proper burial and of having notice of his death recorded in the local newspaper. Since Roth has betrayed her and Ike lives in total isolation, Mollie must turn to an outsider for help—to a young, educated, guilt-ridden, white lawyer named Gavin Stevens.

Mollie visits Stevens in his office in the town. She holds Roth Edmonds responsible for her grandson's fate, for Roth Edmonds had driven Butch, then nineteen, off his property for breaking into a commissary store; as Mollie has it, he has " 'sold [Butch] in Egypt.' "

> "Beauchamp?" Stevens said. "You live on Mr Carothers Edmonds' place."
> "I done left," she said. "I come to find my boy." Then, sitting on the hard chair opposite him and without moving, she began to chant. "Roth Edmonds sold my Benjamin. Sold him in Egypt. Pharaoh got him—"
> "Wait," Stevens said. "Wait, Aunty." Because memory, recollection, was about to mesh and click. "If you dont know where your grandson is, how do you know he's in trouble? Do you mean that Mr Edmonds has refused to help you find him?"
> "It was Roth Edmonds sold him," she said. "Sold him in Egypt. I dont know whar he is. I just knows Pharaoh got him. And you the Law. I wants to find my boy."
> "All right," Stevens said. "I'll try to find him. If you're not going back home, where will you stay in town? It may take some time, if you dont know where he went and you haven't heard from him in five years."
> "I be staying with Hamp Worsham. He my brother."[*34]

Mollie's speech is quite different from her own speech in "The Fire and the Hearth" and from the speech of the other black characters in the novel. It is distinguished by an extended biblical allusion and by its incantatory, almost "gospel" musicality. Mollie uses the form of the Negro spiritual to compare the plight of black Americans to the biblical story of the oppression of the Jews. The short sentences and ritualistic patterning add dignity and articulation to Mollie's expression of her grief; yet here is a language to which the

---

*Pronunciation Features
  None.

Grammatical Features
Verbs
  1. Lack of subject-verb agreement: *I just knows; I wants.*
  2. Zero copula: *I come; And you the law; I be staying; He my brother.*
Pronoun
  1. Omission of relative pronoun: *It was Roth Edmonds sold him.*

highly educated and articulate Gavin Stevens cannot respond. The separation between the races is now so great as to prevent verbal intercourse.

Later, when Gavin visits her, Mollie's chanting has become a shared verbal act; now her brother, Hamp Worsham, joins her, and their incantatory dialogue helps to ritualize their shared anguish.

> "Sold my Benjamin," she said. "Sold him in Egypt."
> "Sold him in Egypt," Worsham said.
> "Roth Edmonds sold my Benjamin."
> "Sold him to Pharaoh."
> "Sold him to Pharaoh and now he dead."[35]

And, later,

> "Sold him in Egypt and now he dead."
> "Oh yes, Lord. Sold him in Egypt."
> "Sold him in Egypt."
> "And now he dead."
> "Sold him to Pharaoh."
> "And now he dead."[36]

This shared act of verbal communication acknowledges what no white in *Go Down, Moses* has been able to acknowledge, the human condition that the black and white share. Mollie and Hamp's gospel chant—like so many of the spiritual songs identifying the suffering of the black people with that of the Old Testament Jews—looks to a similar salvation and addresses a similar leader, presumably a leader yet to be born, who can lead black and white together out of the dehumanizing proprietary assumptions of their civilization.[37] Thus their verbal act is not only an articulation of private and communal grief, but a redemptive act as well. After all the silences it is the only really meaningful verbal act in the novel.

Since Gavin Stevens cannot penetrate Mollie's trancelike state, frustrated, he runs from the house. Accepting Mollie's blame, he tries to alleviate his own guilt and that of the white community by organizing a ritual funeral for Butch to which various townspeople contribute.

Yet the funeral is not the only ritual that Gavin has to offer. After the funeral Gavin returns to town with the editor of the local newspaper, who reports Mollie's request for an obituary notice of Butch's death. Not content with her own effort at mythic memorializing, Mollie demands verbal acknowledgement of Butch's humanity in keeping the white man's rituals. As the black makes song, so the white makes newspapers.

> "Do you know what she asked me this morning, back there at the station?" he said.
> "Probably not," Stevens said.
> "She said, 'Is you gonter put hit in de paper?'"

"What?"

"That's what I said," the editor said. "And she said it again: 'Is you gonter put hit in de paper? I wants hit all in de paper. All of hit.' And I wanted to say, 'If I should happen to know how he really died, do you want that in too?' And by Jupiter, if I had and if she had known what we know even, I believe she would have said yes. But I didn't say it. I just said, 'Why, you couldn't read it, Aunty.' And she said, 'Miss Belle will show me whar to look and I can look at hit. You put hit in de paper. All of hit.' "[38]

Now it is not Mollie's speech that Faulkner records, but rather the white newsman's parody of it. His parody suggests the incongruousness of Mollie's request; for Mollie's black dialect speech and her inability to read the white man's Standard English set her apart from the white ritual of communal recording that is the newspaper. Butch died neither naturally nor with dignity and Mollie cannot even read the notice of his death. The white man's insensitive imitation of the black woman's dialect reinforces the thematic idea that understanding between blacks and whites is desperately absent in the community. Only Gavin Stevens, the sensitive but ineffective intellectual, understands, and the story and the novel end with his recognition of what has happened. Unfortunately, it is not to Mollie to whom he communicates this recognition. Yet Gavin's recognition is all there is in the way of tragic catharsis.

> *Yes*, he thought. *It doesn't matter to her now. Since it had to be and she couldn't stop it, and now that it's all over and done and finished, she doesn't care how he died. She just wanted him home, but she wanted him to come home right. She wanted that casket and those flowers and the hearse and she wanted to ride through town behind it in a car.* "Come on," he said. "Let's get back to town. I haven't seen my desk in two days."[39]

Faulkner uses dialect in *Go Down, Moses* in ways that are quite different from those of other writers. Instead of being used primarily as a means of characterization, dialect is used rather to reinforce main themes of the novel. Faulkner recognizes that verbal communication is implicit in human community; his sense of the violation of community is manifest in his awareness of differences in speech acts. This awareness gives rise to experimentation with various methods of dialectal representation to accommodate thematic intent. Faulkner's radical experiment in the final story comes very close to a tacit acknowledgement of the possibility of Black English as a potential medium for creative expression.

Both Eudora Welty and William Faulkner published their best work before *Brown* v. *Board of Education* in 1954. William Styron published the most controversial of his five novels, *The Confessions of Nat Turner*, in 1967, at the end of the Civil Rights Movement and at the climax of the Black Power-Black Pride Movement. The timing was brilliant commercially but less fortunate critically, for the book immediately became the subject of politically motivated literary controversy. Despite the fact that the novel was awarded the Pulitzer Prize for 1968, it was vigorously attacked by black critics.[40]

Styron based his novel on events involving a nineteenth-century historical figure, Nat Turner, the leader of a slave rebellion in Southeastern Virginia in 1831. Although the event itself can be authenticated historically, Styron's account is fictionalized; it is written in the first person, with Nat Turner himself as the recording perceiver. Styron presents Nat as a self-educated man of superior intelligence who was regarded by his peers as a leader and as a religious prophet. Commanded by God to "slay the serpent," Nat prepares his band of discontented slaves for an insurrection. His plan is for the slaves to kill every white man, woman, and child they can find; before they are captured, they kill fifty-nine people. Sixteen of the captured slaves, including Nat Turner, are hanged in the county seat, ironically (but historically) named Jerusalem.

Styron's remarks in an interview with George Plimpton, first published in the New York *Times,* indicated his awareness of the problems the language of the book posed for him. Styron, who had chosen to write a fictional account of an early nineteenth-century historical event from a black protagonist's point of view some 130 years later, was aware not only of changes of narrative method over the years, but also of the distinct possibility that the dialectal language that his protagonist used, both in thought and in speech, might have changed as well, and in ways that may well have been obscured by time. In his interview with Plimpton, Styron considered but confused these two problems.

> The language of the book is in my own literary style, 20th-century *literary* style, which after all is not too different from 19th-century *literary* style. . . . when I set out to write the book, I didn't strive to write like a 19th-century preacher. I tried to write as spontaneously as I could in the form and language I would have written a contemporary novel, at every point, of course, trying to avoid obvious anachronisms like slang phrases and figures of speech which are peculiarly 20th-century. It was a risk, call it arrogance.[41]

Narrative method (which Styron refers to interchangeably as "style" and "form") is not of concern here, but Styron's representation of the black dialect of his protagonist is critical. The assertions in the Plimpton interview suggest that Styron adroitly sidestepped the historical problem in his novel. He simply assumed that the dialect with which Styron himself was familiar from his youth in the Virginia Tidewater was also spoken by Nat Turner.

> There's enough on record to show that Negroes in the early part of the 19th century spoke very much as rural Negroes in the South speak today. It is a distinct dialect and I believe that with some modifications

it has remained frozen for several hundred years. Fanny Kemble, Frederick Law Olmsted and other chroniclers of the era set down Negro speech and it sounds very much like the rhythms of the speech I heard as a boy when I grew up in the Virginia Tidewater. It's with the urban class that the language evolves. As soon as you learn to spell and write, the language becomes educated American English, whatever one might call it, and the dialect disappears. I'm not speaking, of course, of the "hip" sub-language that rises in the city.[42]

Styron here also assumed a regional distinctiveness in his characters' use of Black English dialect. And since all the slaves in the novel come from the same region, one would expect that they would speak in a definable dialect and that their speech would be represented according to a uniform system. But an examination of the speech of two of the black characters will reveal that that assumption is not true.

Will's speech will be considered first. Will is the volatile, somewhat unbalanced black man who joins Nat's band just before the insurrection begins. Unlike Nat, who finds it difficult to kill, he actually seems to enjoy killing the whites. When he appears on the eve of the uprising, Nat is uneasy about accepting him into the group, until he realizes that Will's propensity for violence—both in speech and in action—is the result of his mistreatment as a slave. Will says,

> "Don' *shit* me, preacher man!". . . His voice was the hiss of a cornered cat. "You try an' shit me, preacher man, an' you in *bad* trouble. I isn't run in de woods all dis yere time fo' nothin'. I'se tired of huckaberries. I gwine git me some meat now—*white* meat. I gwine git me some dat white cunt too.". . . "You shit me, preacher man," he said hoarsely, "an' I fix yo' preacher ass! I knock you to yo fuckin' black knees! I isn't gwine hang out in de swamp no mo' eatin' huckaberries. I gwine git me some *meat*. I gwine git me some *blood*. So, preacher man, you better figger dat Will done jined be ruction! You maybe is some fancy talker but you isn't gwine talk Will out'n dat!"*[43]

Will's dialect is represented by both pronunciation and grammatical fea-

---

Pronunciation Features
1. Reduction of consonant clusters: *huckleberries > huckaberries; and > an'*.
2. *th > d: this > dis; that > dat; the > de.*
3. Loss of *r: for > fo'; your > yo'; more > mo'*.
4. Nasalization: *nothing > nothin'; fucking > fuckin'; eating > eatin'; out of > out'n; going to > gwine.*
5. Loss of glide: *joined > jined.*

Grammatical Features
Verbs
1. Lack of subject-verb agreement: *I isn't; I'se; you maybe is; you isn't.*
2. Zero copula: *you in bad trouble.*
3. Past participle used as helping verb: *done jined.*
Negative
1. Double negative: *I isn't gwine hang out in de swamp no mo'.*

tures. The most frequently used pronunciation features include the pronunciation of voiced *th* as *d*, as in *dis*, *dat*, and *de;* nasalization, which most
frequently appears as the dropping of the final *g* after *n;* and the dropping of
final *r*, as in *fo'*, *yo'*, and *mo'*. Will's speech also includes the most common
grammatical features of Black English—lack of subject-verb agreement,
zero copula, and the double negative.

Furthermore, Will's speech is shot through with highly charged Anglo-
Saxon obscenities. One of Styron's black critics, John A. Williams, has
objected that in the novel only black characters speak obscenely; furthermore, he questions the authenticity of the obscenities they use:

> Only the Negro characters spoke the real earthy language: "fucker,"
> "cunt," "cuntlapper," "shit," "shiteating." Now, I rather like using four-,
> six-, eight-, ten-, and twelve-letter curse words; something really gets
> loose when they are down on paper, something solid about men and
> words. However Anglo-Saxon these words might be, it does not seem
> likely that they were employed in the early nineteenth century among
> the slaves. I don't doubt that there *were* swear words, but not these.
> Like slang, swear words, certain kinds of them, have a vogue in time.
> Styron has transplanted the present back into the past.[44]

Yet the situation is less simple than a distinction between obscene black
speech and nonobscene white. For there are many differences between the
representation of Will's speech and that of Nat. Here is Nat, speaking in
response to Will:

> "Awright," I said, "you can jine up with us. But let me tell you one
> thing good, nigger. *I* is the boss. *I* runs this show. When I says jump
> there, you jump right *there,* not in no still or cider press and *not* in no
> haystack, neither. You ain't goin' to spread no white woman's legs, not
> on this trip you ain't. We got a long way to go and a pile of things to do,
> and if the niggers start a-humpin' every white piece in sight we ain't
> goin' to get half a mile up the road. So brandy and women is *out*. Now
> come on."*[45]

Most obviously, perhaps, Nat, as a preacher and as a leader, does not
use the forbidden Anglo-Saxonisms that Will does. But there are other differences. In the first place, there are many fewer pronunciation features than

---

Pronunciation Features
  1. Reduction of consonant clusters: *All right > Awright.*
  2. Nasalization: *going > goin'; a-humping > a-humpin'.*
Grammatical Features
Verbs
  1. Lack of subject-verb agreement: *I is; I runs; I says.*
Negative
  1. *Ain't.*
  2. Double negative: *not in no cider press; not in no haystack, neither; you ain't goin' to spread no white woman's legs; not on this trip you ain't.*

are evident in Will's speech. In the above passage of Nat's speech there is only one example of the reduction of consonant clusters—*All right* is represented as *Awright*—and there are only two examples of nasalization—*goin'* and *a-humpin'*. Unlike Will, Nat pronounces initial voiced *th* as *th* instead of *d* (as in *this*). The significant features of Nat's dialect are contained in the grammatical features—there are several examples of lack of subject-verb agreement and four examples of the double negative in the above short passage. Here Styron, like Faulkner, has differentiated between social classes and the functions of the black characters within the novel. Will, a "low" and violent character, who is not meant to be entirely acceptable to the reader, speaks a dialect that is not only obscene but is heavily laced with pronunciation features. Nat, on the other hand, the sympathetic protagonist and the "leader," the intelligence behind the uprising, speaks a modified dialect speech, one in which grammatical features clearly predominate over characteristics of pronunciation.

One of Styron's enraged black critics seems to have missed this point. Without differentiating between the ways in which dialect is represented in the novel and, indeed, without any close analysis of the speech of Styron's black characters, John Oliver Killens labels Styron's representation of black dialect "Amos-and-Andy." With further specification, Killens goes on to accuse Styron of failing to recognize

the beauty of Afro-American idiom, which has very little to do with accent, but has everything to do with the rhythms and mannerisms of black language, the manners of formulations and of thinking through and the special way of saying things, the unique-to-our-blackness methods of expression; the Afro-American psyche. Amos-and-Andy dialect is easy, too easy. On the other hand, black idiom, Afro-Americanese, is more difficult to achieve, but it is also more authentic, more rewarding and profound; it is historic and creative. Styron, in attempting to write Afro-Americanese, is like a man who tries to sing the blues when he has not paid his dues.[46]

Killens has not defined what he means by "Amos-and-Andy," by "the mannerisms of black language," or by "Afro-Americanese," and his "blues-dues" rhyme, while musical, is hardly logically analogous. Actually, the two passages discussed above indicate that Styron's representation of dialect speech is quite versatile.

A more serious flaw exists in Styron's representation of Nat Turner's language in the novel than in the simple representation of his speech. It was identified by Stanley Kauffman in his review of the novel; his point was reiterated by Richard Gilman and Killens also touched upon it. For there is a disturbing difference in Styron's representation of Nat's thoughts recorded in formal, ornate, rhetorical language and his distinctly dialectal speech (recorded though it is with some restraint). In the last chapter of the novel, just before Nat is hanged, Styron records the recurrence of a symbolic vision that opened the novel. Nat imagines himself in a little boat, drifting gently toward the sea.

> *Surely I Come Quickly . . .*
>   Cloudless sunlight suggesting neither hour nor season glows down upon me, wraps me with a cradle's warmth as I drift toward the river's estuary; the little boat rocks gently in our benign descent together toward the sea. On the unpeopled banks the woods are silent, silent as snowfall. No birds call; in windless attitudes of meditation the crowd of green trees along the river shore stands drooping and still. This low country seems untouched by humanity, by past or future time. Beneath me where I recline I feel the boat's sluggish windward drift, glimpse rushing past eddies of foam, branches, leaves, clumps of grass all borne on the serene unhurried flood to the place where the river meets the sea. Faintly now I hear the oceanic roar, mark the sweep of sunlit water far-near, glinting with whitecaps, the ragged shoulder of a beach where sea and river join in a tumultuous embrace of swirling waters. But nothing disturbs me, I drowse in the arms of a steadfast and illimitable peace. Salt stings my nostrils. The breakers roll to shore, the lordly tide swells back beneath a cobalt sky arching eastward toward Africa. An unhurried booming fills me not with fear but only with repose and slumbrous anticipation—serenity as ageless as those rocks, in garlands of weeping seaweed, thrown up by the groaning waves.[47]

Certainly it is difficult to imagine the same character who thinks in such language speaking in the dialect in which Nat speaks. It is the sort of inconsistency that Mark Twain never permits in *Huckleberry Finn*. Yet here it is a result of Styron's confusion of language and literary method, the confusion manifest in the Plimpton interview. This inconsistency seriously damages the authenticity and believability of Nat as a character. And, of course, if Nat's character is not believable, the novel as a whole is severely flawed.[48]

The three white writers whose representation of Black English dialect has been discussed in this chapter concentrated on characterizing rural, never urban, black characters. Despite their sophisticated awareness and abilities, and their subtlety in recording character and class distinctions within a specific geographical locale, they avoided any attempt to enter the complex, more contemporary, more volatile world of the city. That would be the province of black writers who had grown up in an urban setting after World War II, who understood the diversified culture within the city and attempted to record the speech they associated with black urban experience.

Certainly one of the most significant influences on the literary representation of Black English speech in the years after World War II was a new awareness of the cultural significance of black music, specifically of the blues and of jazz. Blues, which had begun primarily as an expression of a rural people, moved North and to the cities. New York City, the cultural locus of the newly deprovincialized, racially aware, and radicalized black, became the center for jazz as well. Billie Holiday in the 1940s, Charlie Parker and Bud Powell in the 1950s, Thelonius Monk, Miles Davis, John Coltrane, and Charlie Mingus in the 1960s, changed the shape of jazz and reclaimed for it a black identity.

In the 1950s Duke Ellington spoke of jazz as representative of "Negro music" (though he had experimented with white sidemen);[49] by 1963 Amiri Baraka was describing blues and jazz as unique forms of Afro-American expression:

> Blues is the parent of all legitimate jazz, and it is impossible to say exactly how old blues is—certainly no older than the presence of Negroes in the United States. It is a native American music, the product of the black man in this country: or to put it more exactly the way I have come to think about it, blues could not exist if the African captives had not become American captives.[50]

Later, in identifying the characteristic features of this "black" music that he traces to an African past, Baraka recognizes them as essentially rhythmic.

> The most apparent survivals of African music in Afro-American music are in its rhythms; not only the seeming emphasis in the African music on rhythmic, rather than melodic or harmonic, qualities, but, also the use of polyphonic, or contrapuntal, rhythmic effects.[51]

Baraka's remarks are typical; in the 1950s and 1960s jazz was coming to be perceived as a black cultural possession. With rhythmic experiments rife and new developments in jazz in the be-bop and "modern" years of the late 1940s and early 1950s, new interest also arose in the rhythms of black speech as culturally distinguishing features. And, because rhythm was now seen as a positive feature of black culture, writers soon came to be aware that rhythmic qualities of Black English could be represented without generating the negative connotations that pronunciation and even syntactic features seemed to provoke in the minds of black and white readers alike. The representation of rhythmic features was a way out for writers trapped in the nationalist-assimilationist critical struggle of the 1920s and 1930s. Now the speaker of Black English in literature could be both distinctive in his speech and positively represented as an intelligent, creative, and articulate character.

Twentieth-century writers in the years before World War II on occasion undertook to reproduce rhythmic qualities, particularly by means of syntactic repetitions, in the speech of their fictional black characters. Gertrude Stein, in "Melanctha," was probably the first, but there were also Langston Hughes (who explored these possibilities more in his poetry than in his prose) and Zora Neale Hurston. More recently, William Faulkner used the rhythms of black religious music to define black cultural values in the title story of *Go Down, Moses*. But the fiction writer who was perhaps most committed to representing these rhythmic qualities—in reproducing the "music" of black speech—was a black jazz musician and poet turned novelist, Ralph Ellison.

Although it is intensely a "literary" novel, with recognizable allusions to American (Faulkner, T. S. Eliot, Mark Twain, and Melville) and European (Dostoevski, Flaubert, Kafka, and particularly Joyce)[52] literature, Ellison's novel *Invisible Man* (1952) is, at least on one level, a history in two parts of black experience in America. The first half of the novel explores the unnamed protagonist's education as a black in the South—his disillusionment with southern life, with his "Negro" college, with racism, and with capitalism. The second recounts his experience as a black in the North, his disillusionment with the North, and his rejection of Communism and of Black Nationalism as alternatives to white American capitalist culture. The novel concludes with the protagonist's existential recognition that identity for himself and the American black man paradoxically lies in his "invisibility," a condition necessitated by the refusal on the part of whites to acknowledge the existence of individuated black humanity. In disappearing into a manhole during a riot in Harlem at the end of the novel, in retiring from the chaos of racial and class conflict above him, the protagonist achieves full invisibility; only underground, where he is free of any assigned identity, can he begin the work of establishing the authentic identity so long denied him. Invisible Man promises at the end of the novel that he will return later to the "surface," still "invisible," but with "a socially responsible role to play."[53]

One of the distinctive capabilities of Ellison's writing—in this respect he is much like Faulkner—is to represent the speech of a variety of black characters. Faulkner's black characters are, for the most part, of rural origin, but Ellison's are not always so. *Invisible Man* is distinguished by the variety of black character types that Ellison represents, rural and urban, educated and uneducated, upper class and lower class. There is a southern sharecropper, a "Negro" college president, a black preacher, a southerner-come-North, a Black Nationalist leader, a black Communist activist, and various urban street types. In individuating these characters, Ellison is careful to record the distinguishing features of each one's speech. And his methods of dialect representation are also various. But in nearly every case, Ellison attempts to render the particular musical qualities of the various Black English vernaculars he represents.

Ellison's fascination with music began before he committed himself to writing as a career. Having performed as a jazz trumpeter and having shown an interest in musical composition in his youth, he did not abandon his music completely when he turned to fiction. Instead, as he said in an interview with John Hersey, he approached writing "through *sound*."

My sense of form, my basic sense of artistic form, is musical. As a boy I tried to write songs, marches, exercises in symphonic form, really before I received any training, and then I studied it. I listened constantly to music, trying to learn the processes of developing a theme, of expanding and contracting and turning it inside out, of making bridges, and working with techniques of musical continuity, and so on. I think that basically my instinctive approach to writing is through *sound*. A change of mood and mode comes to me in terms of sound. That's one part of it, in the sense of composing the architecture of a fiction.[54]

The structure of *Invisible Man* has been compared to musical form by a number of critics; as Robert Bone says of Ellison, "he writes a 'melody' (thematic line) and then orchestrates it."[55] Larry Neal goes as far as to suggest that Louis Armstrong's music provides "the over-all structure for the novel." Neal continues, "If that is the case, the subsequent narrative and all of the action which follows can be read as one long blues solo."[56] Albert Murray, a friend of Ellison who is quoted by Neal, is more specific:

Invisible Man was *par excellence* the literary extension of the blues. Ellison had taken an everyday twelve-bar blues tune (by a man from down South sitting in a manhole up North in New York, singing and signifying about how he got there) and scored it for full orchestra. This was indeed something different and something more than run-of-the-mill U.S. fiction. It had new dimensions of rhetorical resonance (based on lying and signifying). It employed a startlingly effective fusion of narrating realism and surrealism, and it achieved a unique but compelling combination of the naturalistic, the ridiculous, and the downright hallucinatory.[57]

But it is not only the structure of the novel that has been labeled as musical. The novel is interspersed with allusions to blues lyrics (most notably to Louis Armstrong's "Black and Blue"). What is more significant is Ellison's recognition of the musicality of dialect. He spoke about this subject to John Hersey:

one of the things I work for is to make a line of prose *sound* right, or for a bit of dialogue to fall on the page in the way I hear it, aurally, in my mind. The same goes for the sound and intonation of a character's voice. When I am writing of characters who speak in the Negro idiom, in the vernacular, it is still a real problem for me to make their accents fall in the proper place in the visual line.[58]

And in his acceptance speech for the National Book Award in 1953, Ellison pointed out the inadequacy of conventional literary language and the need, as he saw it, of recording not only the rhythms of spoken language but its imagery.

For despite the notion that its rhythms [those of twentieth-century American writing] were those of everyday speech, I found that when compared with the rich babel of idiomatic expression around me, a language full of imagery and gesture and rhetorical canniness, it was embarrassingly austere. Our speech I found resounding with an alive language swirling with over three hundred years of American living, a mixture of the folk, the Biblical, the scientific and the political. Slangy in one stance, academic in another, loaded poetically with imagery at one moment, mathematically bare of imagery in the next.[59]

But it is not only Ellison's consistent concern for the musicalities of black speech that distinguishes the dialects of *Invisible Man*. For in the novel Ellison atypically uses Black English as validating speech. Although other novelists have assigned Black English to demeaned characters, Ellison in *Invisible Man* assigns black dialect only to those characters who are to be taken seriously. The protagonist of Ellison's novel is, of course, an existential hero, and as such can achieve his own authenticity only by and for himself. Although none of the Black English speakers has any exclusive access to truth, each does have something to teach Ellison's protagonist, so consistently so in the novel that the very presence of Black English seems to carry with it a certain validation, even if that validation is qualified. Indeed, Ellison's Black English speakers seem almost the very representatives of those positive characteristics of Black American culture to which Ellison would have his protagonist attend.

The first example of Black English in the novel proper (if one for the moment looks past the prologue and its references to Louis Armstrong) is to be found in words uttered by Invisible Man's grandfather on his deathbed—words that, as Invisible Man is aware, initially "caused the trouble."

"I want you to overcome 'em with yeses, undermine 'em with grins, agree 'em to death and destruction, let 'em swoller you till they vomit or bust wide open."[60]

Although the Black English features of his statement are minimal, the grandfather's words are clearly in dialect and as such are in clear contrast to the Standard English that surrounds them. And they are the only words of advice to the protagonist in the first chapter that are at all to be taken seriously. For although they are the deathbed utterance of a frustrated man, they are words that set Invisible Man on his way and that stage his behavior in the Battle Royal section.

The dominant metaphor of the Battle Royal section, the blindfold, is visual. Invisible Man speaks only occasionally in the chapter and his only significant speech is his repetition—in Standard English—of his graduation speech to the men who had recently tormented him with physical violence. But the speech, with its Standard English, is met only with ridicule and with adverse consequences for its speaker. Here is the first evidence of Invisible

Man's invisibility, and here is the first evidence as well that authenticity (to use again the existentialist's term) is not to be achieved by a black who speaks Standard English.

After the Battle Royal section there exists in each division of the novel that follows at least one Black English speaker. The next to appear—in the college episode—is the tormented Jim Trueblood, who describes how he came to impregnate his own daughter. Jim Trueblood is a rural southern sharecropper, an uneducated man, one whose speech, if represented traditionally, would be expected to contain both pronunciation and grammatical features. And indeed it does, although Ellison's phonetic spelling is reduced to a minimum.

> "That's the way it was," he said. "Me on one side and the ole lady on the other and the gal in the middle. It was dark, plum black. Black as the middle of a bucket of tar. The kids was sleeping all together in they bed over in the corner. I must have been the last one to go to sleep, 'cause I was thinking 'bout how to git some grub for the next day and 'bout the gal and the young boy what was startin' to hang 'round her. I didn't like him and he kept comin' through my thoughts and I made up my mind to warn him away from the gal. It was black dark and I heard one of the kids whimper in his sleep and the last few sticks of kindlin' crackin' and settlin' in the stove and the smell of the fat meat seemed to git cold and still in the air just like meat grease when it gits set in a cold plate of molasses. And I was thinkin' 'bout the gal and this boy and feelin' her arms besides me and hearing the ole lady snorin' with a kinda moanin' and a-groanin' on the other side. I was worryin' 'bout my family, how they was goin' to eat and all, and I thought 'bout when the gal was little like the younguns sleepin' over in the corner and how I was her favorite over the ole lady. There we was, breathin' together in the dark. Only I could see 'em in my mind, knowin' 'em like I do. In my mind I looked at all of 'em, one by one. The gal looks just like the ole lady did when she was young and I first met her, only better lookin'. You know, we gittin' to be a better-lookin' race of people.*[61]

The dominant pronunciation feature here is nasalization—there are thirteen

---

Pronunciation Features
    1. Reduction of consonant clusers: *old > ole.*
    2. Loss of *th: them > 'em.*
    3. Nasalization: *starting > startin'; coming > comin'; kindling > kindlin'; cracking > crackin'; settling > settlin'; thinking > thinkin'; feeling > feelin'; snoring > snorin'; moaning > moanin'; a-groaning > a-groanin'; worrying > worryin'; knowing > knowin'; looking > lookin'.*
    4. Loss of initial unstressed syllable: *because > 'cause; about > 'bout: around > 'round.*

Grammatical Features
Verbs
    1. Lack of subject-verb agreement: *kids was.*
Pronouns
    1. Objective pronoun as subject: *me on one side.*
    2. Nominative instead of possessive pronoun form: *in they bed.*

examples in this passage. The grammatical features are less frequent: a single example of lack of subject-verb agreement—*kids was*—and two examples of black pronoun usage. The most distinctive syntactic characteristic of Trueblood's speech and of his narrative style is his tendency to use verbless and almost identifiably "metric" sentence fragments at the beginning of the passage—*Black as the/ middle of a/ bucket of/ tar*—and later, the long, rambling, and dominantly "dactylic" sentences in which ideas are loosely connected by the conjunction *and*.

Although there are perhaps fewer qualities that can be identified as "musical" in Trueblood's speech than can be found in some of the examples that follow, a few other features can also be pointed out here. There is, to begin with, repetition of syntactic patterns; the most obvious is a number of sentences that begin with "I" and are followed by a verb. Also, a number of significant words are repeated—"black" and "I" and "gal" and "ole lady." Furthermore, there is rhyme—"moanin' and a-groanin'" and, finally, a dominantly poetic figure, the simile, is used twice in the passage: " 'Black as the middle of a bucket of tar' " and " '. . . the smell of the fat meat seemed to get cold and still in the air just like meat grease when it gits set in a cold plate of molasses.' "

Ellison's presentation of Trueblood's speech, then, appears to be a combination of the traditional representation of pronunciation and grammatical features to indicate the speech of a rural black southerner and the use of musical-poetic techniques—of figuration, of meter, and even of rhyme. For it is significant—of central significance to the novel—that Trueblood, despite social disapproval by his community (ironically the whites see him as one who has acted out their own fantasies and thus regard him with a kind of perverse reverence), has not lied. The truth he utters, the assertion he makes of the realities of black life, are of real importance to the protagonist if he is to come to terms with the actualities of his own identity.

Some Black English is spoken in the Golden Day, although the educated blacks from the asylum, wearing gray clothes, for the most part, speak Standard English. Back at the College, of course, the mode of communication is decidedly Standard English. The only utterance resembling Black English at the College is the chapel sermon of the Reverend Homer A. Barbee. The Reverend Barbee's speech is not Black English, but it is highly rhythmical.

"this barren land after Emancipation," he intoned, "this land of darkness and sorrow, of ignorance and degradation, where the hand of brother had been turned against brother, father against son, and son against father; where master had turned against slave and slave against master; where all was strife and darkness, an aching land. And into this land came a humble prophet, lowly like the humble carpenter of Nazareth, a slave and a son of slaves, knowing only his mother. A slave born, but marked from the beginning by a high intelligence and princely personality; born in the lowest part of this barren, war-scarred land, yet somehow shedding light upon it where'er he passed through.[62]

The rhythm that is achieved here is largely that of the repetitive repre sentation of syntactic units, particularly of nouns linked together by *and (of dárkness and sórrow, of ignórance and degrádation)* and by the repetition of specific key words—*brother, father, son, master.* These repetitions are characteristic of almost any preacherly style,

And Barbee's sermon, with its highly artificial rhetoric, is not uniquely Black English; rather, it is intended as a sermon in the tradition of Joyce or Melville. For in both *A Portrait of the Artist as a Young Man* and in *Moby-Dick,* as Ellison is certainly aware, there appears, fairly early in each book, a parodied sermon in which the worst aspects of the hypocrisy of the culture are held up to the protagonist's view. Given the pervasive pun that recurs throughout the College section—in which the reader is repeatedly reminded of the protagonist following "the white line" in the highway—and given the initial description of Barbee—"his white collar gleaming, like a band between his black face and his dark garments, dividing his head from his body"[63]—Ellison's parodic intentions are unmistakable.

But a critical discovery is made when it is revealed that Barbee is blind. For blindness is a recurrent metaphor in *Invisible Man.* In the first section of the novel, blindfolded black boys were duped into a Battle Royal; later a one-eyed Party leader will emerge. And blindness seems in *Invisible Man* always associated with an inability to see beyond language to truth. When he becomes aware of Barbee's blindness, Ellison's protagonist comes to know the preacher's hypocrisy in his artificial manipulation of the language of his profession.

It is only when Invisible Man leaves the South and finds himself in New York City that he is exposed to the various realities of Black English speech. As he walks through the streets of Harlem, the protagonist meets a rather insouciant man who is pushing a cart filled with blueprints. " 'Folks is always making plans and changing 'em,' "[64] says this vendor. This black man of the city, a Harlemite, speaks an encoded variety of Black English; he speaks in rhyming slang.

> "All it takes to get along in this here man's town is a little shit, grit and mother-wit. And man, I was bawn with all three. In fact, I'maseventhsonofaseventhsonbawnwithacauloverbotheyesandraisedonblackcatboneshighjohntheconquerorandgreasygreens—" he spieled with twinkling eyes, his lips working rapidly. "You dig me, daddy?"
> "You're going too fast," I said, beginning to laugh.
> "Okay, I'm slowing down. I'll verse you but I won't curse you— My name is Peter Wheatstraw, I'm the Devil's only son-in-law, so roll 'em! You a southern boy, ain't you?" he said, his head to one side like a bear's.[65]

Neither pronunciation nor grammatical features (there is one example of *ain't*) are distinctive here, but rather rhymes and omitted spacing to indicate rapidity in speech delivery *(I'maseventhsonofaseventhsonbawnwithacaul-overbotheyesandraisedonblackcatboneshighjohntheconquerorandgreasy-greens)*. "Peter Wheatstraw" could only be speaking Black English, and it is a variety that depends for its effect on a rhythm produced in part by rhyme and rapidity rather than on pronunciation and grammar. And Peter Wheatstraw, in his acceptance of life in contemporary culture, offers an important truth noted by the protagonist. After Wheatstraw leaves, Invisible Man remarks to himself, "God damn . . . they're a hell of a people!"[66]

When Invisible Man innocently relies on the written recommendation of Dr. Bledsoe, the president of his college, to find a job, he soon becomes aware that white mastery is maintained through white control of language. Since Bledsoe has condemned him in "white English," he will not be able to find white-collar work. And, as young Mr. Emerson tells him the truth about Bledsoe's letter, Invisible Man learns his lesson through his memory of his grandfather's black dialect words:

> *Don't let no white man tell you his business, 'cause after he tells you he's liable to git shame he tole it to you and then he'll hate you. Fact is, he was hating you all the time.*[67]

Invisible Man finally finds a blue-collar job in a paint factory, where his immediate superior, Lucius Brockway, is the only Black English speaker. Brockway, suspicious of college graduates and of labor unions, has mastered his job and his white superiors. He is the only one who knows how to run the machines. He is the indispensable color-mixer. And he utters the truths of his situation in Black English.

> "They thinks 'cause everything down here is done by machinery, that's all there is to it. They crazy! Ain't a continental thing that happens down here that ain't as iffen I done put my black hands into it! Them machines just do the cooking, these here hands right here do the sweeting. Yes, sir! Lucius Brockway hit it square on the head! I dips my fingers in and sweets it!"[68]

Brockway's position is ultimately a compromise; loyal to the owners of the factory, he resists the organizing activities of a labor union, and, infuriated at his union contacts, diverts the protagonist from his duties. Thus, when Invisible Man fails to control the boiler "pressure," the boiler in the paint factory blows up and the paint factory is destroyed in an apocalyptic, prophetic (and heavily symbolic) "explosion."

In the hospital, where Invisible Man finds himself after the explosion, no Black English is spoken. For here is a world of whiteness, a world without black truth, a world in which the protagonist is again invisible. Now

Invisible Man, in a half-conscious state, remembers black songs from his childhood. They are for him the saving remnants of a nearly lost identity.

Back in Harlem, Invisible Man is fortunate to find Mary, another Black English speaker, who kindly provides a home for him. Mary is a simple, traditional figure who is no theorizer, but who gives the protagonist the motherly love that he finds nowhere else in the novel. Mary's genuine warmth and human decency in the midst of the impersonal hordes of the modern city are recognized by the protagonist as real cultural strengths.

Given the validity that Ellison attributes to Black English utterances, it is interesting to note that up to this point in *Invisible Man,* Ellison's protagonist—who like Styron's Nat Turner is also his narrator—has not himself employed Black English, either in narration or in recorded utterance. It is not until he delivers his extemporaneous speech at the Harlem eviction that Invisible Man uses Black English, and on this occasion and thereafter his use of dialect is infrequent. His narration in the novel is also dominantly in Standard English. There are moments in which Ellison's delight in irony leads him to experiment with certain rhetorical devices, notably with a rather heavy narrative punning, as in the "white line" motif in the College section. But Ellison is at heart a conventional novelist, and in 1952 there was little or no tradition of experiment with Black English narration.

Nevertheless, there are occasional moments, moments of great importance, in which Invisible Man allows himself a line or two of Black English, and the first of these comes only after a critical moment of insight in the novel, in the scene in which Invisible Man takes food from the hand of the Black English-speaking yam seller in Harlem and, like Stephen Daedalus on the beach, formulates a phrase of central thematic and dramatic significance—" 'I yam what I am.' "[69]

" 'I yam what I am' " is a comically profound and multi-signative statement of identity for Invisible Man. Not only is it a recognition of the essentially deterministic nature of his identity—on one level of meaning it can signify "I am what I eat"—but it is a recognition that as a man the protagonist is in God's likeness; " 'I yam what I am' " is, of course, a dialect translation of "Jahweh," the Hebrew name of God. And perhaps of most importance, " 'I yam what I am' " is a simple, unapologetic assertion of being. But whatever its meaning, " 'I yam what I am' " is an assertion which, if not obviously so, shows itself as Black English through impaction of the verb.

Obviously, such a triumphant assertion is not enough; things are not so simple any more. Invisible Man immediately discovers that the yams are frost-bitten and taste bitter up North. Some sort of role and some fuller means of self-definition must be found. And that role is to be achieved through speech. But here at least is the protagonist's first explicit assertion of self. Invisible Man speaks in Black English; therefore he is.

It is in the Harlem eviction scene that follows that the protagonist finds what is apparently a role for himself, a role in which his identity is to be recognized. In his impromptu speech which results in his employment by the "Brotherhood," Invisible Man allows himself a phrase or two of Black English.

> "They ain't *got* nothing, they cain't *get* nothing, they never *had* nothing."[70]

Here again is the highly patterned double negative, the verb manipulation, the musicality that Ellison so often employs.

Of course the new-found role is an illusory one; all the characters associated with the Brotherhood speak Standard English. When the protagonist, caught up in his new identity, tries to discard his blackness with his briefcase and its symbolic contents, it is characteristically a Black English speaker who forces it back upon him:

> "Man, don't tell me! I *seen* you. What the hell you mean?" he said, furtively removing the package from his pocket. "This here feels like money or a gun or something and I know damn well I seen you drop it."[71]

Later, when Brother Jack, the Communist leader, warns Invisible Man to " 'stay completely out of Harlem,' "[72] the warning seems almost to apply to the dialect identified with Harlem as well as to the place itself. Even when Invisible Man eventually returns to Harlem, the language of the Brotherhood is Standard English; in a manner reminiscent of the union workers at the paint factory, the Brotherhood opposes the nationalist interests of blacks. And the Brotherhood's use of Standard English seems an *indicium* of that organization's inadequacy as a source of truth—at least for the blacks it pretends to serve.

On the other hand, the Black Nationalist leader, Ras the Exhorter (later Ras the Destroyer), does speak a black dialect. His dialect, however, is not American Black English, but rather a West Indian variety. Ellison seems to treat Ras somewhat differently from other black dialect speakers. For Ras is a foreigner, a West Indian demagogue bent ultimately and simply on expression of destructive anger. Although he is no more to be trusted than the Standard English speakers of the Brotherhood, the protagonist must at least recognize Ras's anger as real.

Increasingly now the protagonist narrator makes use of puns and rhymes, especially in expository passages. Invisible Man witnesses the police murder of a black friend, Tod Clifton, a former Brother who has disappeared and then has reappeared as an illegal street vendor of black dolls. Clifton, who thus seems to have become only a parody of himself as former organizer for the Brotherhood, assaults an overbearing white officer in a moment of rage and is immediately shot. Invisible Man escapes from the scene by walking to a subway, where he notices three elegantly dressed black youths. He thinks of the young men as "outside of historical time."

> For they were outside, in the dark with Sambo, the dancing paper doll; taking it on the lambo with my fallen brother, Tod Clifton (Tod, Tod) running and dodging the forces of history instead of making a dominating stand.[73]

But even in this moment of sadness and speculation, the protagonist's impulse toward the musical play of Black English is again evidence of his expanded self-knowledge and understanding of his situation.

As Invisible Man's awareness of and sympathy for Tod and his blackness increase, Ellison's rhythmic devices increase in frequency. And in Invisible Man's final oration in the novel, his eulogy for Tod (a speech that is not acceptable to the Brotherhood), the language is not palpably dialectal; still, rhythmic devices and syntactic repetitions have a mesmerizing effect.

> "His name was Clifton and he was tall and some folks thought him handsome. And though he didn't believe it, I think he was. His name was Clifton and his face was black and his hair was thick with tight-rolled curls—or call them naps or kinks. He's dead, uninterested, and, except to a few young girls, it doesn't matter. . . . Have you got it? Can you see him? Think of your brother or your cousin John. His lips were thick with an upward curve at the corners. He often smiled. He had good eyes and a pair of fast hands, and he had a heart. He thought about things and he felt deeply. I won't call him noble because what's such a word to do with one of us? His name was Clifton, Tod Clifton, and, like any man, he was born of woman to live awhile and fall and die. So that's his tale to the minute. His name was Clifton and for a while he lived among us and aroused a few hopes in the young manhood of man, and we who knew him loved him and he died. So why are you waiting? You've heard it all. Why wait for more, when all I can do is repeat it?"[74]

Two four-beat questions *("Háve yóu gót it? Cán yóu sée him?")* are at the center of the speech and set a pattern for various other syntactic units *("Yoủ've héard it all. Whý wáit for móre . . .").* Recurrences of short syntactic units, such as short appositional clauses joined by "and," reinforce the intensely musical quality of the passage. The clause *"His name was Clifton,"* occuring four times in the passage, functions as a rhythmic refrain. All of these devices—of repetition and of variation in sentence length—give power and movement to the passage. And the fact that these are legitimately Black English rhythms is manifest, for they reiterate other Black English rhythms earlier in the novel. Although Ellison makes use of musical or poetic features rather than pronunciation or grammatical features, here there is no parody. This, to Ellison's mind, is "the Negro idiom," the learned and inherited "sound" of black speech; here, in Standard English dress, is Black English still in touch with truth.

In the great riot that follows, the protagonist suddenly finds himself in a world of emergent Blackness—a world of Black English. Wearing reflective sunglasses and mistaken for Rinehart (whose reflexive identity is embodied in his own reflecting sunglasses), the protagonist finds himself safe in the black community. But when Invisible Man loses his own reflecting glasses and with them his disguise (his surrogate identity), he is forced to flee from the marauding Ras. The protagonist first seeks to escape to Mary's apartment, to the simpler world of the past. In his search he again hears Black English spoken, but this time by winos, who observe but do not participate in the action. When the briefcase containing Invisible Man's badges of inherited identity becomes the object of attention by the police, Invisible Man escapes down a manhole into a coal chute and an underground world of total blackness. It is only here that he can safely surrender his briefcase and its contents, the material of an outgrown self.

Significantly, after this descent into full invisibility, no more of the characteristics that identify speech as black dialect are to be seen in the novel. But although, in its apocalyptic conclusion, other symbolic systems become significant, the identifying metaphor of utterance remains important. Indeed, in the novel's final sentence, Invisible Man reminds the reader, "Who knows but that, on the lower frequencies, I speak for you?"[75]

For all its narrative punning, allusion, complexity of symbol, and dialectal innovation, *Invisible Man* remains essentially a conventional modern novel, a *bildungsroman,* much in the tradition of *Huckleberry Finn* or *A Portrait of the Artist as a Young Man.* And for the most part Ellison controlled his impulse toward the ultimately radical experiment, the novel narrated in Black English. But in his recognition of Black English as a language of valid utterance, a language with a potential for truth, a language that has gained that capacity through its relationship to the rhythms and recurrences of black music, Ellison took a critical step. Without *Invisible Man,* the novels of Ernest J. Gaines or Ishmael Reed would not have been possible.

While for many, Ellison is a spokesman of the black experience in the postwar years, for others a younger, more prolific writer, James Baldwin, fills that position.[76] Raised in Harlem, he was the product of a northern city; in the fifties he lived abroad. Thus Baldwin had no firsthand experience in the South until after his return from Europe when, during the Civil Rights Movement, he made a tour of the southern states.[77] Until that time his knowledge of southern dialects, black as well as white, was limited to what he had observed and heard in a northern city. His first novel, *Go Tell It on the Mountain* (1953), is the story of a fourteen-year-old boy's religious experience.[78] In the novel the cast of characters is much less diverse than Ellison's in *Invisible Man.* Because in Baldwin's novel the main characters are either related to someone in the protagonist's family or are members of their church in Harlem, one would not expect their dialect speech to be particularly varied. And it is not. Although the older people in the novel migrated to Harlem from the South while the children were born in Harlem, these differences are not manifest in Baldwin's recording of dialect. Instead of experimenting with the varieties of Black English as Ellison had done, Baldwin has simplified his representation of the single dialect that all of his characters speak. The dialect he records is one sharply affected by religious rhetoric. Baldwin tends to minimize pronunciation and grammatical features and to emphasize repetitive syntactic and rhythmic patterns.

In the following passage, Roy (the half-brother of the protagonist, John Grimes, and favorite son of his father, Gabriel Grimes) speaks with bitter irony about his father to his mother:

> "Yeah," said Roy, "we don't know how lucky we *is* to have a father what don't want you to go to movies, and don't want you to play in the streets, and don't want you to have no friends, and he don't want this and he don't want that, and he don't want you to do *nothing*. We so *lucky* to have a father who just wants us to go to church and read the Bible and beller like a fool in front of the altar and stay home all nice and quiet, like a little mouse. Boy, we sure is lucky, all right. Don't know what I done to be so lucky."[79]

Except for the addition of final *r* in *beller,* the passage contains no significant pronunciation features, and the syntactic features are limited. The dominant grammatical features are the regularization of third person singular present tense: *what don't* and *he don't;* lack of subject-verb agreement in *we is;* double negative: *don't want you to have no friends; he don't want you to do nothing;* substitution of the past participle for the past tense in *I done;* and substitution of *what* for the relative pronoun *who.* But more significant than Roy's grammar is the fact that by parodying the highly patterned rhetoric of his preacher-father, Roy ridicules him.

First there is repetition of the key words, *lucky* and *don't want,* which to a large extent convey the sense of irony in the passage. But Roy also uses a series of parallel syntactic patterns. In the first sentence, for instance, the seven occurrences of *don't* at the beginnings of clauses emphasize the inhibiting, restrictive atmosphere that Roy describes. As Roy continues to describe his father, he parodies his father's pulpit rhetoric; he links together four clauses, each connected by *and:*

> We so *lucky* to have a father who wants us to go to church, and read the Bible and beller like a fool in front of the altar and stay home all nice and quiet, like a little mouse.

Baldwin's representation of Roy's speech, however, is characterized not only by the repetition of syntactic patterns, but also by rhythmic emphasis. The passage is metrically patterned—spondaic *dón't wánt* recurs, punctuated by dactyls and anapests.

```
dón't wánt / yŏu tŏ gó    / tŏ móviĕš      / aňd
dón't wánt / yŏu tŏ pláy / iň tĥe stŕeets   / aňd
dón't wánt / yŏu tŏ háve / nŏ friénds aňd / hĕ
dón't wánt / thĭs aňd hĕ
dón't wánt / tháт ˣ ˣ
```

Baldwin's later representations of Black English are also often marked by repetitions and rhythmical characteristics. At one point in the novel, Gabriel, Roy's father, recalls the events of his past, including a sermon that he, a preacher who has lived "sinfully," delivered. The passage illustrates how well Roy, in the first passage, was able to parody the characteristics of an actual sermon.

> "For let us remember that the wages of sin is death; that it is written, and cannot fail, the soul that sinneth, it shall die. Let us remember that we are born in sin, in sin did our mothers conceive us—sin reigns in all our members, sin is the foul heart's natural liquid, sin looks out of the eye, amen, and leads to lust, sin is in the hearing of the ear, and leads to folly; sin sits on the tongue, and leads to murder. Yes! Sin is the only heritage of the natural man, sin bequeathed us by our natural father, that fallen Adam, whose apple sickens and will sicken all generations living, and generations yet unborn! It was sin that drove the son of the morning out of Heaven, sin that drove Adam out of Eden, sin that caused Cain to slay his brother, sin that built the tower of Babel, sin that caused the fire to fall on Sodom—sin, from the very foundations of the world, living and breathing in the heart of man, that causes women to bring forth their children in agony and darkness, bows down the backs of men with terrible labor, keeps the empty belly empty, keeps the table bare, sends our children, dressed in rags, out into the whore-houses and dance halls of the world!"[80]

There are no Black English pronunciation or grammatical features represented here. However, because of the syntactic patterning and rhythm, the passage seems dialectal. The subject of the sermon is sin, and as if to keep the audience clearly focused on the subject, the word is repeated—sixteen times in the above paragraph.[81] The effect is of a bell regularly tolling out the message and accentuating Gabriel's hypocrisy. But, as in the example of Roy's speech, not only are single words repeated, but whole clauses. In the last part of the second sentence, for instance, five successive clauses begin with *sin;* the first two are "simple" statements having a single subject and verb. In the last three, the verbs are compounded—and linked together by *and*. The three final balanced statements help the preacher to build toward an emotional crescendo:

> sin reigns in all our members, sin is the foul heart's natural liquid, sin looks out of the eye, amen, and leads to lust, sin is in the hearing of the ear, and leads to folly, sin sits on the tongue, and leads to murder.

In the final, exceedingly long sentence of the paragraph, there is a similar syntactically and lexically repetitive pattern,

> It was sin that drove the son of the morning out of Heaven, sin that drove Adam out of Eden, sin that caused Cain to slay his brother, sin that built the tower of Babel, sin that caused the fire to fall on Sodom— sin, from the very foundations of the world, living and breathing in the heart of man, that causes women to bring forth their children in agony and darkness, bows down the backs of men with terrible labor, keeps the empty belly empty, keeps the table bare, sends our children, dressed in rags, out into the whore-houses and dance halls of the world!

As in Roy's speech, clearly defined accents—generally a combination of iambic and dactyllic rhythms—accentuated by occasional alliteration emphasize the message.

In the third passage, which is an excerpt from the narrator-protagonist's third person internal monologue just before he is "saved," the same repetition of words, of syntactic patterns, and of rhythms is clearly evident.

> They wandered in the valley forever; and they smote the rock, forever; and the waters sprang, perpetually, in the perpetual desert. They cried unto the Lord forever, and lifted up their eyes forever, they were cast down forever, and He lifted them up forever, No, the fire could not hurt them, and yes, the lion's jaws were stopped; the serpent was not their master, the grave was not their resting-place, the earth was not their home. Job bore them witness, and Abraham was their father, Moses had elected to suffer with them rather than glory in sin for a season.[82]

Thus Baldwin, with a frequency that must be seen as significant, seems in his representation of Black English dialect often to be engaged in ironic parody, a parody through rhythmical representations of the hypocritical piety of the black pulpit. One is reminded of Ralph Ellison's Homer Barbee, and, before him, of Herman Melville.

To some extent, the literary sophistication of Ralph Ellison and the benignly retrospective realism of James Baldwin seemed to be directed at a white rather than a black audience. During the 1960s, however, certainly years of open struggle and sometimes of near revolutionary violence in the history of American race relations, years marked not only by the enactment of Civil Rights legislation but also by the violent deaths of Malcolm X and Martin Luther King and by rioting in major American cities from Watts to Washington, there surfaced a writer whose periodically changing views are regarded by some as a barometer of black American thought of the last twenty years.

Described as the "symbolic heir to Malcolm,"[83] Amiri Baraka, who followed many blacks in replacing his "white" name by an African one, has, according to his most recent biographer, Werner Sollors, passed through four major phases—aesthetic protest (1958–1961); political/ethnic protest (1960–1965); Black Cultural Nationalism (1964–1974); and Marxist-Leninist-Maoism (1974–)[84]—in his development as political activist and writer, two roles that, to Baraka, are indistinguishable.

In *Tales* (1967), Baraka's most recent prose fiction, the tension between the conflicting claims of "white" literary standards and black "separatism" is clearly evident.[85] *Tales* contains sixteen short pieces, linked together by theme, characters, and language. Theodore Hudson, who regards *Tales* as a novel rather than a collection of short stories, particularly admires its use of language; as he says, "One may read *Tales* just to see what it is possible to do with language."[86]

The early *Tales* concern the narrator-protagonist as child and youth, isolated, alienated, and out of place among whites and middle-class blacks committed to "white" modes of expression. In "The Screamers," a later story about a jazz saxophonist, Lynn Hope, who plays at a dance in Newark and leads his followers from the dance hall into the street and back, Baraka contrasts the sense of cohesion and unity among the black marchers with the chaos and racial violence that results at the end of the story when the police provoke violence.

Baraka, a historian of jazz and a poet, is acutely sensitive to aural values of language. In "The Screamers" he describes the effect of the music on the patrons of the dance hall as they eagerly follow Hope and his side-men, who are "screaming" a single note. Baraka attempts to depict the musical and rhythmic quality of the event by his choice of words, his manipulation of sentence structure, and his typography. He first sets Hope within the scene:

> And Newark always had a bad reputation, I mean everybody could pop their fingers. Was hip. Had walks. Knew all about The Apple. So I suppose when the word got to Lynn what Big Jay had done, he knew all the little down cats were waiting to see him in this town. He knew he had to cook. And he blasted all night, crawled and leaped, then stood at the side of the stand, and watched us while he fixed his sky, wiped his face.

Next he describes the reaction of his audience to the music.

> "Okay, baby," we all thought, "Go for yourself." I was standing at the back of the hall with one arm behind my back, so the overcoat could hang over in that casual gesture of fashion. Lynn was moving, and the camel walkers were moving in the corner. The fast dancers and practic-ers making the whole hall dangerous. "Off my suedes, motherfucker."

And then Hope and his audience are melded into perfect complements of one another—both mesmerized by the "scream" of the trumpet.

> And he screamed it so the veins in his face stood out like neon. "Uhh, yeh, Uhh, yeh, Uhh, yeh," we all screamed to push him further. . . . And we strutted back and forth pumping our arms, repeating with Lynn Hope, "Yeh, Uhh, Yeh, Uhh."

Finally, Hope leads the musicians and the audience out into the street, where the music binds together the musicians and the community.

> Five or six hundred hopped-up woogies tumbled out into Belmont Avenue. Lynn marched right in the center of the street. Sunday night traffic stopped, and honked. Big Red yelled at a bus driver, "Hey, baby, honk that horn in time or shut if off!" The bus driver cooled it. We screamed and screamed at the clear image of ourselves as we should always be.[87]

Werner Sollors denies that the language of "The Screamers" can be described as Black English "since Baraka was far more concerned with fusing the impulse of Black music and the ethnic milieu with the prose language of *The Moderns*,[88] with merging Beat writing and Rhythm & Blues, and with combining the theme of violent struggle against oppression and the literary model of dadaism."[89] Perhaps, however, the "impulse of Black music" of which Sollors speaks is a characteristic of Black English frequently represented in and central to Baraka's style here. Although other influences on Baraka's style can be isolated, its essential reflection of black culture seems intentionally dominant.

As Sollors admits, the diction and vocabulary of "The Screamers" are clearly "black," as in the colloquial asides—" 'Okay, baby,' we all thought, 'Go for yourself,' " and " 'Hey, baby, honk that horn in time or shut it off!' " or " 'Off my suedes, motherfucker,' " and in the slang words—"cook" and "sky" and "down cats" and "woogies." But the rhythm of the sentences and nonsentences—usually subjectless statements such as "Was hip. Had walks. Knew all about The Apple"—can also be regarded as efforts of "black" expression. After all, the audience in the story is responding to black music, and Baraka has not lost an opportunity to try to suggest the rhythm of that music in his prose. " 'Uhh, yeh, Uhh, yeh,' " is a strongly rhythmic utterance, as is " 'Yeh, Uhh, Yeh, Uhh.' " There is a strong metric beat to the passage as a whole.

"The Screamers" is a politically committed story, a kind of "Socialist Realism" to the Marxist critic. Here Baraka dramatizes the narrative engagement in a communal experience, an experience that, although taking the form of a militancy (a march), is essentially rhythmic and aesthetic in its quality. To represent that engagement, Baraka's narrator employs an idiomatic and intensely rhythmic language, a language that is certainly intended by Baraka to be perceived as "black."

At other points in *Tales,* Baraka undertakes to represent pure, nonsyntactic sound, the sound of jazz or of "black" music. In "Answers in Progress," the final story in *Tales* (which concerns "blue people" from outer space who have come to earth to obtain Art Blakey records), the following passage occurs:

> I talked with Pinball and the blue leader about Ben Caldwell's paintings . . . the one where the guy is smoking the reefer. We thought about the changing reference, of our new world. As it stood already in the old ruins. And we all felt like Bird. The old altosaxophonist . . . but the limits opened out into the pure lyric tone of powerful beings. But when the Sun-Ra tape came on this blue dude really opened up. He dug the hell out of it. Perfect harmony these cats had too. Boooooo-Iiiiiiiiiooooooooooooooo . . . daaaaa ahhhhhhhh aaaaahhhhhh . . . booooo OOOOOOOOOOOOOO ooooooooooaaaaaaaaaooooaaaaa.[90]

Baraka's representation of black speech and music and his use of "black" language as a narrative medium set into motion an experimental phase in the representation of Black English dialect in black American fiction. Committed to writing for a black rather than a white audience, Baraka, the poet, the blues and jazz critic, the political activist, refuses to be bound by the rules of "white" literature and language. Instead, he expresses himself (or his narrators express themselves) in a normative but distinctive black speech. Black speech is now no longer to be conceived as a dialect but rather as the natural medium of a varied and versatile and imaginative literary style. Baraka is experimenting with a new "aesthetic," a "black aesthetic"—a medium for black literary expression that for black writers is to replace the more traditional "white" language and thus is to offer new and exciting possibilities of literary expression.

With this experimental and radically revolutionary commitment, Baraka undertook literary work in a number of literary genres—in poetry, and the drama as well. He organized the Black Arts Theatre Movement in Harlem in 1964 and, when this failed, he founded a black community theater in Newark. Thus Baraka was at the vanguard of what he likes to regard as "revolutionary" black art during the late 1960s and early 1970s. Out of this movement, which came to be known as the Black Arts Movement, was developed a "Black Aesthetic," a set of values that have been described in a variety of ways but are usually linked with the assertion of black nationalism and envision the creation of a black art directed at a black audience. Writing in 1968, Larry Neal defined the movement as a more successful Harlem Renaissance.

> The Black Arts Movement represents the flowering of a cultural nationalism that has been suppressed since the 1920's. I mean the "Harlem Renaissance"—which was essentially a failure. It did not address itself to the mythology and the life-styles of the Black community. It

failed to take roots, to link itself concretely to the struggles of that community, to become its voice and spirit. Implicit in the Black Arts Movement is the idea that Black people, however dispersed, constitute a *nation* within the belly of white America.[91]

Another Black Arts advocate, Addison Gayle, Jr., writing in 1970, asserted the necessity for the black writer to assume a black nationalist point of view.

> The black writer at the present time must forgo the assimilationist tradition and redirect his art to the strivings within the race—those strivings that have become so pronounced, here, in the latter half of the twentieth century. To do so, he must write for and speak to the majority of black people; not to a sophisticated elite fashioned out of the programmed computers of America's largest universities.[92]

Gayle concluded his discussion by quoting the poet Don L. Lee:

> "Black art will elevate and enlighten our people and lead them towards an awareness of self, i.e., their blackness. It will show them mirrors. Beautiful symbols. And will aid in the destruction of anything nasty and detrimental to our advancement as a people."[93]

Renewed respect, appreciation, and pride in the distinctiveness of oral black expression were some of the more creative results of the Black Arts Movement. Although there was a certain arbitrary quality in the characteristics of black speech that Black Arts writers chose to reproduce in their fiction, there was in general a departure from traditional modes of dialect representation and an exhilaration in the experimental modes that Baraka had been instrumental in initiating.

Baraka's experimentation was to lead him away from the purely expressive to a didactic and even polemic art—away from fiction and to drama—to see an art in the service of a politics of black separatism. Yet other black artists remained seriously committed to the problems that the effort for a distinctive black literary expression—in the language and modes of a dominant and nonblack culture—were to pose. One of the more seriously creative and stylistically innovative of the Black Arts-influenced writers is Ishmael Reed. Reed defines his role as a writer independent of the Western literary tradition. For Reed,

> the Afro-American artist is similar to the Necromancer (a word whose etymology is revealing in itself!). He is a conjuror who works JuJu upon his oppressors; a witch doctor who frees his fellow victims from the psychic attack launched by demons of the outer and inner world.[94]

The writer, according to Reed, practices hoodoo; as necromancer, he works a spell on his reader; among other things, he "write[s] about a time like the present or use[s] the past to prohesy about the future."[95]

Reading Reed is somewhat analogous to switching a T.V. set from channel to channel; the characters and situations change abruptly and without warning; plot line is often interrupted. Chronological sequentiality is distorted; historical figures are recalled from the dead to attend parties and to answer questions. The prose often has a psalmic quality, whereby statement is reuttered. This technique is part of what Reed calls "necromancy."

Reed's "necromancy" consists in his awareness of his own role as the negotiator of two systems of reality, that apprehended and uttered by the black consciousness and that apprehended and uttered by the white. The two consciousnesses do not converge, and Reed's ironic awareness is generated out of their divergence. For Ishmael Reed as narrator stands apart from both consciousnesses, often recording reality—event or description—in the language of first one then the other consciousness, in Standard and then Black English. In one of his early novels, *The Free-Lance Pallbearers,* Reed's narrator, Bukka Doopeyduk, does not usually speak Black English, but he does use it to articulate *sotto voce* evaluations in internalized asides. At one point, while he is waiting his turn to apply for an apartment in a housing project, he first describes the interviewer, then comments on him—in *sotto voce* Black English, phonetically represented.

> They were interviewed by a roly-poly man in 90 per cent rayon Sears and Roebuck pants, mod tie and nineteen-cent ball-point pen sticking from the pocket of his short-sleeve shirt, and hush puppy shoes. (No shit. Da kat must have been pushing forty and he wore hush puppy shoes and a polka-dot mod tie. Why da man looked ridiculous!)[96]

Reed's use of eye dialect in *kat* and *d* for *th* in *da* are indeed phonetic representations of Black English, but they occur in an alternate description, here contained in parentheses. It is as though there is not one text here but two, one directed at white (Standard English) readers, the other at a black (Black English) audience. And this doubling of text generates an intertextuality in which is to be found meaning.

But it is not only language that is divergent here. For the items recorded for white consumption by the narrator—and thus the presumed matter of white consciousness—are the products and indicators of white culture: ball-point pens, Sears and Roebuck, rayon, percentages, and money ("nineteen-cent"). Yet those indicators recorded for the black audience are different: human age ("pushing forty") and emotional value ("ridiculous"). It is in the contrast of choice that one finds meaning. Reed's "necromancy" here consists in the juxtaposition of culturally induced awareness out of which is generated a distancing and ironic awareness for both audiences—black and white.

Reed also uses phonetic spelling—the substitution of *d* for *th* and other indicators, even eye-dialect, in his representation of working-class *white* New York dialect in the passage that immediately follows Doopeyduk's ironic observation. This is an excerpt from a phone-in radio program, which the narrator overhears while he is waiting to be interviewed:

> Typical: "Hello Frank? Dis Frank? Been trying to get ya ever since you come on da air. Geez kids, it's Frank. Come and say hello to ya Uncle Frank. Hiya Frank. We sure like to hear toy talk out here in Queens and Brooklyn, which brings me to the point about what I wrung ya up. You see we tink dey got too much already, running around in da streets like monkies. Why can't dey behave demselves like da res of us 'mericans. And as far as bussing wit um goes—we don't tink it'ul 'mount to much for da very simple reason dat we don't tink it's too good. Dey should help demselves like we did when we come over on da manure dumps. Take my ol man for an instant. Worked hisself up and now he is a Screw. Killed fourteen hoods last week what was comin' at um wit a knife. And my son jess shipped overseas to put down dem Yam riots what's gettin' ready to break loose. As you can see we are all doin' our part. Why can't *dey?*"[97]

Thus he turns the tables on the white dialect writers who have used phonetic spellings to denigrate Black English-speaking characters. In Reed's dialect representation, in neo-hoodoo necromancy, all speech is created equal, at least in its potential as text.

Later, in the same novel, after Bukka Doopeyduk marries Fannie May, he comes home one night, opens the door of the refrigerator, and complains about the filth. Fannie May reacts with fury:

> "MOTHAFUKAAAAAAAAAAAAAAA. What do you think I am, some kind of bowlegged pack animal who's gone empty your slops dat you can keek and give orders to? If you want somebody to clean dis place, why don't you get somebody to come in and do daywork." She waved her hands and screeched like the real scourge of a scrounge she was.[98]

The initial burst of highly phoneticized Black English that opens this passage is used by Reed solely to represent Fannie May's emotional state. But the words—even the radically phoneticized and capitalized metaphor with which Fannie May's outburst opens—are not words in the symbolic sense. They are not conventionally textual; they are representations of expressive sound, or, if you will, of dialectal "black" music.

Loudness and stress, suggested by the capital letters, and the resounding sound of the word suggested by the lengthening of the final vowel, communicate Fannie May's uncontrolled anger. In addition to the radical syntactic distortion, there are a few dialectal features in the remainder of Fannie May's response, primarily a substitution of *d* for *th* and a lengthening of the vowel in *keek*—features that are used with satiric intent to detextualize her utterance and to satirize Fannie May and the marital relationship. The narrator's comment in the last sentence of the passage, marked by alliteration of *sc* and a near-rhyme in *scourge-scrounge* is a rhythmic aside which is again a *sotto voce* evaluation.

   Mumbo Jumbo (1972), Reed's third novel, takes his awarenesses a step
farther. Here he explicitly recognizes the nontextual, or oral quality of black
consciousness and simultaneously enacts a search for the text that will em-
body it as art. Neil Schmitz proceeds from a similar assumption when, in his
consideration of *Mumbo Jumbo,* he says,

> The recitative as a narrative form [is] . . . a composite narrative contain-
> ing a variety of texts, the most important of which (the sacred text—the
> Book of Thoth) is never revealed. Indeed that is Reed's thesis in
> *Mumbo Jumbo. "So Jes Grew is seeking its words. Its text. For what
> good is a liturgy without a text?"* Jes Grew is the Osirian/Dionysian
> phenomenon of the Dance recurring in New Orleans around the 1890s.
> Reed takes the term from James Weldon Johnson's *The Book of Ameri-
> can Negro Poetry.* "The earliest Ragtime songs," Johnson wrote, "like
> Topsy, 'jes grew' " (*MJ,* p. 11). In his narrative Reed concentrates on
> the Harlem Renaissance of the twenties (Langston Hughes, Countee
> Cullen, et al), the first significant adaptation of the idiomatic energies
> present in Jes Grew by Black artists in the United States, and his fiction,
> except for the epilogue, is set in that period.[99]

   In *Mumbo Jumbo* a more idiosyncratic use of black speech is evident than in
Pallbearers. In the passage that follows, Papa LaBas, the high priest of
Mumbo Jumbo Kathedral and originator of HooDoo psychiatry, lectures to
a group of students on the origins of "Jes Grew."

> "It belonged to nobody," [James Weldon] Johnson said. "Its words
> were unprintable but its tune irresistible." Jes Grew, the Something or
> Other that led Charlie Parker to scale the Everests of the Chord. Riff fly
> skid dip soar and gave his Alto Godspeed. Jes Grew that touched John
> Coltrane's Tenor; that tinged the voice of Otis Redding and compelled
> Black Herman to write a dictionary to Dreams that Freud would have
> envied. Jes Grew was the manic in the artist who would rather do
> glossolalia than be "neat clean or lucid." Jes Grew, the despised enemy
> of the Atonist Path, those Left-Handed practitioners of the Petro Loa,
> those too taut to spring from sharp edges, wiggle jiggle go all the way
> down and come up shaking. Jes Grew is the lost liturgy seeking its
> litany.[100]

The passage, which can hardly be characterized as dialectal, is filled with
elaborate rhetorical and poetic devices—pun and metaphor: *scale the Ever-
ests of the Chord;* reduplications: *wiggle jiggle;* alliteration: *that touched
John Coltrane's tenor; that tinged; lost liturgy seeking its litany;* and *diction-
ary to Dreams;* and an almost palpable periodicity. These devices, and the
passage's sharply aural and rhythmic quality, give it an incantatory effect; a
spell seems to be being cast on the students, especially when we are told that
Papa LaBas cannot end his lecture and that no one interrupts him. The

incantation here—and it is only this intensely aural and incantatory quality that suggests it as Black English—seems to cast a necromancer's spell.

One is reminded of the peculiarly incantatory quality of Mollie Beauchamp's chant in "Go Down, Moses." Mollie seems to achieve an alleviation of grief through incantation of language, through its utterance as expressive music more than as a means of symbolic communication. But Ishmael Reed's awareness of the expressive and the incantatory in the speech of the black has set him on another course. Reed would seek the "lost text" for this incantation, which would make it possible for the black writer to undertake to establish that incantation as a means of conjuring a reader, and to "elevate" mystique to the timelessness of "art." Reed's own "art" here is a prose that demands to be read aloud; yet it is prose and is textually rendered. Thus rendered, it seems to offer itself as a text for a Black English to conjure with. For Schmitz this raises another problem.

Schmitz points out that Jes Grew's mystique is closely to be identified with the "mystique of the oral tradition [which] is compelling—particularly for Black writers" and that it will be lost precisely at the moment when a text is found.[101] Papa LaBas's relation of the history of Neo-HooDoo art is an assertion of the primacy of text, and it is precisely this textualization that will destroy mystique.

Ishmael Reed's exploration of the expressive potential in the representation of black speech has thus brought him to questions concerning the very dimensions of symbolic communication and of language written and spoken. He has also moved beyond the traditional literary notion of language as a communicative and symbolic medium, the fundamental convention of Western fiction, to consider alternative possibilities and paradoxes, at least for the black writer. For Reed black literary expression in English, even as it seeks its text, must mirror the incantatory and the magical intention implicit in the act of utterance in black culture.

Amiri Baraka, who has since rejected prose fiction as a political tool and therefore as a medium of artistic expression, and Ishmael Reed represent two directions in which experimentation with black speech to achieve a distinctive "black expression" has moved in recent years. But other writers—Ernest J. Gaines, Alice Walker, and Toni Morrison are distinguished examples—continue in their fiction to represent black speech more traditionally. They are the heirs of the main lines of development of that tradition. They have reduced the pronunciation features and rely on grammatical and lexical, rhythmical and poetic features to carry the burden of rendering black dialectal speech. It is perhaps this line of development, the tradition of dialectal simplification, that offers the greatest flexibility for future writers who wish to represent Black English dialect in the traditional novel. As Toni Morrison, in speaking of dialect writing, said in a lecture at American University in the Spring of 1979, "The action and passion of a language is never in its spelling."

In the two hundred years in which American fiction has been written, and in which the speech of black Americans has been represented in it, the conventions of representing that speech have undergone many changes. Some characteristics of Black English dialect came to be acceptable for representation; others developed unwanted connotations. And the very act of the representation of Black English speech was seen by some to be a part of a hidden agenda. In certain periods, any effort to represent the distinctiveness of the speech of black Americans was criticized by black cultural leaders. In recent years, however, as blacks have gained a positive image of themselves, their culture, and their mode of expression, black writers have been able to use Black English in strikingly original ways, which sometimes penetrate to the very foundation of cultural assumptions concerning speech utterance. Contemporary black writers are now using dialect with pride, for they recognize that representation of Black English speech is central to an expression of their identity. Although recent white writers, perhaps intimidated by Styron's experience with Nat Turner, have not often used Black English dialect when they represented the speech of black characters, it is possible that when the really distinguishing characteristics of black utterance are identified and are fully accepted as a proper subject for literary representation, white as well as black writers will again confront the problems implicit in its representation. What is clear is that dialect has now become respectable—at least for black writers. With such acceptability almost anything is possible. As Fats Waller so aptly put it, "One never knows, do one?"

NOTES

1. Richard Kluger, *Simple Justice* (New York: Vintage Books, 1975), p. 218.
2. C. Vann Woodward, *The Strange Career of Jim Crow*, 2d rev. ed. (New York: Oxford University Press, 1966), p. 128.
3. Kluger, *Simple Justice*, p. 227.
4. Woodward, *The Strange Career of Jim Crow*, p. 188.
5. Ibid., p. 191.
6. See Harold Cruse, *The Crisis of the Negro Intellectual* (New York: William Morrow, 1967) and Alphonso Pinkney, *Red, Black, and Green: Black Nationalism in the United States* (Cambridge: Cambridge University Press, 1976).
7. Eudora Welty, "Place in Fiction," *The Eye of the Story* (New York: Random House, 1977), p. 132.
8. Ibid., p. 118.
9. Ibid., p. 121.
10. Katherine Anne Porter, Introduction to Eudora Welty, *A Curtain of Green* (Garden City, N.Y.: Doubleday, Doran, 1941), pp. xvii–xviii.
11. Eudora Welty, "A Worn Path," *A Curtain of Green*, pp. 282–84.
12. Cleanth Brooks, R. W. B. Lewis, Robert Penn Warren, *American Literature: The Makers and the Making,* (New York: St. Martin's Press, 1973), 2: 2559.
13. Edmond L. Volpe, *A Reader's Guide to William Faulkner* (London: Thames and Hudson, 1964), p. 232. In an interesting examination of Faulkner's revisions, Joanne Creighton

argues that in *Go Down, Moses* Faulkner was struggling toward a new form, a form that she calls the "short story composite." See Joanne V. Creighton, *William Faulkner's Craft of Fiction* (Detroit: Wayne State University Press, 1977).

14. One other black man speaks in the story; he brings a piece of red ribbon from Miss Sophonsiba's neck to Uncle Buck:

"She just sont hit to you," the nigger said. "She say to tell you 'success.' "
"She said what?" Uncle Buck said.
"I dont know, sir," the nigger said. "She just say 'success.' "

William Faulkner, "Was," *Go Down, Moses* (New York: The Modern Library, 1942), p. 16.

15. Perhaps he contributes most significantly to the plot and to the determination of his own future when he silently deals the cards in the game of poker and, without uttering a word, fixes the game so that he and his girl, Tennie, can live together at Uncle Buddy's.

16. Faulkner, "Was," *Go Down, Moses*, p. 13.

17. Faulkner, "The Fire and the Hearth," *Go Down, Moses*, p. 97.

18. Ibid., pp. 67–68.

19. In this connection one remembers Huck's curiously ambiguous, dialectal double negative in *Huckleberry Finn:* " 'I was stealing a poor old woman's nigger that hadn't ever done me no harm. . . .' " Samuel Langhorne Clemens, *Adventures of Huckleberry Finn*, 2d ed., ed. Sculley Bradley, Richmond Croom Beatty, E. Hudson Long, and Thomas Cooley (New York: W. W. Norton, 1977), p. 168.

20. Faulkner, "The Fire and the Hearth," *Go Down, Moses*, pp. 101–2.

21. Ibid., p. 111.

22. Faulkner, "Pantaloon in Black," *Go Down, Moses*, p. 136.

23. Ibid., p. 139.

24. Faulkner, "The Bear," *Go Down, Moses*, p. 215. For a full discussion of Sam Fathers's racial origins and their influence on his life, see Lewis M. Dabney, *The Indians of Yoknapatawpha* (Baton Rouge: Louisiana State University Press, 1974).

25. Faulkner, "The Old People," *Go Down, Moses*, p. 172.

26. Faulkner, "The Bear," *Go Down, Moses*, p. 198.

27. Ibid., p. 229.

28. Fonsiba's name is, of course, an important reference again to "Was"; Ike's mother is named Sophonsiba. It is interesting to note (and certainly a subject for later study) that in *Go Down, Moses*, the possessory presumption of the male whites extends to women as well as to blacks.

29. Faulkner, "Delta Autumn," *Go Down, Moses*, p. 360.

30. Ibid., p. 361.

31. Ibid., p. 363.

32. When Mollie appears in "The Fire and the Hearth," her name is spelled "Molly."

33. Like Rider in "Pantaloon in Black," and like Bigger Thomas as well, "Butch" has apparently expressed himself not in words but in violent actions, and his fate is similar to that of Rider and of Bigger.

34. Faulkner, "Go Down, Moses," *Go Down, Moses*, p. 371.

35. Ibid., p. 380.

36. Ibid., p. 381.

37. After Issac McCaslin's failed and inarticulate prophecy, *"Not now!"* in "Delta Autumn," only one child born to the blacks and whites (Pharaoh's descendant as well as the Jews') is offered; the child in the arms of the black woman in "Delta Autumn" (who, like his mother and Fonsiba's husband, remains unnamed) could be the "Moses" of the title and of Mollie's allusion.

38. Faulkner, "Go Down, Moses," *Go Down, Moses*, p. 383.

39. Ibid.

40. Interestingly enough, Styron's next and latest novel, *Sophie's Choice*, avoids depicting black characters entirely.

41. George Plimpton, "A Shared Ordeal: Interview with William Styron," in *William Styron's "The Confessions of Nat Turner,"* ed. Melvin J. Friedman and Irving Malin (Belmont, Calif.: Wadsworth, 1970), p. 37.

42. Ibid.

43. William Styron, *The Confessions of Nat Turner* (New York: Random House, 1967), p. 377.

44. John A. Williams, "The Manipulation of History and Fact: An Ex-Southerner's Apologist Tract for Slavery and the Life of Nat Turner," in *William Styron's Nat Turner: Ten Black Writers Respond,* ed. John Henrik Clarke (Boston: Beacon Press, 1968), pp. 48–49.

45. Styron, *The Confessions of Nat Turner,* p. 378.

46. John Oliver Killens, "The Confessions of Willie Styron," *William Styron's Nat Turner: Ten Black Writers Respond,* pp. 43–44.

47. Styron, *The Confessions of Nat Turner,* p. 421.

48. For further discussion of this problem in the work of other writers, see chapter 6.

49. Leonard Feather, *The Book of Jazz* (New York: Horizon Press, 1965), p. 45.

50. LeRoi Jones (Amiri Baraka), *Blues People* (New York: William Morrow, 1963), p. 17.

51. Ibid., p. 25.

52. Robert A. Bone, *The Negro Novel in America* (New Haven, Conn.: Yale University Press, 1958), pp. 198–203.

53. Ralph Ellison, *Invisible Man* (New York: The Modern Library, 1952), p. 439.

54. John Hersey, "Introduction: 'A Completion of Personality,' " *Ralph Ellison,* ed. John Hersey (Englewood Cliffs, N.J.: Prentice-Hall, 1974), p. 11.

55. Robert A. Bone, *The Negro Novel in America,* p. 200.

56. Larry Neal, "Ellison's Zoot Suit," in Hersey, *Ralph Ellison,* p. 71.

57. Ibid.

58. Hersey, Introduction, *Ralph Ellison,* p. 11.

59. Ralph Ellison, "Brave Words for a Startling Occasion," *Shadow and Act* (New York: Random House, 1964), pp. 103–4.

60. Ellison, *Invisible Man,* pp. 19–20.

61. Ibid., p. 42.

62. Ibid., p. 92.

63. Ibid., pp. 106–7.

64. Ibid., p. 133.

65. Ibid., p. 134.

66. Ibid., p. 156.

67. Ibid., p. 164.

68. Ibid., p. 191.

69. Ibid., p. 201.

70. Ibid., p. 242.

71. Ibid., p. 286.

72. Ibid., p. 305.

73. Ibid., p. 333.

74. Ibid., pp. 343–44.

75. Ibid., p. 503.

76. There are, of course, many blacks, particularly those who consider themselves Black Nationalists, who do not consider either one politically radical enough.

77. See "Nobody Knows My Name," *Nobody Knows My Name* (New York: Dell, 1961), p. 87.

78. Roger Rosenblatt, in *Black Fiction* (Cambridge, Mass.: Harvard University Press, 1974), pp. 36–54, gives a stimulating analysis of the novel.

79. James Baldwin, *Go Tell It on the Mountain* (New York: Dell, 1953), p. 24.

80. Ibid., pp. 103–4.

81. In addition, *sinneth* appears once.

82. Baldwin, *Go Tell It on the Mountain*, pp. 204–5.

83. Werner Sollors, *Amiri Baraka/LeRoi Jones: The Quest for a "Populist Modernism"* (New York: Columbia University Press, 1978), p. 1.

84. Ibid., p. 8.

85. For a discussion of this conflict, see Larry G. Coleman, "Le Roi Jones' *Tales:* Sketches of the Artist as a Young Man Moving Toward a Blacker Art," in *Imamu Amiri Baraka (LeRoi Jones)*, ed. Kimberly W. Benston (Englewood Cliffs, N.J.: Prentice-Hall, 1978), pp. 84–95.

86. Theodore R. Hudson, *From LeRoi Jones to Amiri Baraka* (Durham, N.C.: Duke University Press, 1973), p. 123.

87. LeRoi Jones (Amiri Baraka), "The Screamers," *Tales*, in *Three Books by Imamu Amiri Baraka* (New York: Grove Press, 1967), pp. 77–79.

88. An anthology of contemporary prose writers edited by Baraka and published in 1963.

89. Sollors, *Amiri Baraka/LeRoi Jones: The Quest for a "Populist Modernism,"* p. 166.

90. Jones-Baraka, "Answers in Progress," *Tales*, in *Three Books by Imamu Amiri Baraka*, p. 131.

91. Larry Neal, "The Black Arts Movement," *The Black Aesthetic*, ed. Addison Gayle, Jr. (Garden City, N.Y.: Doubleday, 1972), p. 273.

92. Addison Gayle, Jr., "The Function of Black Literature at the Present Time," *The Black Aesthetic*, p. 393.

93. Ibid., p. 394.

94. Ishmael Reed, Introduction to *19 Necromancers From Now* (Garden City, N.Y.: Doubleday, 1970), p. xvii.

95. Ishmael Reed, "The Writer as Seer: Ishmael Reed on Ishmael Reed," *Black World* 23 (June 1974): 22.

96. Ishmael Reed, *The Free-Lance Pallbearers* (Garden City, N.Y.: Doubleday, 1967), p. 7.

97. Ibid., pp. 7–8.

98. Ibid., p. 24.

99. Neil Schmitz, "Neo HooDoo: The Experimental Fiction of Ishmael Reed," *Twentieth Century Literature* 20 (April 1974): 135.

100. Ishmael Reed, *Mumbo Jumbo* (Garden City, N.Y.: Doubleday, 1972), p. 211.

101. Schmitz, "Neo HooDoo," p. 137.

6
Black English and Narrative Structure:
Some Conclusions

OVER the past two centuries the speech of American blacks has been repeatedly represented by American writers of fiction. These representations have often betrayed political and social assumptions and strategies. But fiction is not mere representation. It is a complex structure comprehending many relationships—among author, narrator, speaker, and reader. A consideration of these relationships is necessary if one is to understand fully the acts of representation of Black English in American fiction.[1]

In fiction the relationship of the author and-or his agent, the narrator, to the characters whose actions are described and whose speech is recorded is shaped in part by the extent to which that author or narrator sets down language that is to be attributed to himself as opposed to the extent to which he simply records the quoted language of others. For any author or narrator—whether he be a historian (who primarily reports past events), a journalist (who primarily reports immediately past, present, and immediately future events), a prophet (who primarily reports future events), or a fictionist (who primarily reports imagined events)—there is the possibility of linguistic declaration on a potentially infinite number of "levels." The author or narrator may simply report directly the speech of characters without intervening comment, or he may engage in a written discourse with the reader in language chosen by himself—as "teller"—and delivered without an overt *persona* or agent. Or he may employ a mediating agent—a character in a frame narrative who then reports the central story (Marlow in Joseph Conrad's fiction), a second-person narrator ("you said"—this is rare in formal fiction[2]), or even a *persona* who enters the story, an observer and-or actor who becomes an "I" narrator. With so many narrative possibilities, and with the added possibility that any narrator may directly or indirectly quote the speech, thoughts, or stream of consciousness of characters in the fiction, any fiction may be conducted in several "languages." The "language" referred to here is not only a language in the traditional sense (English,

French, Italian), but a particular variety or dialect of a given language, a particular level of diction, even a consistent "style." For most fiction there is an established "language-style" chosen by the author, who transmits the fiction directly or through the mediation of a narrating character. That established "language-style" functions as a standard to which other utterances directly quoted in the narration are compared or contrasted. Variations from that established language provoke the reader to evaluate that variant utterance and its utterer.

Of course, there are gray areas and borderline cases. There is language that is not clearly to be attributed to author, narrator, or to character; indirect reporting of speech and records of unuttered "thoughts" or "stream of consciousness" of characters are only two of myriad possibilities. And, of course, there is a whole range of relationships—from absolute agreement to absolutely ironic opposition between author and narrator. The concern here, however, is with language, and with how the choice of narrative method affects the implications of language choice in novels employing Black English.

Seymour Chatman uses the term *unmediated* fiction to refer to a fiction that "records nothing beyond the speech or verbalized thoughts of the characters."[3] In unmediated fiction there is no established language of narration, but only directly reported speech. Characters speak directly and to one another, like characters in a play.[4] In fact, the only difference in such a fiction from a play lies in its ultimately textual nature. Although this method is difficult to sustain in a long work, it can be effective in a short piece. In his "Simple" columns, which he originally wrote for the Chicago *Defender,* Langston Hughes has occasionally employed this unmediated method. In the selection that follows from "Dear Dr. Butts—," a *Defender* column collected in *Simple Takes a Wife* (1953), except for a speech ascription in the first line quoted in which Simple is identified as the first speaker, no narrator intrudes in Simple's conversation with his friend.

"Do you know what has happened to me?" said Simple.
"No."
"I'm out of a job."
"That's tough. How did that come about?"
"Laid off—they're converting again. And right now, just when I am planning to get married this spring, they have to go changing from civilian production to war contracts, installing new machinery. Manager says it might take two months, might take three or four. They'll send us mens notices. If it takes four months, that's up to June, which is no good for my plans. To get married a man needs money. To stay married he needs more money. And where am I? As usual, behind the eight-ball."[5]

The first speaker in this passage speaks a modified Black English dialect; the second speaks Standard English. This fact establishes that one speaker is black, while the racial identity of the other character is not so clear. Certainly his language defines him as more highly educated than Simple, the Black English speaker. Since there is no language established by a narrator, since all the language here is directly quoted, only the juxtaposition of two slightly different varieties of English is evident. However, since Simple speaks more than his friend, Black English in the passage is dominant.

The next passage, from Warren Miller's *The Cool World* (1959), is narrated by an "I" narrator who has established himself (whether as observer or participant) as a "character" in the fiction and who employs a dialect that conforms to that of other characters.

> They call him Priest because he always wear black. Black suits with thin tight pants. One day some body see him an they say. "Man you always in black. Like a priest. You the hep priest Man." So that how come he is call priest.
>
> Priest say to me. "Man I tellin you. You aint gonna find anything good as this for the kind of bread I askin for. You can go up an down this street a thousan times an you aint gonna find it."
>
> I say to Priest. "Man I dont have time to go up and down this street a thousan times. I in a big hurry. But shitman that aint worth no 15 dollas."
>
> Priest he laugh. He taken the piece out of the draw again. It a short-barl 45 with that crisscross lines on the butt. Priest dont flip it around like a cowboy. He cool. He hold it in his big hand like it somethin sweet an he smile at it.
>
> "It aint gonna smile back at you Man," I say. An Priest he laugh an not lookin smash a roach under his heel. He say. "Only 9 hundred and 99 thousan left in Harlem now Man. I killin em all. I leavin rats an mice to the City but I killin the roaches myself."[6]

Here both the narrator and the characters communicate in Black English; as a result there is no disparity between the established language of narration and the speech of quoted characters.

The same remains true when the "I" narrator reports his thoughts, without quotation marks and in dialect. The dialect language is ascribed to the "I" narrator and is the established language of narration. An example can be found in Ernest J. Gaines's "A Long Day in November," a story from *Bloodline* (1968). Here, the "I" narrator is a child; this fact in itself releases a certain irony, but the irony is dramatic, not verbal. After a day of adventure in which the narrator's parents have fought and then made up, the child-narrator before he falls asleep is comforted by his observation of the renewed love between his mother and father.

> I hear the spring. I hear Mama and Daddy talking low, but I don't know what they saying. I go to sleep some, but I open my eyes again. It's some dark in the room. I hear Mama and Daddy talking low. I like Mama and Daddy. . . . I hear the spring on Mama and Daddy's bed. I get 'way under the cover. I go to sleep little bit, but I wake up. I go to sleep

some more. I hear the spring on Mama and Daddy's bed. I hear it plenty now. It's some dark under here. It's warm. I feel good 'way under here.[7]

Yet the situation is changed when Standard English is intruded within the Black English dialect of the "I" narrator. In Lucille Clifton's children's story, *All Us Come Cross the Water* (1973), the "I" narrator is a schoolboy and the narration is in Black English. At one point the boy remembers and reports in quotation marks the speech of his teacher. Although the teacher is pictured as black in an illustration, she speaks a Standard English appropriate to her profession. There is a clear contrast between the two types of languages used. The language that has been established for narration here is Black English, so the teacher's directly quoted speech, although it is recognizable to the reader as the Standard English of the educated, seems, within a fictional world realized through the medium of Black English, to be somewhat artificial, or at best atypical. The teacher has defined herself to the narrator by her Standard English and the established medium of narration generates a linguistic irony that serves complexly the purposes of the author.

> I got this teacher name Miss Wills. This day she come asking everybody to tell where they people come from. Everybody from over in the same place suppose to stand up by theirselves. When it come to me I don't say nothing so she get all mad, cause that make all the other brothers not say nothing too.
> "Won't you please cooperate with us, Jim?" she say. I didn't say nothing cause my name is Ujamaa for one thing. So when the bell ring she ask me to stay a little after, so we can talk.
> "We must not be ashamed of ourselves, Jim," she say. "You are from a great heritage and you must be proud of that heritage. Now you know you are from Africa, don't you?" she say.
> I say, "Yes, mam," and walk on out the place.[8]

Yet if the "I" narrator does not narrate consistently in dialect, another kind of discordance, one that generates inconsistency within the conception of the central character, can be the disturbing result. William Styron's *The Confessions of Nat Turner,* considered in chapter 5, is the obvious example. Nat Turner, the "I" narrator of that novel, reports his own thoughts and visions in a highly rhetorical Standard English, sets forth events in a somewhat flatter Standard English, and reports in direct quotations his own speech in Black English. A character in a fiction—whether of historical or of imaginative origins—is entirely a linguistic construction, and a narrator-character thus gives the illusion of being self-created, narrationally *sui generis*. Yet if the construction is not consistently built of the same material, a curiously incongruous creation results. Nat Turner, a narrator-character who transmits in three varieties of English, seems to create three Nat Turners, not one; yet they all occupy the same imaginative space. The result is a blurred image.

It is also possible for more than one variety of dialectal English—one black, one nonblack—to occur in a fiction narrated by a first person dialect speaker. *Huckleberry Finn* is an example. Here all of the language of the book is aggressively dialectal; it contrasts sharply with the reader's expectation of the Standard English in which fiction is usually written. But since all the dialects are equally nonstandard, no discordance *among them* results. One of them, Huck's, emerges clearly as the established medium of narration, the variety of English employed consistently by the "I" narrator. Yet in a totally dialectal novel the reader comes to realize that Standard English simply has no place.

One can see from this brief and preliminary examination how rich are the possibilities and how real are the dangers when an "I" narrator employs a Black English dialect. Yet the "I" narrator was not often used by the early American dialect novelists. Only recently has there been active experimentation with this method in dialect novels, and that experimentation has been conducted for the most part by black novelists.

There is yet another possibility—that in which the author-narrator transmits directly. Some students of fictional structures have minimized the distinction between this possibility and that in which the "I" narrator is employed;[9] nevertheless, in dialect fiction the difference is a significant one. It is generally true, whether dialect is used or not, that this sort of narrator—the "teller"—tends to be more omniscient than an "I" narrator.[10] Also, whether dialect is used or not, there seems to be a greater distance between the teller and his subject than between the "I" narrator and his. The teller is not usually (except when a frame is employed) an actor in his own story; the "I" narrator seems to be assumed to be an actor in his. Thus this narrator seems to assume a "reportorial voice" as an outside commentator and interpreter who does not participate in the action.

Although the teller's assumption of his position may allow him somewhat more "objectivity" as an interpreter of what he observes than the position of an "I" narrator allows, certain problems arise in dialect fiction when he transmits in Standard English and the characters he describes are directly quoted as speaking in Black English. The established language of narration here is different from that of the directly quoted speech of Black English-speaking characters; the reader (whose communication is from the narrator) finds himself at considerable distance from the Black English-speaking characters. With an "I" narrator (especially a Black English-speaking one), who functions as a *persona* for the author, the reader's relationship to a Black English-speaking character is immediate. However, the teller intrudes between reader and character. The reader is always aware of his presence.[11]

Of course, the discrepancy between Black English dialect and the established language of narration only increases this distance. Yet there are ways in which the distance can be diminished and linguistic discrepancy minimized. Some writers, particularly in the latter years of the nineteenth century, found the frame story a satisfactory way to introduce the reader to dialect speech or narration. The "frame," transmitted by the author-narrator, usually in a variety of Standard English, frequently introduced explicitly a third person narrator who was a Black English speaker. In his collection of short stories, *The Conjure Woman,* Charles W. Chesnutt employs such a frame. In other words, a narrator, here an "I" narrator employing Standard English, incites the ex-slave, Uncle Julius, a third person narrator, to tell his story and does not again intrude until Uncle Julius has completed his dialect transmission. Thus, in the first story of the collection, "The Goophered Grapevine," the first person narrator concludes his introduction and Uncle Julius begins his story:

> We assured him that we would be glad to hear how it all happened, and he began to tell us. At first the current of his memory—or imagination—seemed somewhat sluggish; but as his embarrassment wore off, his language flowed more freely, and the story acquired perspective and coherence. As he became more and more absorbed in the narrative, his eyes assumed a dreamy expression, and he seemed to lose sight of his auditors, and to be living over again in monologue his life on the old plantation.
> "Ole Mars Dugal' McAdoo," he began, "bought dis place long many years befo' de wah, en I 'member well w'en he sot out all dis yer part er de plantation in scuppernon's. De vimes growed monst'us fas', en Mars Dugal' made a thousan' gallon er scuppernon' wine eve'y year.[12]

In *The Conjure Woman* all the stories share a common frame, a continuing narrative that reintroduces Uncle Julius in each successive story. The reader's attention is on the mediate figure of the dialect narrator, and the fact that he is the common agent for the transmission of several stories causes the reader to attend more to the fact of the transmission than to the discrepancy between Uncle Julius's dialect and the narrative standard briefly established in the frame and not reasserted within the story. Inside each frame Black English holds exclusive sway.

Perhaps the best-known example of the use of the frame technique in American dialect writing is in the stories in Joel Chandler Harris's *Uncle Remus*. After introducing Uncle Remus, the third person narrator, in the first story, Harris reintroduces him in later stories with only a fragment of a frame, a mere allusion to the earlier frame, sometimes in no more than a single Standard English sentence. Thus Harris takes care to avoid disharmonious violation of Uncle Remus's language of transmission, Black English. One of the more delightful of Harris's tales, "Miss Cow Falls a Victim to Mr. Rabbit," for instance, begins with a question by the little boy that links what has gone before with what is yet to come:

> "Uncle Remus," said the little boy, "what became of the Rabbit after he fooled the Buzzard, and got out of the hollow tree?"

Immediately after the little boy's opening question, Uncle Remus begins to narrate his story in Black English:

> "Who? Brer Rabbit? Bless yo' soul, honey, Brer Rabbit went skippin' 'long home, he did, des ez sassy ez a jay-bird at a sparrer's nes'."[13]

Although Uncle Remus's narration is occasionally punctuated by questions in Standard English from the little boy, the narrative burden is assumed by Uncle Remus, who speaks consistently in Black English.

Of course, not all writers of dialect fiction employ a frame and introduce a dialect narrator. By far the more usual situation today is that in which the author-narrator "tells" the story in his own variety of language, which is clearly established as the language of narration. In this case all language for which the author-narrator does not assume responsibility is assigned to characters and identified as their dialect speech by quotation marks. This sort of narration has been variously identified by critics; here it will be called "basic" narration. Yet in dialect fiction obvious discrepancies in the varieties of language occur when this most usual of narrative methods is employed.

In a great deal of fiction Black English is transmitted directly by a narrator who employs Standard English. It is in this situation that critical problems of linguistic disunity arise. If the majority of characters in a story are directly quoted as speaking Standard English and only one speaks in Black English, then the presence of a teller using Standard English as the language of transmission is expected and the question of linguistic unity is not at issue. Edgar Allan Poe's story "The Gold Bug" is an example. However, if all, or the majority of the characters, are Black English speakers, the presence of a teller transmitting in Standard English is quite awkward. In the following example from *Uncle Tom's Cabin* by Harriet Beecher Stowe, there is a troublesome and distancing discrepancy between the English of the teller, the standard of narration, and that of the dialect-speaking characters:

> "Lor, Pete," said Mose, triumphantly, "han't we got a buster of a breakfast!" at the same time catching at a fragment of the chicken.
>   Aunt Chloe gave him a sudden box on the ear. "Ther now! crowing over the last breakfast yer poor daddy 's gwine to have to home!"
>   "Oh, Chloe!" said Tom gently.
>   "Wal. I can't help it," said Aunt Chloe, hiding her face in her apron; "I 's so tossed about, it makes me act ugly."
>   The boys stood quite still, looking first at their father and then at their mother, while the baby, climbing up her clothes, began an imperious, commanding cry.[14]

In a more recent work, *Howard Street* (1968), by black writer Nathan Heard, there is a similar discrepancy between the language of the teller and that of the characters.

A long silence was finally broken by Franchot's embarrassed cough. "Well," he said, "maybe all that'll change once he gits some hard work in his back." He smiled at them. "Be too damn tired to do much arguin' then."

No one made any reply and he got down from the television shell. "I see you don't need no money, Lonnie. . . ."

"Naw, I'm doin' good, bro," Hip answered.

"Well, I guess I'll be goin' then. Take it easy."[15]

In both of the above examples, and indeed in any work of fiction in which the teller transmits in Standard English and a majority of the characters he quotes directly use Black English, the discrepancy between the varieties of English is disconcerting. Moreover, the establishment of Standard English by the author as the language of narration imposes upon the reader the suggestion that the narrator is an intruder in an intimate relationship between the dialect-speaking characters. Thus the reader, who perceives the situation through the intrusive teller, becomes an uncomfortable bystander, listening to an exchange to which he is not privy. The establishment of Standard English in this situation has a more detrimental effect, however. The contrast between the dialects makes an implicit evaluative statement. The dialect speakers are put on view; attention is called to their speech and the extent to which it differs from the narrative standard. The result is an inevitable diminishment of these characters.

And in this situation, the characters, because they speak differently from the teller, can be caricatured, stereotyped, and made humorous, or in the extreme, ridiculous. Thus it is often the case that in fiction in which the teller speaks in Standard English, the blacks are portrayed as simple and naive, even uneducable and foolish. Or they are presented in caricature, as in Thomas Dixon's *The Clansman* or in Margaret Mitchell's *Gone With the Wind*. In polemic fiction black characters may be portrayed sentimentally, as they are in *Uncle Tom's Cabin*. In all these examples differences between blacks and whites are emphasized, for the language established by the teller and the directly quoted speech of the black characters are deliberately set in vivid contrast. Even in *Howard Street* a certain attitude of superiority toward the dialect-speaking characters is conveyed by the teller because he records the events in Standard English and thus establishes it as the norm.

There are occasions in directly narrated dialect fiction in which a Standard English narrator presents a dialect-speaking character whose thoughts are reported—yet not directly quoted—in Standard English. Here there is the possibility of a characterological discordance similar to that identified in the "I" narrated *Confessions of Nat Turner,* with the added complication that the language in which those thoughts are transmitted is uncertainly attributed. Is the language to be taken as that of the teller, or is yet another sort of record, that of the consciousness of the character, here being transmitted? Is the character deliberately speaking in dialect as a social strategy?

Such a situation occurs in Carl Van Vechten's *Nigger Heaven,* when Anatole Longfellow, the "Creeper," whose dialect speech was discussed in chapter 4, reflects on his position in Harlem. Here, although his reflection is not attributed to him by the use of quotation marks, the language, which is Standard English rather than dialect, seems to have been generated somehow by the character rather than by the teller.

> Was there another sheik in Harlem who possessed one-tenth his attraction for the female sex? Was there another of whose muscles the brick-pressers, ordinarily quite free with their audible, unflattering comments about passers-by, were more afraid?[16]

Zora Neale Hurston seems aware of the ambiguity here described in *Their Eyes Were Watching God,* a novel directly narrated in Standard English. She there takes steps to modify the characterological discrepancy. In the novel Hurston carefully places a dialect speech within quotation marks. She omits quotation marks when she records the thoughts of Black English-speaking characters, yet she transmits those thoughts in a modified Black English.

> "Ah didn't aim tuh let on tuh yuh 'bout it, leastways not right away, but Ah ruther be shot wid tacks than fuh you tuh act wid me lak you is right now. You got me in de go-long."
> At the newel post Janie whirled around and for the space of a thought she was lit up like a transfiguration. Her next thought brought her crashing down. He's just saying anything for the time being, feeling he's got me so I'll b'lieve him. The next thought buried her under tons of cold futility. He's trading on being younger than me. Getting ready to laugh at me for an old fool. But oh, what wouldn't I give to be twelve years younger so I could b'lieve him![17]

Hurston has conditioned this transmission by another difference; unlike the "Creeper" in Van Vechten's novel, when Janie thinks here, she does so in the first person. Nevertheless, the difference between the clearly dialectal representation of Janie's quoted speech and the less dialectal transmission of her unquoted thoughts generates an uncertainty as to the attribution of the thought-language; the result, while less discordant than the Van Vechten passsage, is still somewhat disconcerting.

If, unlike both the "Creeper" and Janie, a character clearly thinks in the same Black English dialect as that in which his speech is directly quoted, the harmony resulting does a great deal to overcome the problems caused by the presence of a Standard English-speaking teller. Richard Wright, in "Big Boy Leaves Home," a short story from his collection *Uncle Tom's Children* (1940), employs this method of dialect narration with great skill.

> But shucks, nobody couldnt see im here in this hole . . . But mabbe theyd seen im when he wuz comin n had laid low n wuz now closin in on im! Praps they wuz signalin fer the others? Yeah, they wuz creepin up

on im! Mabbe he oughta git up n run . . . Oh! Mabbe tha wuz Bobo! Yeah, Bobo! He oughta clim out n see if Bobo wuz lookin fer im . . . He stiffened.[18]

Most of the events in this story occur within the imagination of the dialect-speaking character and are thus reported as thought-language, although not directly quoted. The success of Wright's characterization here is to a considerable degree the result of the fact that there is no dialectal discrepancy between directly quoted speech and thoughts indirectly reported, yet in dialect, by the narrator.

Alice Walker, in *The Third Life of Grange Copeland* (1974), records the ongoing thoughts of the wife, Mem, in Black English, as a domestic argument is in process.

> "You hear that, Woman!" Brownfield swung up and placed his feet with a stamp on the floor. "We moving exactly when and where I say we moving. Long as I'm supporting this fucking family we go where I says go." He bullied his thin wife murderously with his muddy eyes. "I may not be able to read and write but I'm still the man that wears the pants in this outfit!" He towered over her in rage, his spittle spraying her forehead.
>
> I don't have to stand here and let this nigger spit in my face, she thought more or less calmly, and for the first time very seriously. Who the hell he think he is, the President or somethin'.[19]

Here again a characterological discrepancy is avoided by maintaining dialectal consistency between a character's thoughts and contiguous, directly quoted speech. Nevertheless, a problem of uncertainty of language attribution seems to persist.

It was this uncertainty that Gertrude Stein, with a prescience really extraordinary for 1909, adroitly avoided in her "Melanctha." The story is radically experimental; its commitment is centrally to point of view, to a representation of a character by means of the transmission of her consciousness as it records perceived events. The story's teller primarily records the consciousness of Melanctha as indirectly recorded thought process. Gertrude Stein here maintains linguistic consistency and a coherence of point of view and thus avoids an inconsistency in character by transmitting in a sharply modified dialect language. The transcription, as indicated in chapter 4, is original, and provokes no formulaic response. The teller, although he or she employs Standard English, establishes a level of diction and a style that do not clash with the directly quoted speech of the black characters. Thus the characters are presented intimately and sympathetically; they are distinguished, but not distanced.

> "Oh, I certainly shall go crazy now, I certainly know that," Melanctha moaned as she sat there, all fallen and miserable and weak together.

Jeff came and took her in his arms, and held her. Jeff was very good then to her, but they neither of them felt inside all right, as they once did, to be together.

From now on, Jeff had real torment in him.

Was it true what Melanctha had said that night to him? Was it true that he was the one had made all this trouble for them? Was it true, he was the only one, who always had had wrong ways in him? Waking or sleeping Jeff now always had this torment going on inside him.[20]

Although the passage contains basic narration, and although characters speak and think in Black English, there is no real discordance between an established language of narration and directly quoted dialect speech or indirectly reported thought-language. For really no language of narration is ever established. What appears here is actually quite close to unmediated transmission.

The ultimate discordance generated by the presence of Black English in American fiction concerns the attitude of the author and the reader toward the dialect. For, as Gertrude Stein's avoidance of establishing a language of narration might suggest, there seems a certain shared awareness on the part of American writers and their readers that, when all is said and done, Black English is a "subliterary" dialect, not properly a language appropriate as an established language of narration. This discordance—the sense on the part of the reader that he is reading a fiction written in two varieties of English, one "established," the other "subliterary"—is not to be overcome until the teller, ultimately the author, establishes Black English as the language of narration—in effect, until the fiction is directly narrated in Black English. Now finally—and with more insistent clarity than in an "I" narrated fiction—Black English becomes unambiguously a literary language, not only the language of narration, but also the language of the text. For the teller is always to a greater extent than the "I" narrator clearly and primarily a narrator. He is distinctively not a "character," whether as observer or as actor. He does not merely "speak" Black English; he "tells" in Black English. His linguistic act is purely a literary act.

Curiously, one of the earliest undertakings in this method of dialect narration can be found in dialect parodies of Bible stories, like those collected in Roark Bradford's *Ol' Man Adam an' His Chillun*. One of these stories, "Steamboat Days," tells the story of Noah and the flood. The story is narrated by a black man in Black English. In the story, and in all the other stories in the collection, Black English is the narrative standard. The following selection presents "de Lawd" forecasting the weather for Noah.

Well, when de people got so low down to de Lawd couldn't stand 'em, he decided to flood de yearth and drown ev'ybody 'ceptin' old man Noah. So he told Noah to build a ark and ride de flood down.

"'Cause from what I got in my mind," say de Lawd, "hit look like she's gonter be a mighty wet spring, Noah."

"Gonter bust de levees, is you, Lawd?" say Noah.

"When de levees bustes," say de Lawd, "dat's just gonter be de startin' of de wet weather. I got my mind set on rain, Noah, and when I gits my mind set, I mean to tell you I makes hit rain."

So Noah got de hammer and de saw and de nails and de lumber and things and went out on de hillside wid his boys to build de ark.[21]

Here the Black English, transcribed with extreme, almost grotesque phonetic orthography, and generating the connotations of such transcription fully, seems itself unreal, caricatured, absurd. Because of this awareness on the part of the reader and because of the unavoidable comparison to the biblical text that is implicit here, the result is diminution and ridicule. But linguistically, the fact remains that in Bradford's tales there is no disturbing dialectal discrepancy. Black English is being used here as a literary language, almost in spite of itself.

Yet, although Black English seems to be the language of basic narration here, the result is parody. Black English is the language of the text, but there is a subtext, a subtext that is absolute in its textuality, the Old Testament. And here the apparent text is detextualized by its comparison with its predecessor. Roark Bradford, the author, refusing responsibility for his teller's choice of language, nevertheless seems to hover beyond him, pointing the finger of ridicule at him.

There have been few writers of American fiction who have been willing to narrate directly and nonparodically in Black English. Few writers, black or white, have attempted to establish the dialect as the language of narration, as the language of an autonomous text, and thus to assert for the dialect a standing as a literary language. Occasionally, very self-conscious and highly intellectualized undertakings of this sort in experimental novels of the 1960s and 1970s were attempted—notably by Ishmael Reed. In the more traditional novel, attempts have been rarer still. The two novels yet to be considered represent only the earliest of tentative beginnings.

One of the most successful recent writers of dialect fiction, a writer who has used basic narration, has established Black English as the standard of narration, and has thereby carefully unified her novel, is June Jordan. Her *His Own Where* (1971) is a love story of two black teenagers. As would be expected, they speak in Black English. But so does the teller.

You be different from the dead. All them tombstones tearing up the ground, look like a little city, like a small Manhattan, not exactly. Here is not the same.

Here, you be bigger than the buildings, bigger than the little city. You be really different from the rest, the resting other ones.

Moved in his arms, she make him feel like smiling. Him, his head an Afro-bush spread free beside the stones, headstones thinning in the heavy air. Him, a ready father, public lover, privately at last alone with her, with Angela, a half an hour walk from the hallway where they start out to hold themselves together in the noisy darkness, kissing, kissed him, kissed her, kissing.

Cemetery let them lie there belly close, their shoulders now undressed down to the color of the heat they feel, in lying close, their legs a strong disturbing of the dust. His own where, own place for loving made for making love, the cemetery where nobody guard the dead.[22]

There is not much dialogue in this novel, so it is crucially important that the teller, in order to present the characters sympathetically, transmit in a dialect close to that of the directly quoted speeches of the characters. By doing this, and by thus reducing the aesthetic distance between teller and characters, June Jordan exploits the potential that Black English possesses as a literary language, as a vehicle for the communication of ideas and emotions. Now Black English as text is something more than a mere indicator that a black character is speaking or as a device of parody or caricature.

In 1979 Ellease Southerland followed June Jordan's lead. In her novel *Let the Lion Eat Straw,* she explores other possibilities with basic narration in Black English. Here, as in June Jordan's novel, the fact that the teller transmits directly in Black English establishes his community with his characters. *Let the Lion Eat Straw* opens thus:

Jackson didn't have good sense. He had all the sense he was born with, but that wasn't enough. He was a great big boy, sixteen years old and what'd he do all day? Go on up the road to the midwife's place and play just as content with the little girl there. Playing tea party. That ain't no way for a grown boy to be. Just two years ago, the little girl fix mud cakes and all. Took weeds and fixed it sos it looked like greens and laid a twig beside the dinner for a fork then called Jackson to the table to eat and that great big boy picked up the little mud cakes and bit right into them. And Abeba Williams, that's the little girl, put her hand on her hip just as she see the midwife do and said, "Jackson, you to play eat, not to eat mud sure enough." And Jackson got it straight after that.

And Jackson quick to tell people, "Me and Abeba going to get married."[23]

It is, of course, not yet possible to predict with authority whether or how Black English will become an autonomous literary language for American writers. Certainly it functions with great force when set in contrast to Standard English—as it is in Alice Walker's provocative novel, *The Color Purple* (1982, a novel published too late for consideration here). But no dialects have ever been so established in American fiction. Indeed, no dialect, not even that of the urban Jew, has been the subject of such varied and consistent experimentation over the history of the American literary undertaking. Certainly there is something unusually compelling about the dialect of the black American, something that has seemed to fascinate both black and white American writers. With the resurgence of black cultural awareness in the 1960s and 1970s there was a striking increase in experimentation. Yet, because of a tradition that assumes a standard among the varieties of American English and that identifies Black English—indeed, identifies all ethnic American English dialects—as "substandard" and therefore subliterary, there remain many problems. Those problems reenact the great American cultural ambiguity as regards freedom and nonconformity.

Even after Black English is freed from this tradition and from the shackles of its particular past, problems still remain. As yet Black English may be too syntactically rigid, too rhetorical, too dynamic, and not of sufficient lexical variety to serve as an adequate medium for the complex task of the imaginative writer. And yet it has already shown a significant and unique literary potential—a striking richness in metaphor, a reflective awareness of its own development, an incredible freshness. Its potential extends to the manipulation of literary irony, the exploration of relationships between narrators and speakers, authors and readers, and as a metaphor in itself through which to examine the meaning of black, and more generally, American, experience and culture. With such literary potential and with the notable success that some very recent writers have achieved by experimenting with dialectal expression, the use of Black English in American fiction today appears significantly and strikingly alive.

NOTES

1. Lubomir Dolezel, *Narrative Modes in Czech Literature* (Toronto: University of Toronto Press, 1973), p. 15. Here Dolezel has said:
> One of the most important tasks in the structural study of narrative prose is a thorough investigation of the relationship between the narrator's discourse (DN) and the characters' discourse (DC). The opposition of the two discourses can be said to represent the "deep" level of the verbal structure in every narrative text.

2. Wayne Booth managed to find one example of a second-person novel, Michel Butor's *La Modification* (Paris, 1957). See *The Rhetoric of Fiction* (Chicago: University of Chicago Press, 1961), p. 150, n. 3.

3. See Seymour Chatman, *Story and Discourse: Narrative Structure in Fiction and Film* (Ithaca, N.Y.: Cornell University Press, 1978), p. 166.

4. Norman Friedman calls this the "Dramatic Mode." See *Form and Meaning in Fiction* (Athens: University of Georgia Press, 1975), pp. 155–56.

5. Langston Hughes, *Simple Takes a Wife* (New York: Simon and Schuster, 1953), p. 223.

6. Warren Miller, *The Cool World* (Boston: Little Brown and Company, 1959), pp. 1–2.

7. Ernest J. Gaines, *Bloodline* (New York: The Dial Press, 1968), pp. 78–79.

8. Lucille Clifton, *All Us Come Cross the Water* (New York: Holt, Rinehart, and Winston, 1973), n.p.

9. Wayne Booth asserts that in discussions of the function of the narrator, "perhaps the most over worked distinction is that of person." See *The Rhetoric of Fiction*, p. 150.

10. Norman Friedman has demonstrated that there are varying degrees of "omniscience." See *Form and Meaning in Fiction*, pp. 145–55.

11. Franz K. Stanzel discusses this issue in "Towards a 'Grammar of Fiction,'" *Novel* (Spring 1978), pp. 247–64.

12. Charles Waddell Chesnutt, *The Conjure Woman* (Ridgewood, N.J.: The Gregg Press, 1968), pp. 12–13.

13. Joel Chandler Harris, *Uncle Remus: His Songs and His Sayings* (New York: The Heritage Press, 1957), p. 24.

14. Harriet Beecher Stowe, *Uncle Tom's Cabin,* ed. Kenneth S. Lynn (Cambridge, Mass.: The Belknap Press of Harvard University Press, 1962), pp. 100–101.

15. Nathan C. Heard, *Howard Street* (New York: The Dial Press, 1968), p. 108.

16. Carl Van Vechten, *Nigger Heaven* (New York: Octagon Books, 1973), p. 6.

17. Zora Neale Hurston, *Their Eyes Were Watching God* (Urbana: University of Illinois Press, 1937, 1965), p. 159.

18. Richard Wright, "Big Boy Leaves Home," in *Uncle Tom's Children* (New York: Harper and Row, 1936), p. 45.

19. Alice Walker, *The Third Life of Grange Copeland* (New York: Harcourt, Brace, Jovanovich, 1970), p. 87.

20. Gertrude Stein, "Melanctha," in *Three Lives* (New York: The Modern Library, 1909, 1933), p. 173.

21. Roark Bradford, *Ol' Man Adam an' His Chillun* (New York: Harper and Brothers, 1928), pp. 26–27.

22. June Jordan, *His Own Where* (New York: Thomas Y. Crowell, 1971), p. 1.

23. Ellease Southerland, *Let the Lion Eat Straw* (New York: Charles Scribner's Sons, 1979), p. 3.

Works Cited

I. Linguistic Studies

Bennett, John. "Gullah: A Negro Patois." *South Atlantic Quarterly* 7 (1908): 332–47; 8 (1909): 39–52.

Bickerton, Derek. *Dynamics of a Creole System*. Cambridge: Cambridge University Press, 1975.

Brooks, Cleanth. *The Relation of the Alabama-Georgia Dialect to the Provincial Dialects of Great Britain*. Baton Rouge: Louisiana State University Press, 1935.

Burling, Robbins. *English in Black and White*. New York: Holt, Rinehart, and Winston, 1973.

Crum, Mason. *Gullah*. Durham: Duke University Press, 1940.

De Camp, David, and Hancock, Ian F. *Pidgins and Creoles: Current Trends and Projects*. Washington, D.C.: Georgetown University Press, 1974.

Dillard, J. L. *Black English*. New York: Random House, 1972.

——. *Black Names*. The Hague: Mouton, 1976.

Fasold, Ralph W. "Decreolization and Autonomous Language Change." *Florida Foreign Language Reporter* 10 (1972): 9–12, 51.

——, and Shuy, R. W., eds. *Teaching Standard English in the Inner City*. Washington, D.C.: Center for Applied Linguistics, 1970.

Fickett, Joan. *Aspects of Morphemics, Syntax, and Semology of an Inner-City Dialect (Merican)*. New York: Meadowood Publishers, 1972.

Hall, Robert A., Jr. *Pidgin and Creole Languages*. Ithaca: Cornell University Press, 1966.

Herskovits, Melville J. *The Myth of the Negro Past*. New York: Harper and Brothers, 1941.

Hymes, Dell. *Pidginization and Creolization of Languages*. Cambridge: Cambridge University Press, 1971.

Kochman, Thomas. *Rappin' and Stylin' Out*. Urbana: University of Illinois Press, 1972.

Krapp, George Philip. "The English of the Negro." *American Mercury* 2 (June 1924): 190–95.

Labov, William. *Language in the Inner City: Studies in the Black English Vernacular*. Philadelphia: University of Pennsylvania Press, 1972.

——. *The Social Stratification of English in New York City*. Washington, D.C.: Center for Applied Linguistics, 1966.

McDavid, Raven I., Jr. "American Social Dialects." *College English* 26 (January 1965): 254–60.

———. "New Directions in American Dialectology." *Studia Anglica, Poznaniensia* 5 (1973): 9–25.

McDowell, Tremaine. "The Use of Negro Dialect by Harriet Beecher Stowe." *American Speech* 6 (1931): 322–36.

Mencken, H. L. *The American Language*. New York: Alfred A. Knopf, 1937.

Shuy, Roger W.; Wolfram, Walter A.; and Riley, William K. *Field Techniques in an Urban Language Study*. Washington, D.C.: Center for Applied Linguistics, 1968.

Smith, Reed. *Gullah*. Columbia: Bureau of Publications, University of South Carolina, 1926.

Smitherman, Geneva. *Talkin and Testifyin*. Boston: Houghton Mifflin, 1977.

Todd, Lorenzo. *Pidgins and Creoles*. London: Routledge and Kegan Paul, 1974.

Turner, Lorenzo Dow. *Africanisms in the Gullah Dialect*. Ann Arbor: University of Michigan Press, 1949, 1973.

Twiggs, Robert D. *Pan-African Language in the Western Hemisphere*. North Quincy, Mass.: The Christopher Publishing House, 1973.

Williams, Robert. *Ebonics: the True Language of Black Folks*. St. Louis: The Institute of Black Studies, 1975.

Williamson, Juanita V. *A Phonological and Morphological Study of the Speech of the Negro of Memphis, Tennessee*. Publications of the American Dialect Society 50 (1968).

———, and Burke, Virginia M., eds. *A Various Language: Perspectives in American Dialects*. New York: Holt, Rinehart, and Winston, 1971.

Wolfram, Walter A. *A Sociolinguistic Description of Detroit Negro Speech*. Washington, D.C.: Center for Applied Linguistics, 1968.

———, and Clarke, Nona H., eds. *Black-White Speech Relationships*. Washington, D.C.: Center for Applied Linguistics, 1971.

Woofter, T. J., ed. *Black Yeomanry*. New York: Henry Holt, 1930.

II. Primary Sources

Aptheker, Herbert, ed. *Book Reviews by W. E. B. DuBois*. Millwood, N.Y.: KTO Press, 1977.

Baldwin, James. *Go Tell It on the Mountain*. New York: Dell, 1953.

———. *Nobody Knows My Name*. New York: Dell, 1961.

Baraka, Imamu Amiri. See also Jones, LeRoi.

———. *Three Books by Imamu Amiri Baraka (LeRoi Jones)*. New York: Grove Press, 1967.

———, and Fundi [Billy Abernathy]. *In Our Terribleness*. Indianapolis: Bobbs-Merrill, 1970.

Brackenridge, Hugh Henry. *Modern Chivalry*. Edited by Lewis Leary. New Haven: College and University Press, 1965.

Bradford, Roark. *Ol' Man Adam an' His Chillun*. New York: Harper and Brothers, 1928.

Brooks, Cleanth; Lewis, R. W. B.; and Warren, Robert Penn. *American Literature: The Makers and the Making.* 2 vols. New York: St. Martin's Press, 1973.

Brown, William Wells. *Clotel, or, The President's Daughter.* New York: Arno Press and The New York Times, 1969.

Cable, George W. *The Grandissimes.* New York: Scribner's Sons, 1880.

Chesnutt, Charles Waddell. *The Conjure Woman.* Ridgewood, N.J.: The Gregg Press, 1968.

Chopin, Kate. *Bayou Folk.* Boston: Houghton Mifflin, 1934.

Clemens, Samuel Langhorne [Mark Twain]. *Adventures of Huckleberry Finn.* 2d ed. Edited by Sculley Bradley, Richmond Croom Beatty, E. Hudson Long, and Thomas Cooley. New York: W. W. Norton, 1977.

Clifton, Lucille. *All Us Come Cross the Water.* New York: Holt, Rinehart, and Winston, 1973.

Cohen, Octavus Roy. *Highly Colored.* New York: Dodd, Mead, 1921.

Crane, Stephen. *Tales of Whilomville.* Edited by Fredson Bowers. Charlottesville: The University Press of Virginia, 1969.

Cullen, Countee. *One Way to Heaven.* New York: Harper and Brothers, 1932.

Dixon, Thomas. *The Clansman.* New York: A. Wessels, 1907.

DuBois, W. E. B. *The Quest of the Silver Fleece.* College Park, Md.: McGrath, 1969.

Ellison, Ralph. *Invisible Man.* New York: The Modern Library, 1952.

————. *Shadow and Act.* New York: Random House, 1964.

Faulkner, William. *Go Down, Moses.* New York: The Modern Library, 1942.

Gaines, Ernest J. *Bloodline.* New York: The Dial Press, 1968.

Gonzales, Ambrose. *The Black Border.* Columbia, S.C.: The State College, 1922.

Harris, Joel Chandler. *Nights with Uncle Remus.* Boston: Houghton Mifflin, 1881.

————. *Uncle Remus: His Songs and His Sayings.* New York: Heritage Press, 1957.

Harrison, James A., ed. *The Complete Works of Edgar Allan Poe.* 17 vols. New York: Thomas Y. Crowell, 1902.

Heard, Nathan C. *Howard Street.* New York: The Dial Press, 1968.

Hughes, Langston. *The Big Sea.* New York: Hill and Wang, 1940.

————. *Good Morning Revolution.* Edited by Faith Berry. New York: Lawrence Hill, 1973.

————. *Not Without Laughter.* New York: Knopf, 1930.

————. *Simple Takes a Wife.* New York: Simon and Schuster, 1953.

Hurston, Zora Neale. "Story in Harlem Slang." *American Mercury* 55 (July 1942): 84–96.

————. *Their Eyes Were Watching God.* Urbana: University of Illinois Press, 1937, 1965.

Jackson, Bruce. "Get Your Ass in the Water and Swim Like Me." Cambridge, Mass.: Harvard University Press, 1974.

Johnson, James Weldon. *The Autobiography of an Ex-Coloured Man.* New York: Knopf, 1927.

Jones, LeRoi. See also Baraka, Imamu Amiri.

————. *Blues People*. New York: William Morrow, 1963.

————. *The Moderns*. New York: Corinth Books, 1963.

Jordan, June. *His Own Where*. New York: Thomas Y. Crowell, 1971.

McKay, Claude. *Home to Harlem*. Chatham, N.J.: The Chatham Bookseller, 1928.

Melville, Herman. *Moby-Dick or The Whale*. Edited by Charles Feidelson. New York: Bobbs-Merrill, 1964.

Miller, Warren. *The Cool World*. Boston: Little Brown and Company, 1959.

Mitchell, Margaret. *Gone With the Wind*. New York: Macmillan, 1936.

Morrison, Toni. *Song of Solomon*. New York: Knopf, 1977.

Oliver, Clinton F., and Sills, Stephanie. *Contemporary Black Drama*. New York: Charles Scribner's Sons, 1971.

Page, Thomas Nelson. *In Ole Virginia*. Chapel Hill: University of North Carolina Press, 1969.

Poe, Edgar Allan. *The Complete Poems and Stories of Edgar Allan Poe*. 2 vols. New York: Alfred A. Knopf, 1946.

Reed, Ishmael. *The Free-Lance Pallbearers*. Garden City, N.Y.: Doubleday, 1967.

————. *Mumbo Jumbo*. Garden City, N.Y.: Doubleday, 1972.

————. *19 Necromancers From Now*. Garden City, N.Y.: Doubleday, 1970.

Southerland, Ellease. *Let the Lion Eat Straw*. New York: Charles Scribner's Sons, 1979.

Stein, Gertrude. *Three Lives*. Norfolk, Conn.: New Directions, 1909, 1933.

Stockton, Eric, and Campbell, Killis, eds. *Poe's Short Stories*. New York: Harcourt, Brace, 1927.

Stowe, Harriet Beecher. *Uncle Tom's Cabin*. Edited by Kenneth S. Lynn. Cambridge, Mass.: The Belknap Press of Harvard University Press, 1962.

Styron, William. *The Confessions of Nat Turner*. New York: Random House, 1967.

————. *Sophie's Choice*. New York: Random House, 1979.

Toomer, Jean. *Cane*. New York: Boni and Liveright, 1923.

Van Vechten, Carl. *Nigger Heaven*. New York: Octagon Books, 1973.

Walden, Daniel. *W. E. B. DuBois: The Crisis Writings*. Greenwich, Conn.: Fawcett, 1972.

Walker, Alice. *The Color Purple*. New York: Harcourt Brace Jovanovich, 1982.

————. *The Third Life of Grange Copeland*. New York: Harcourt, Brace, Jovanovich, 1970.

Welty, Eudora. *A Curtain of Green*. Garden City, N.Y.: Doubleday, Doran, 1941.

————. *The Eye of the Story*. New York: Random House, 1977.

Wright, Richard. *Native Son*. New York: Harper and Row, 1940.

————. *Uncle Tom's Children*. New York: Harper and Row, 1936.

III. Literary Criticism, History, and Commentary

Benston, Kimberly W., ed. *Imamu Amiri Baraka (LeRoi Jones)*. Englewood Cliffs, N.J.: Prentice-Hall, 1978.

Bone, Robert. *The Negro Novel in America*. New Haven, Conn.: Yale University Press, 1958.

————. *Richard Wright*. Minneapolis: University of Minnesota Press, 1969.

Booth, Wayne. *The Rhetoric of Fiction*. Chicago: University of Chicago Press, 1961.

Brasch, Walter M. *Black English and the Mass Media*. Amherst: University of Massachusetts Press, 1981.

Brown, Sterling. *The Negro in American Fiction* and *Negro Poetry and Drama*. New York: Arno Press, 1969.

Chatman, Seymour. *Story and Discourse: Narrative Structure in Fiction and Film*. Ithaca: Cornell University Press, 1978.

Clarke, John Henrik, ed. *William Styron's Nat Turner: Ten Black Writers Respond*. Boston: Beacon Press, 1968.

Coleman, Leon. "Carl Van Vechten Presents the New Negro." *Studies in the Literary Imagination* 7 (Fall 1974): 85–104.

Cook, Raymond A. *Thomas Dixon*. New York: Twayne, 1974.

Creighton, Joanne V. *William Faulkner's Craft of Fiction*. Detroit, Mich. Wayne State University Press, 1977.

Dabney, Lewis M. *The Indians of Yoknapatawpha*. Baton Rouge: Louisiana State University Press, 1974.

Dolezel, Lubomir. *Narrative Modes in Czech Literature*. Toronto: University of Toronto Press, 1973.

Emanuel, James A., and Gross, Theodore L., eds. *Dark Symphony*. New York: The Free Press, 1968.

Friedman, Melvin J., and Malin, Irving, eds. *William Styron's "The Confessions of Nat Turner."* Belmont, Calif.: Wadsworth, 1970.

Friedman, Norman. *Form and Meaning in Fiction*. Athens: University of Georgia Press, 1975.

Gayle, Addison, Jr. *The Black Aesthetic*. Garden City, N.Y.: Doubleday, 1972.

Giles, James R. *Claude McKay*. Boston: Twayne, 1976.

Hemenway, Robert E. *Zora Neale Hurston*. Urbana: University of Illinois Press, 1977.

Hersey, John, ed. *Ralph Ellison*. Englewood Cliffs, N.J.: Prentice-Hall, 1974.

Hudson, Theodore R. *From LeRoi Jones to Amiri Baraka*. Durham: Duke University Press, 1973.

Huggins, Nathan Irvin. *Harlem Renaissance*. New York: Oxford University Press, 1971.

Hurston, Zora Neale. "Stories of Conflict." Review of Richard Wright, *Uncle Tom's Children*. *The Saturday Review,* April 2, 1938, p. 32.

Jackson, Blyden. *The Waiting Years*. Baton Rouge: Louisiana State University Press, 1976.

Kinnamon, Keneth. *The Emergence of Richard Wright*. Urbana: University of Illinois Press, 1972.

Lewis, David Levering. *When Harlem was in Vogue*. New York: Alfred A. Knopf, 1981.

Locke, Alain. *The New Negro*. New York: Arno Press, 1968.

McCall, Dan. *The Example of Richard Wright*. New York: Harcourt Brace, and World, 1969.

Reed, Ishmael. "The Writer as Seer; Ishmael Reed on Ishmael Reed." *Black World* 23 (June 1974): 20–34.

Rosenblatt, Roger. *Black Fiction*. Cambridge, Mass.: Harvard University Press, 1974.

Rubin, Louis D. *George W. Cable*. New York: Pegasus, 1969.

Schmitz, Neil. "Neo HooDoo: The Experimental Fiction of Ishmael Reed." *Twentieth Century Literature* 20 (April 1974): 126–40.

Sollors, Werner. *Amiri Baraka/LeRoi Jones: The Quest for a "Populist Modernism."* New York: Columbia University Press, 1978.

Stanzel, Franz K. "Towards a 'Grammar of Fiction.'" *Novel* (Spring 1978): 247–64.

Volpe, Edmond L. *A Reader's Guide to William Faulkner*. London: Thames and Hudson, 1964.

IV. Other

Blassingame, John W. *The Slave Community*. New York: Oxford University Press, 1972.

Cruse, Harold. *The Crisis of the Negro Intellectual*. New York: William Morrow, 1967.

Douglass, Frederick. *My Bondage and My Freedom*. New York: Miller, Orton, and Mulligan, 1855.

Feather, Leonard. *The Book of Jazz*. New York: Horizon Press, 1965.

Fisher, Miles Mark. *Negro Slave Songs in the United States*. New York: Citadel Press, 1953.

Haley, Alex. *Roots*. New York: Doubleday, 1976.

Kluger, Richard. *Simple Justice*. New York: Vintage Books, 1975.

Kunitz, Stanley J., and Haycraft, Howard. *Twentieth-Century Authors*. New York: The H. H. Wilson Co., 1942.

Martin Luther King Junior Elementary School Children v. *Ann Arbor School District Board. United States Law Week (U. S. L W.)* 48 (July 24, 1979): 2058.

Myrdal, Gunnar. *An American Dilemma*. New York: Harper and Row, 1944, 1962.

Pinkney, Alphonso. *Red, Black, and Green: Black Nationalism in the United States*. Cambridge: Cambridge University Press, 1976.

Ramsey, David. *History of South Carolina, from Its First Settlement in 1670 to the year 1808. . . .* 2 vols. Newberry, S.C., 1858.

Woodward, C. Vann. *The Strange Career of Jim Crow*. 2d rev. ed. New York: Oxford University Press, 1966.

Index